The New Politics of Social

The New Politics of Social Work

Edited by

Mel Gray and Stephen A. Webb

© Selection, editorial matter: Mel Gray and Stephen A. Webb 2013
Individual chapters © contributors 2013

All rights reserved. No reproduction, copy or transmission of this
publication may be made without written permission.

No portion of this publication may be reproduced, copied or transmitted
save with written permission or in accordance with the provisions of the
Copyright, Designs and Patents Act 1988, or under the terms of any licence
permitting limited copying issued by the Copyright Licensing Agency,
Saffron House, 6–10 Kirby Street, London EC1N 8TS.

Any person who does any unauthorized act in relation to this publication
may be liable to criminal prosecution and civil claims for damages.

The authors have asserted their rights to be identified
as the authors of this work in accordance with the Copyright, Designs
and Patents Act 1988.

First published 2013 by
PALGRAVE MACMILLAN

Palgrave Macmillan in the UK is an imprint of Macmillan Publishers Limited, registered
in England, company number 785998, of Houndmills, Basingstoke, Hampshire RG21
6XS.

Palgrave Macmillan in the US is a division of St Martin's Press LLC,
175 Fifth Avenue, New York, NY 10010.

Palgrave Macmillan is the global academic imprint of the above companies
and has companies and representatives throughout the world.
Palgrave® and Macmillan® are registered trademarks in the United States,
the United Kingdom, Europe and other countries

ISBN: 978-0-230-29678-7

This book is printed on paper suitable for recycling and made from fully
managed and sustained forest sources. Logging, pulping and manufacturing
processes are expected to conform to the environmental regulations of the
country of origin.

A catalogue record for this book is available from the British Library.

A catalog record for this book is available from the Library of Congress.

Contents

List of Tables

Acknowledgements

The issues motivating our narrative are political, and we come at them from our professional background in social work. A commitment to social and economic justice first galvanised this book's journey. We hope the book proves to be a bold challenge to the orthodox, mainstream and conservative elements of social work, as many social workers continue to acquiesce in the face of the neoliberal capitalist onslaught of austerity, injustice, violence and virulent greed. If we could achieve a better understanding of the destruction and disruption wrought by neoliberalism to which we are currently exposed in social work, we would have a better chance of doing something about it. We believe a massive disappointment sits at the heart of what is happening in social work today and more broadly in liberal democracies. An ethics of commitment and community is required to inform a new politics of social work. We need to find each other to undertake this important task.

This venture has been some time in the making and reached fruition through the commitment, hard work and dedication of our brilliant contributors and the supportive staff at Palgrave Macmillan, including Katie Rauwerda, India Annette-Woodgate and our excellent publishing editor Catherine Gray, who believed in the project from the start and encouraged us every step of the way. Not only did she help guide and polish the text but she also provided us with creative inspiration. We thank Juanita Bullough for her excellent work on copy-editing our manuscript.

It has been a real privilege to work with such a fine and outstanding line-up of international scholars on this book, with each of them, in different ways, creatively mapping the terrain for a new politics for social work. This blend of outstanding radical thinkers in social work really did feel like it gelled over the time in producing this book. There are many other good scholars in social work whose progressive writings opened up new perspectives for us or provided outstanding analyses of issues that we could not hope to cover here. Some of these have not seen this work, some we have never met, and some might even disown what is written here. Regardless of their political position, we will venture to acknowledge some intellectual debt to them: Jim Albright, Willem Blok, Linda Briskman, Malcolm Carey, John Coates, Lena Dominelli, Brid Featherstone, Jan Fook, Nancy Fraser, Howard Goldstein, Karen Healy, Jim Ife, Bill Jordan, Diana Kennedy, Fabian Kessl, Declan Kuch, James Ladwig, Michael Lavellete, Michael Lipsky, Jim

Midgley, Carolyn Noble, Joan Orme, Hans Uwe Otto, Christine Phillipon, David Philpott, Brian Relph, Dennis Saleebey, Sandy Schram, Elaine Sharland, Paul Stepney, Heinz Sunker and Sue White.

Mel would like to thank all those around her who provided support in the production of this book. Thanks to Dave for his generosity and practical wisdom, and to all the contributors, who often put aside other work to meet our deadlines and were extremely patient and diligent in responding to our many editorial requests.

Stephen, as ever, owes a great debt to the insight, virtue and loving companionship of Penni. As always she subtly referees his struggles with the politics of institutions, cultures and people. He is also indebted to the wisdom of Jenny Backwell, a practice teacher (among many other things) in Brighton, England, who long ago pointed out the need for critical engagement with students and practitioners in developing a political stance.

Notes on Contributors

Viviene E. Cree is Professor of Social Work Studies at the University of Edinburgh, Scotland. She is a qualified social worker and youth and community worker. She has written and researched extensively on the social work profession, on children and HIV, and on higher education. Her recent book is *Becoming a Social Worker: Global Narratives* (Routledge, 2013). She is co-editor of the Social Work in Practice series published by Policy Press and BASW.

Harry Ferguson is Professor of Social Work at the University of Nottingham, England. He is a qualified social worker and has taught, researched and published on social work and social theory; child abuse and protection; domestic violence; and fatherhood, men and masculinities. His books include *Child Protection Practice* (Palgrave Macmillan, 2011).

Iain Ferguson is a Professor of Social Work at University of West Scotland and a Research Fellow at the University of the Witwatersrand, South Africa. His most recent book is *Radical Social Work in Practice* (with Woodward, Policy Press, 2009). He is one of the authors of the Manifesto for Social Work and Social Justice (www.socialworkfuture.org) and a member of the Steering Committee of the Social Work Action Network. He is editor of the journal *Critical and Radical Social Work*.

Tammy Findlay teaches Canadian Studies, Political Studies and Women's Studies at the Mount Saint Vincent University in Halifax, Nova Scotia, Canada. Her research interests include Canadian politics, gender and politics, gender and public policy, social policy, community engagement, multi-level governance and representation. She is currently working on projects related to childcare policy in Canada and is completing a book on women's representation in the Ontario public service.

Paul Michael Garrett works at the National University of Ireland (NUI) Galway in the Republic of Ireland. He is the author of several books, including most recently *'Transforming' Children's Services?* (McGraw Hill, 2009) and *Social Work and Social Theory* (Policy Press, 2013). His work has appeared in academic journals across a range of disciplines and he has presented papers at a number of international conferences. He is a member of the editorial boards of *Critical Social Policy* (where he edits the Reviews section) and the *European Journal of Social Work*.

Mel Gray is Professor of Social Work in the School of Humanities and Social Science at the University of Newcastle, New South Wales, the highest ranked social work research programme in Australia. She has published extensively on international social work and social development. Recent books include the *Sage Handbook of Social Work* (with Midgley and Webb, 2012), *Environmental Social Work* (with Coates and Hetherington; Routledge, 2013), *Social Work Theories and Methods* (2nd edn with Webb; Sage, 2013), and *Decolonizing Social Work* (with Coates, Yellow Bird and Hetherington; Ashgate, 2013).

Stan Houston qualified as a social worker in 1981. He then spent the following sixteen years practising in a range of child and family social work settings in Belfast, Northern Ireland. In 1997, he entered higher education. Since then, his interests have focused on the application of critical social theory and moral philosophy to social work practice and research, particularly in the field of child welfare.

Richard Hugman is Professor of Social Work at the University of New South Wales, Sydney, Australia. His work on social work ethics is widely known and he is chair of the International Federation of Social Workers' permanent committee on ethics. Also renowned for his international work, he acted as a consultant for UNICEF Vietnam to advise the Vietnamese government on the establishment of professional social work there. His most recent book is *Understanding International Social Work: A Critical Analysis* (Palgrave Macmillan, 2010).

John Lawler (Ph.D.) is Senior Lecturer Public Sector Management in the School of Development and Economic Studies at the University of Bradford, England. His research interests include management and leadership development, especially in the public services. He has researched and published in a variety of related areas, including change in organizations; management development; user views of health and social care services; evidence in health and social care; and existential thinking in relation to management and leadership.

Greg Marston (Ph.D.) is Professor of Social Policy in the Faculty of Health, School of Public Health and Social Work, Queensland University of Technology, Brisbane, Australia. He has published widely in the field of social policy analysis, the future of the welfare state, citizenship and identity, contemporary social theory, unemployment, income support, social housing and refugee settlement.

Bob Pease is Chair of Social Work in the School of Health and Social Development at Deakin University, Melbourne, Australia. His recent books include *Migrant Men, Critical Studies of Masculinities and the Migration Experience* (Routledge, 2010); *Men and Masculinities Around the World: Transforming Men's Practices* (Palgrave Macmillan, 2010); and *Undoing Privilege: Unearned Advantage in a Divided World* (Zed Books, 2010).

Carolyn Taylor is Senior Lecturer in Applied Social Science at the University of Lancaster, England. She has published widely in major social work journals and her research interests include the study of the ways in which professional practice is enacted in health and welfare bodies and the historical study of social work and welfare organizations.

Stephen A. Webb is Professor of Social Work at Glasgow Caledonian University, Scotland. His recent books include *Evidence-based Social Work* (with Gray and Plath; Routledge, 2009), *Social Work Theories and Methods* (with Gray; Sage, 2013), and the *Sage Handbook of Social Work* (with Gray and Midgley; Sage, 2012). Webb's critical analysis 'Considerations on the Validity of Evidence-based Practice in Social Work' (2001) is the world's most cited article in the field and 'the most influential publication in social work over the last ten years' (Hodges et al., 2011).

PART I
New Agendas for Social Work

1
Towards a 'New Politics' of Social Work

Mel Gray and Stephen A. Webb

Undoubtedly, one of the great virtues of social work is that it continues to think politically in these difficult times of crisis and austerity. Its foundational values of equality and justice have always been compounded with freedom as core political ideals and 'right principles'. The search for structures that might realize these moral standards has been a consistent feature of critical social work. Taking a political stance in defence of these values is the risk that social work must take. The objective would be twofold: a renewal of a progressive Left agenda in social work and, secondly, articulating social work's role in contributing to the abolition of exploitative and despotic regimes maintained by the capitalist class and its neoliberal economic order (Badiou, 2012). As Warren Buffett, 'The Sage of Omaha', has observed, 'there's class warfare, all right but it's *my class*, the rich class, that's making war, and we're *winning*'.

Collectively, the contributors to this book seek to devise a 'new politics' for social work in the belief that it bears a public responsibility to confront injustice while seeking justice for all. While the chapters which follow speak for themselves, and deliberately, do not speak in the same voice, we explicitly adopt justice as a normative value. The point, of course, is partly exhortatory, a call to social workers to take a stance, but partly a matter of necessity in defining how this might be mobilized. A new politics involves redefining the project of the Left in social work in terms of a 'radicalization' of theory and practice (see Chapter 13). This requires a militancy which confronts the system of capitalist power that redefines, limits and rejects the core values of social work. These ultimately are the central objectives of a renewed social work politics, which begins with grappling with ideas about what a 'just society' might look like and how injustice manifests itself in everyday relationships and institutional structures. This political project confronts, unsettles and agitates, and seeks to transform capitalist relations of domination, oppression, marginalization and exclusion that lead to injustice (see Chapter 8). Critical social work is the primary method for framing a new politics of social work with its conceptual and historical tools significantly informing our perspective on a new politics. However, there has been a proliferation of post-Marxist perspectives that have moved us beyond critical social work, freeing social work up from its postmodern influences and reconfiguring it more closely with the Frankfurt School Marxist traditions. Moreover, contemporary political mobilization through new social movements in a post-global financial crisis scenario has significantly changed responses to the neoliberal juggernaut and welfare austerity, seen *inter alia* with the Occupy Movement, the Turkish protesters in Taksim Square, the Greek resurgence of the Left and the Arab Spring. Although the inspiration for this book falls within the critical and radical tradition described by Bob Pease in Chapter 2, our notion of a new politics encompasses new perspectives and issues within the contemporary political environment of social activism.

The Long Night of the Left is Coming to a Close

The starting point for conceiving a renewed politics of social work hinges on two important contemporary developments within the social sciences: one from social theory, the other from political philosophy. The fact that they crisscross in instantiating new forms of political possibility is particularly helpful in advancing our new politics in social work. The former focuses exclusively on debates in theoretical sociology, galvanized chiefly by Nancy Fraser and Axel Honneth (2003) and often referred to as the integrated model of social justice debate (permeating discussions throughout this book – see Chapters 2, 4, 8, 10 and 11). The latter is derived from French political philosopher Alain Badiou, particularly his reworking of the communist hypothesis as part of his larger project of reconstructing a theory of political action derived from Marx's historical materialism (see Chapter 3). Taken together, they have the potential to galvanize a new politics of social work by innovatively reworking agendas on social justice and solidarity, of political possibility, and transformative ideas relating to universal emancipation and freedom.

This agenda situates the push towards a new politics within a lively and much invigorated New Left grouping of thinkers that coalesce around critical considerations of community and progressive political agendas with the work of Badiou, including Slavoj Žižek, Jacques Rancière, Chantal Mouffe, Jean-Luc Nancy, Antonio Negri, Peter Hallward, Costas Douzinas, Gianni Vattimo, Susan Buck-Morss, Alberto Toscano, Roberto Esposito and Giorgio Agamben. It involves radical New Left online journals, such as the *International Journal for Communisation, Endnote* and *Tiqqun*. According to this progressive group of thinkers, universal justice is not possible without the abolition of capitalism. Collectively, such radical associations are united in developing a critique of what they call 'post-politics', which refers to the emergence in the post-Cold War climate of a politics of consensus on a global scale, whereby politics simply becomes a concern with the 'facts of politics' or 'the deciding of common affairs' supported by the 'stabilizing class'. Against this politics without hope, this group reinstates the significance of inherent antagonism between competing social classes in an oppressive capitalist-dominated world. As Žižek (1999) argues, a radical stance 'insists on the primacy of inherent antagonism as constitutive of the political' (p. 29). The route politics has historically travelled in social work is self-evident. After abandoning 'class struggle essentialism' for the plurality of anti-racist, feminist and, postmodern resistances, 'capitalism' is now clearly re-emerging as the name of *the* problem (Žižek, 2012). As a consequence we are witnessing today the return of a new theory and practice of resistance.

Taken together, the talented group of New Left thinkers listed above has carved a different path in developing an anti-capitalist political agenda. Their progressive work was showcased at the March 2009 conference, *The Idea of Communism*, organized by the Birkbeck Institute for Humanities in London. This conference had huge political importance, with contributors developing new radical agendas that particularly resonated among young people. It was also the first occasion for bringing together some of the most inspiring philosophers of the Left under the name of communism (Douzinas & Žižek, 2010). 'Communism' here was developed from the idea of 'what we hold in common' and refers to the creation of a common or collective passage for change (e.g. the Occupy Movement's slogan 'We are the 99%' – inspired by the Arab Spring, riots against austerity measures in Europe, occupations by the Spanish *indignados* and Greek activists at Syntagma Square, the movement spread to over 2,556 cities across 82 countries). The key question addressed at the London conference was whether 'communism' was still the name or the 'Idea' to be used to designate and guide radical emancipatory projects. With this debate, communism was not uncritically taken for granted as a solution, but rather treated as a problem to be explored and regarded as a particular process rather than an end point (Noys, 2011). In *The Coming Insurrection*, the Invisible Committee (2008) proclaimed: 'Communism ... as presupposition *and* as experiment. Sharing of a sensibility *and* elaboration of sharing. The uncovering of what is common *and* the building of a force' (p. 4).

The richness of possible trajectories is clear. These can valuably contribute to a progressive militant agenda ranging from Marx to Simmel, Gramsci to Bourdieu, Adorno to Habermas, Fraser to Honneth and Kristeva to Butler (see Chapter 3). This fertile ground of thought can frame the way a critical social work can be instantiated under the banner of a 'New Social Work Left'. This is achieved by taking a political stance that is inherently antagonistic against its adversaries: neoliberalism and parliamentary capitalism, while projecting an emancipatory activism of new social movements without ignoring longstanding problems of economic inequality and social injustice. In adopting the significance of these contemporary forms of thought for social work, an excitingly fresh approach that can construct a New Left political agenda opens up. For the sake of an appropriate designation, the term 'New Social Work Left' is used because it most accurately reflects the radical politics at stake and punctuates the timeliness of the project than does 'critical social work'. It is also an appropriate slogan or rallying cry behind which social workers can unite and find one another.

The drawing together of new insights from sociology and political philosophy is motivated partly by a distinctive and significant shift that is occurring in contemporary times which acts decisively on social work. Broadly, this shift is based on renewal and crisis. *Renewal* is situated largely at the level of political ideas and values, especially as they relate to the development of a progressive left agenda that emphasizes social justice, freedom and equality. *Crisis* refers to the vulnerabilities of neoliberalism and state capitalism on a global scale to the extent that many political commentators believe we are now entering a new phase: a protracted, long downturn in the fortunes of capitalism. These shifts are particularly relevant in considering how we move for a new politics for social work. There is a critical role for social work in confronting the contradictions of the logic of capital accumulation and greed based on the notion of endless growth. It is against this dominant neoliberal world-view that David Harvey's *The Enigma of Capital and the Crises of Capitalism* (2011) urges us to 'constructively rebel if we are to change our world in any fundamental way. The problem of endless compound growth through endless capital accumulation will have to be confronted and overcome. This is the political necessity of our times' (p. 277). Social work owes it as much to itself as to its citizen clients to confront the dominant neoliberal apparatus and capitalist class with every tactic available to it. We have to get organized and find one another.

The chapters that follow demonstrate the distinct sense that we are entering a new phase. It must be stressed from the outset that ideas contained in the introductory and concluding chapters of this book are entirely those of the editors, who certainly have not sought to corral contributors under a single banner of the political 'New Social Work Left'. Having said this, it is necessary to be absolutely clear what is meant by a 'new phase' as it lends itself to politics. As soon as anyone starts talking about a new phase, people automatically assume that what is being proposed is the substitution of one kind of politics for another. However, this book avoids stoking up vain hopes and passions and is unlikely to have people jumping up and down excitedly imagining that the revolution is just around the corner. The 'New Social Work Left' has no manifesto. Manifestos are often written on the assumption that no single idea can convey a political trajectory and are neither compelling nor inspirational. They tend to gather dust like committee-tabled documents.

While we face the difficult challenge of inspiring sympathizers and those already wedded to core progressive values, within social work we face the bigger challenge of convincing the uncommitted – and we assume there are many – that there is something worthwhile to be had in engaging with such a radical project. We are persuaded, often by ourselves that radical politics is futile. So we tend toward compromise, resignation and acquiescence. Mainstream social work discourse can limit and even dislodge our experience of what is important and urgent. It takes over our voice and regulates our actions, such that we behave as ourselves only after hours or post-retirement (Lingis, 2007). Politically, front-line social workers are unorganized and do not usually have the energy, time, resources or assertiveness to take up active political roles. This exposes the weakness of social work as a professional pressure group and helps explain the strength of the capitalist state and its managerial agents in determining our ability to respond with political verve and commitment (Marston & McDonald, 2012).

In times of post-global financial crisis, social work continues to be shaped by political forces (see the video *Greece 2012: Social Work in Austerity* produced by Dora Dimitra Teloni, http://vimeo.com/39398286). It is important not to shrink from these challenges but, most significant of all, to reject the defeatism that has prevailed in certain social work quarters over the last two decades. Indeed, developing a critical approach to politics in social work includes having an awareness of the range of structural and ideological factors underpinning the emergence of policies. A 'New Social Work Left' can inspire core supporters and win over potential – though hesitant – allies. This is best achieved by demonstrating the chain of equivalences that exist among various struggles impacting on social workers – from the ecological crisis to the exploitation of the poor – against different forms of subordination (Standing, 2011). It is also achieved by showing the need to tackle issues of redistribution and recognition as they translate over to social work contexts (see Chapters 2 and 4).

Part of the task at hand with a new politics is to recast a radical identity for the Left under conditions of uncertainty and in the face of such a vicious adversary as neoliberalism. Indeed, as Laclau and Mouffe (2001) note, 'what we have witnessed in the last decade has been the triumph of neo-liberalism, whose hegemony has been so pervasive that it has had a profound effect on the very identity of the Left' (p. xiv). Moreover, there is no sense in which a new phase in critical social work politics is replacing all previous progressive, radical and left politics. If anything, this project is a reactivation of older radical traditions in social work and, if there is a real shift in the point of contestation with this new politics of social work, it is precisely because of the signs of innovation and the constraints that are happening on the wider social, economic and cultural plane under which social work is operating.

Our international organizations – the International Association of Schools of Social Work and the International Federal of Social Workers – have produced a 'global agenda for social work'. In endorsing a critical social work agenda, a challenge for these international social work organizations would be to declare openly their opposition to the malign tendencies of neoliberalism and the destructive nature of state capitalism. Indeed, rather than vainly offering up sanguine diets of 'Global Social Work' through best-practice models, the International Federation of Social Workers should be launching militant agendas, such as 'In Defence of Equality: Social Work Against Neoliberal Capitalism'. We wonder whether our international organizations have the appetite for and courage to lead such a progressive agenda. Are they prepared to stand up in defiance? For us, a new politics is located within social work specifically because of the continuous 'inside' struggles for an ethical politics around social justice. However, this reactivation of the critical project is not merely an internal matter against mainstream social work. Many issues and events central to contemporary understandings of society belong to fields of operation that are *external* to social work and cannot be reconceptualized in terms of social work categories. Indeed, we are working within an opening or discursive rupture that has recently occurred within Progressive Left thought and one which gains salience only through continuous critical discourse about the oppressive and violent regimes we wish to oppose and replace. For certain, social work has been shaped by wider political attitudes towards class, gender and race. Moreover, social work operates in a position of cultural and structural disadvantage, which has been vividly exposed in countries currently undertaking public-sector austerity measures. External structures and processes shape social work decisively. This is one very good reason why social and political theory offers a basis for constructing a new politics. The strands drawn upon, indebted to progressive thought, demonstrate how a 'New Social Work Left' must be concerned with new political forms of resistance, interruption and struggle (see Smith, 2012).

Given our overarching concentration on forging new ways of 'thinking the political', the strategies and tactics for active engagement we propose will be somewhat speculative (see Chapter 13). While any critical social work must be capable of identifying real empirical experiences and attitudes, which demonstrate that its standpoint has a strong basis in social reality, the violence of neoliberalism requires a new critical combination against it at the level of ideas. This is no small point. Very little real debate exists in social work over fundamental principles. As Graham Harman (2005) noted, 'Although I have no wish to be burned at the stake, I would also prefer not to work in a profession in which there is never any real combat over fundamental principles' (p.179).

The desire here is for a testing and proving of critical thought which should be capable of bringing together social work's role in demands for justice and anti-oppression. This book seeks to renew and reactivate the radical tradition of the 1970s and develop a more solid base for political and ethical work. In order to begin this work, it is crucial that certain obstacles and hindrances are cast to one side. Just like all 'Political Springs', this resembles something of a cleaning-out. In the concluding chapter, it is shown how certain trends within social work, notably the 'postmodern turn' on the one hand and the combined push toward a positivist information-based knowledge and public management regulation on the other, militate against the ambitions of critical social work (see Chapter 13).

Outlining Critical Social Work

Critical social work is a generic term for an approach to practice and wage labour that draws upon critical theory to promote social and economic justice through transformational change. It is a committed approach historically situated within the 'radical tradition' of social work that led to the growth of community work and local political action during the 1970s (see Chapter 2). It locates individual experience within wider social structures – the personal is political – and seeks to challenge oppression through progressive welfare policy and practice in the name of social justice and equality (see Chapter 9). However, the absence of an organized political movement for radical change in these neoliberal times makes this an almost impossible task, especially when certain sectors in mainstream social work appear to have accepted global capitalism as 'the only game in town'. As a caricature, mainstream social work is largely about maintenance, fixing and engineering, and not social change. As such, whether mainstream social work were operating in a patriarchal tribal society or under a national socialist regime it would really make very little difference: it would still be fixing attachment bonds, arranging respite care, counselling addictions, conducting risk assessments, and so on.

Critical social work urgently needs a new politics to respond to the vast inequalities generated by contemporary economic policies. The critical social work tradition denotes a set of intellectual and practical representations that breaks with the order of conventional social work – public sector managerialism, protectionist evidence-based social engineering, gross social inequalities and injustices, and so on – and the capitalist state instruments that protect them. Despite the various strands to critical social work – feminism, postcolonialism and anti-oppressivism – its agenda is galvanized by a common set of principles. Thus critical social work reflects a 'zone of political engagement' for students, researchers and practitioners enabling them to take a stance of resistance or defiance. It means taking a stance in support of those who are oppressed, exploited or treated unjustly. Critical social work is 'a perspective that sees itself as part of a progressive political project ... which begins with a rejection of contemporary social arrangements and seeks to establish another more equitable and just state of affairs' (Gray, Stepney, & Webb, 2012, p. 259).

A critical approach to the wage labour of practice generally involves working cooperatively and collectively and building alliances with issue-based groups and movements striving for social change (see Chapter 12). Such activism will involve civil disobedience and social protest, such as protests against unjust austerity measures, state surveillance mechanisms and corporate greed. Armed with a critical understanding of the world, of how social structures impact on human flourishing, critical social workers build people's awareness of the consequences of neoliberal managerialist policies and practices – or any unjust practices, for that matter. In Chapter 8, Greg Marston shows how discourse analysis can be used to generate a political stance on how a moralizing and individualizing discourse of 'bad tenants'– in his example of homelessness – works against the possibility of developing structural problems and long-term solutions. He shows how a critical approach externalizes rather than individualizes social problems. This book pays heed to the way critical social work practice has been deployed as structural, anti-discriminatory, anti-oppressive, transformative, emancipatory, empowering and justice-oriented.

Given that no one preconceived method or set of skills is assumed, it is also useful to think of critical social work as an approach that stresses the reflective aspects of action (see Chapter 5). Critical social work embeds practice in a *cycle of action–reflection–action* that draws crucially on theoretical and practical knowledge (Fook & Gardner, 2007). Knowledge – and the ideas it engenders – increases our critically reflective capabilities and directs attention to the possibilities of emancipatory practice and social transformation. A distinctive politics of social work inheres in a renewed commitment to a progressive agenda for the profession and a resurgent wave of militant thinking aimed at articulating a renewed set of political alternatives (Webb, 2010).

What is a 'New Politics'?

Most definitions associate politics with operations of power or systems of governance in society (see Chapter 8). Foucault's understanding of politics best fits this definition (see Fook, 2002). At another important level, politics is about ideas, principles and values. This is captured in Badiou's elevation of ideas as an avenue for new political forms, suggesting that politics also resides in a revolution of thought. New ways of thinking about politics must be constructed in order to enable people to imagine a different world than one enslaved to capitalism. Politics becomes about *imagining a better future* – one in which justice and equality prevail, in which people have an equal share of Earth's finite resources. For some, the environmental crisis is forcing us to envision and implement a new ecological paradigm because voracious capitalism is no longer tenable or sustainable (Gray, Coates, & Hetherington, 2013). Capitalism has significantly contributed to the crisis over climate change. It is this view of politics that our book addresses, as a way to devise a new politics of social work that will enable us to envision a new future for social work beyond capitalism and its neoliberal economic rationality, austerity measures and managerial control. Though social workers fight daily in their organizations against punitive welfare cuts and oppressive policies, through their acts of resistance and interruption, they also need to envisage alternative ways of thinking about political life, social relations between professionals and citizen clients, and justifications for militant opposition: a new politics is needed. In part, this is why the contributors to this book have been brought together to articulate, in separate ways, but through collective work, a new political agenda for social work.

Critical theory has always sought to diagnose society's illnesses – and to understand their causes – in order to suggest how society might be improved to cure its maladies. As times change and new problems surface, we vacillate between our old, well-worn analyses and the new diagnoses with which we are grappling. As new ideas form, we find merit in the old but all too soon realize that they are not enough to confront the new. It is in this spirit that we approach the 'new politics' of social work, beginning with a historical look at its beginnings in the 1970s and early 1980s when, as Bob Pease claims in Chapter 2, 'radical social work was at the forefront of debates about the future of the profession and its place in modern society'. Pease aptly captures the backward and forward gaze of critical social work today as it faces challenges reminiscent of radical social work in the 1970s and 1980s. Iain Ferguson too, in Chapter 12, seeks to revivify radical social work, seeing its ongoing relevance in contemporary social work. Like most critical social workers, he sees relevance in collectivist-based activism and resistance to oppressive social forces. Ideologically situated on the left, most critical social workers continue to see merit in socialist ideas, though are faced with the need for a reconstructed radical agenda since the demise of European communism.

The 'overtly academic' nature of radical social work has, over the years, enjoyed little support from front-line practitioners (see Carey & Foster,

2011). However, critical social work, as we have shown, is often more a form of critique than a direct emancipatory practice (Delanty, 2005). Its goal is not so much to offer tangible, practical ways of meeting the pressing, crisis-oriented, micro needs of service users (we prefer the designation 'citizen users') and informal carers, which practitioners encounter on a daily basis, but to enlarge their critical thinking so that in applying social work skills and knowledge, they envision better, more effective methods to counter restrictive procedural and managerialist practices. Several critical authors have been at the forefront of these critiques (Ferguson, 2008; Ferguson & Lavalette, 2004a, 2004b; Ferguson, Lavalette, & Whitmore, 2004; Ferguson & Woodward, 2009; Lavalette, 2004). Carey and Foster (2011) best capture the ethos of radical – and critical – social work in noting that its strength has always been its broad, 'often grandiose', general, 'macro' dynamic or onto-logical themes, 'such as the role of social work within a diminishing welfare state apparatus, the underlying causes of greater regulation within social work organisations, [and] the wider impact of globalisation' (p. 577). Despite its best efforts, however, managerial control, loss of professional autonomy and the undermining of practitioner discretion continue to leave practition-ers feeling 'either guilty or helpless' (Howe, 2009, p. 129). It is time to change this. To counter this pessimism, Harry Ferguson sees 'critical best practice' as a reflective medium through which social workers critically address ways in which they have used their powers and capacities in a skil-ful, theoretically informed (critical) way that is deeply respectful to citizen users (see Chapter 7).

When forms of political allegiance are explored, they generally advert to advocacy and lobbying, human rights, anti-oppressive practice, participa-tion and empowerment (see Chapters 4, 9 and 10). In Chapter 9, Viviene Cree argues that empowerment remains a valuable concept for social work today and must be understood as part of a radical response to the problems faced by individuals, groups and communities. It can also be applied to social workers themselves. Overall she is critical of empowerment as under-stood and practised in mainstream social work, which, she says, owes little to the emancipatory aspirations of the collective. She claims that much that passes as empowering practice is individualistic, consumerist and conserva-tive in scope. A truly empowering practice would be unsettling and radical and would likely come from forces outside social work – from citizen users, advocacy groups, community activists and social movements – rather than local government bureaucrats or social work academics. She sees glimpses of what might be possible in the Social Work Action Network (SWAN) in Europe, where practitioners, citizens, academics and students are collec-tively campaigning for 'a profession worth fighting for' (see Chapter 12).

Research repeatedly shows that, rather than participate in mass protests or public dissent, social workers tend to engage in small acts of interruptive resistance, or what Carey and Foster (2011) refer to as 'deviant social work', a concept akin to Lipsky's (1983) notion of the discrete street-level bureaucrat (see Schram, 2012). It is in the nature of such resistance that it must remain surprising and unanticipated, so as to defy managerialism, regulation and control. As John Lawler shows in Chapter 6, in exercising discretion managers, too, resist and undermine hegemonic 'managerial' discourses (Aronson & Smith, 2010; Carey, 2009). Lawler lays out a hefty challenge to social work management: do you wish to continue to connive and contrive for a pernicious system to the advantages of the capitalist class, or do you wish to abjure by exploring ways that can liberate yourselves and those for whom you have oversight?

Carey and Foster's (2011) concept of resistance highlights why radical social work must, to some extent, remain at a level removed from the daily practice of social work. Radical social work's role is to engender a political understanding of how managerial 'prescriptions connect ... with the day-to-day practice of social workers and the organisational conditions of social welfare' (Pearson, 1975, p. 140). Its function lies in the generation of ideas or a language through which practitioners might filter their daily experiences through a critical lens. There is space for separate 'realms of theory' (Althusser, 2003) that are essential in the promotion of progressive social change. It is in this spirit that we would like the reader to approach the 'new politics' of social work, which inevitably will contain something of the old (see Chapter 2) but will also provide new ideas and a new language to help us analyse what is wrong with the world and with its contexts or the policies that drive them. The capacity for critical reflection, so essential to the social worker, is enriched by the types of analyses that writers, like the contributors to this volume, provide. As Taylor notes in Chapter 5, critically reflective practice provides a means by which to wrestle with the contradictions inherent in the work we do and the contexts in which we work.

This critically reflective gaze must, of necessity, extend to the profession itself (see Chapter 2). Critical social work thinkers are up against a profession of social workers prepared to surrender or compromise the loss of their 'technical' and 'ideological' autonomy within a 'highly rationalised care management labour process' (Harris, 2003). Nevertheless, employee resistance and misbehaviour remains common and 'the recalcitrant worker has not disappeared but merely adapted their behaviour or attitudes to accommodate changing circumstances' (Carey & Foster, 2011, p. 583), as they have always done. As Kemshall (2010) points out, even highly regulated systems can be negotiated, circumvented and resisted in myriad ways by skilful social workers. Rather than the 'new politics' of social work then being in grand, over-ambitious ideals, there is a trend which highlights the importance of a 'micro politics' – small deviant acts of resistance going on at the coalface despite lofty schemes and hegemonic discourses. These micro-politics are, however, useless without any overarching set of ethical principles bound by justice, equality and freedom. One might then ask: is a 'micro politics' sufficient for critical social work? Some think not. As Richard Hugman notes in Chapter 10 on human rights, social work must be conceived broadly. It is not just a choice between micro-level, individually-oriented practice confined to small-scale personal change or macro-level, social structural change. It is about both of these things, sometimes separately and sometimes together. Social work is about how the personal connects to the political.

Reassembling the Left

Throughout this book, various authors touch on the centrality of the current debate referred to as the 'politics of recognition and redistribution'. Most important in developing a model of social justice is the reconstruction of a new political project in terms of integrating redistribution and recognition for social work (Garrett, 2010; Houston, 2008, 2010; Houston & Dolan, 2008; Webb, 2010; see Chapters 3, 4, 8, and 10). In outlining the reasons why discourse analysis is an important dimension of critical social work practice, Marston (Chapter 8) brings to the fore the very significant contributions on the politics of recognition and redistribution from Nancy Fraser and Axel Honneth and its importance in establishing a 'new politics' of social work. Rethinking social justice as a set of discursive functions holds out much promise for the understanding of politics and ideology. Fowler (2009) noted that the key issue in the rich exchange between Fraser and Honneth (2003) central to the redistribution/recognition debate was whether we need to distinguish different forms of social suffering: on the one hand, the denial of recognition for certain social groups who are subjected to exploitation and prejudice and, on the other, the consequences for those affected by the vast disparities of stratified wealth and income.

In rethinking social justice in light of the redistribution/recognition debate, Fraser (1995) notes that modern society comprises two empirically interrelated but analytically distinct orders of stratification: (1) an economic order of distributive relations that generate inequalities of social class; and (2) a cultural order of recognition relations – involving gender, ethnicity, age and sexuality – that generate inequalities of status. She argues that, although analytically distinct, these orders are deeply intertwined:

> Even the most material economic institutions have a constitutive, irreducible cultural dimension that are shot through with significations and norms. Conversely, even the most discursive cultural practices have a constitutive, irreducible political economic dimension that are underpinned by material supports. (Fraser, 1995, p. 72)

Honneth's (2007) reconstruction is a combination of what is most fruitful in Foucault and Habermas. From Foucault he takes the embedded nature of conflictual social life, to be understood at the institutional level, and the ever-presence of power relations at the cultural, symbolic and micro-physical level of bodily dispositions. From Habermas he takes the normative preoccupations with morality and inter-subjective aspects of communication to evaluate the prospects for an emancipatory project (Deranty & Renault, 2007). Honneth (2007) deliberately avoids using the term 'a politics of recognition', justifying his reluctance to discuss the political and his focus on the ethical in his theory. As Deranty and Renault (2007) note: 'The driving intuition of his model is that social progress is based on the normative expectations of individuals, which must be construed as moral claims, rather than as socio-economic interests' (p. 92).

Thus for social work's 'new politics', it is Fraser's theory that holds much promise (see also Chapter 8), especially her notion of 'parity of participation' – a normative principle designed to alleviate the inequalities arising from the class structure, which 'institutionalises economic mechanisms that systematically deny some of its members the means and opportunities they need in order to participate on a par with others in social life' (Fraser & Honneth, 2003, p. 49). According to the 'norm of parity of participation – one must have sufficient equality of power and wealth to ensure that the poor have a voice and the wealthy do not monopolise the means of communication' (Blunden, 2004, n.p.) (see Chapter 12).

In Chapter 12, Tammy Findlay provides a case study of macro-level political engagement, which develops the critical notion of citizen-user involvement by taking the highly political notion of care and using two of Fraser's central conceptual pairings: (1) redistribution and recognition and (2) étatism and contra-étatism to construct what a 'femocratic childcare governance' system might look like. Framing childcare as a citizen 'zone of political engagement', Findlay employs a democratic-feminist argument to analyse the gendered contradictions inherent in two models of childcare governance in Canada: school-based and community-based models. She shows how these models exemplify distinct forms of governance, differing in their institutional configurations, ways of involving childcare workers, parents and community.

A Return to the Political

In outlining a political strategy for social work, Webb (2010) drew attention to Badiou and Žižek's presentation at the *On the Idea of Communism* conference in 2009 (see Chapter 3). These key contemporary thinkers maintained that we cannot create political places outside, or at a distance from, the state. So the issue of political determinism is first a question of the state and only secondarily of capitalism. All critical action must, therefore, move from politics to economics and not the other way around. Webb (2010) notes that, in contemporary times, the power of the state is chiefly a function of the neoliberal economy expressed through the repressive apparatus of governmentality, a central concern for any critical social work (Gray & Webb, 2013).

Moving in this terrain of the political relates to our aspirations for social work to experience what Badiou refers to as a collective political moment of truth that endures and shines forth. Badiou wants a *return to the same*, to equality and an essentialist conception of a shared 'good life'. He contends that conceptions of subjectivity that spring from the various forms of an ethics of the Other – as framed in human rights discourses on diversity and difference – rest on an *a priori* designation of the individual as victim. Against the tide of postmodernism, Gray and Webb (2009) proposed that new politics of a transformative social work will be post-Marxist and not postmodern (Eagleton, 2012, see Chapter 13). Indeed, Webb (2009) has argued the 'petite-postmodernist' proselytisers in social work are more an obstacle to real political change than they are enablers, using the term post-Marxist to rail against the postmodern relativism of discursive difference, identity politics and celebrations of diversity. As Terry Eagleton (1981) insightfully noted, 'postmodernism provides you with all the risks of a radical politics while cancelling the subject who might be summoned to become an agent of them' (p. 485). Gray and Webb (2009) outline Badiou's observations of political history and his claim that the type of emancipatory politics required for the present age is very different from classical revolutionary politics (the worker's movement, mass democracy and class politics dictated by the Party) of previous eras: 'The (19th-century) movement and the (20th-century) party were specific modes of the communist hypothesis; it is no longer possible to return to them' (Badiou, 2008, p. 37).

Badiou recognizes that, in the current era, transformative politics are likely to be subdued during an interval dominated by conservative and neoliberal agendas of high finance. As an economic theory, neoliberalism enshrines capital as the sovereign force in the dominant order. The primary agencies it acknowledges explicitly are property-owning individuals, who are 'free' to engage in a constant and competitive race for improvement, with the market as sole regulator of the quest (van Der Pijl, 2006). Capitalism in its neoliberal guise is entirely growth-dependent. As Harvey (1989) shows, a steady rate of growth is essential for the health of a capitalist economic system, since it is only through growth that profits can be assured and the accumulation of capital sustained. Badiou wants to construct a politics that is not in the 'service of wealth' – one that involves a new relation between political movements and at the level of the ideological. During the present reactionary era, a new radical leftist politics must concentrate on the *struggle for ideas* prefigured in the May 1968 French notion of a 'revolution of mind'. Badiou's (2008) goal is straightforward: 'We need to re-install the communist hypothesis – the proposition that the subordination of labour to the dominant class is not inevitable – within the ideological sphere' (p. 37).

It remains an open question how much today's dominant neoliberal order might be genuinely vulnerable to incursions from a radical political attack. Yet a definition of politics for social work as a collective form, organized by key principles that aim to unleash a series of new possibilities currently repressed by the dominant order, would necessarily have to engage with this question. In this regard, the enemy is acutely visible and ever-present in the perverse expression of calculating reason and the manner in which it is ideologically mobilized in the name of managerialism, racism, scientism, neoliberalism, globalization, advanced capitalism, and so forth (Butler & Drakeford, 2001). Badiou is interested in a revolution in theory and practice, and social work can learn much from his conceptions of truth and politics that turn so strongly against the fashionable tide of postmodern relativism, identity politics and asinine celebrations of diversity (Webb, 2009). As Erik Olin Wright (2012) argues, any transformative politics pitted against existing institutions and social structures has the potential to substantially reduce human suffering and expand the possibilities for human flourishing. He suggests an emancipatory social work faces four broad tasks in undertaking this transformative role: (1) specifying the moral principles for judging social institutions; (2) using these moral principles as the standards for diagnosis and critique of existing institutions; (3) developing an account of viable alternatives in response to the critique; and (4) proposing a theory of transformation for realizing those alternatives. The idea of a new politics is a decisive way of thinking about such alternatives.

Badiou's characterization of the political times in which we live underscores the need for courage, not as an innate quality but as something that practically constructs itself in the face of formidable opposition. The virtue of courage involves understanding our natural and logical fears and the ability to keep the act of overcoming fear – of being courageous – between a lack of political judgement, on the one hand, and excesses of political judgement on the other. In calling for radicals to be courageous during these oppressive times, Badiou (2008) argues that courage 'manifests itself through endurance' (p. 41). His conception of politics rightly affirms the *primacy of commitment* as the basis of a 'new politics'. In solidarity with Badiou, we conclude that for social work, and for the people it serves, nothing less than a revolution of thought will suffice. We hope that this book will contribute to that revolution as we grapple with thinking about what a politics of the past entailed in order to envision what a politics of the future can bring.

References

Althusser, L. (2003). *The humanist controversy and other writings*. London: Verso.

Aronson, J., & Smith, K. (2010). Managing restructured social services: Expanding the social? *British Journal of Social Work, 40*, 530–547.

Badiou, A. (2008). The communist hypothesis. *New Left Review, 37*, 29–42.

Badiou, A. (2012). *The rebirth of history: Times of riots and uprisings*. London: Verso.

Blunden, A. (2004). Nancy Fraser on recognition and redistribution. Retrieved 10 April 2012 from http://home.mira.net/~andy/works/fraser-review.htm.

Butler, I., & Drakeford, M. (2001). Which Blair project? Communitarianism, social authoritarianism and social work. *Journal of Social Work, 1*, 7–19.

Carey, M. (2009). The order of chaos: Exploring agency care managers' construction of social order within fragmented worlds of state social work. *British Journal of Social Work, 39*(3), 556–573.

Carey, M., & Foster, V. (2011). Introducing 'deviant social work': Contextualising the limits of radical social work whilst understanding fragmented resistance within the social work labour process. *British Journal of Social Work, 43*(1), 576–593.

Carniol, B. (2005). *Case critical: Social services & social justice in Canada* (5th edn). Toronto: Between the Lines.

Delanty, G. (2005). *Social science* (2nd edn). Milton Keynes: Open University Press.

Deranty, J.P., & Renault, E. (2007). Politicizing Honneth's ethics of recognition. *Thesis Eleven, 88*, 92–111.

Douzinas, C., & Žižek, S. (eds) (2010). *The idea of communism, vol. 1*. London: Verso.

Eagleton, T. (1981). Marxism and deconstruction. *Contemporary Literature, 22*(4), 477–488.

Eagleton, T. (2012). *Why Marx was right*. New Haven, CT: Yale University Press.

Ferguson, I. (2008). *Reclaiming social work: Challenging neo-liberalism and promoting social justice*. London: Sage.

Ferguson, I., & Lavalette, M. (2004a). Beyond power discourse: Alienation and social work. *British Journal of Social Work, 34*(3), 297–312.

Ferguson, I., & Lavalette, M. (2004b). 'Another world is possible!' Social work and the struggle for social justice. In I. Ferguson, M. Lavalette, & E. Whitmore (eds), *Globalisation, global justice and social work*. London: Routledge.

Ferguson, I., Lavalette, M., & Whitmore, E. (eds) (2004). *Globalisation, global justice and social work*. London: Routledge.

Ferguson, I., & Woodward, R. (2009). *Radical social work in practice: Making a difference*. Bristol: Policy Press.

Fook, J. (2002). *Social work: Critical theory and practice*. London: Sage.

Fook, J., & Gardner, F. (2007). *Practising critical reflection: A resource handbook*. Maidenhead, Berkshire: Open University Press.

Fowler, B. (2009). The recognition/redistribution debate and Bourdieu's theory of practice. *Theory, Culture and Society, 26*(1), 144–156.

Fraser, N. (1995). From redistribution to recognition? Dilemmas of justice in a 'post-socialist' age. *New Left Review, 212*, 68–93.

Fraser, N., & Honneth, A. (2003). *Redistribution or recognition? A political-philosophical exchange*. London: Verso.

Garrett, P.M. (2010). Recognising the limitations of the political theory of recognition: Axel Honneth, Nancy Fraser and social work. *British Journal of Social Work, 40,* 1517–1533.

Gray, M. (2010). Social development and the status quo: Professionalisation and Third Way cooptation. *International Journal of Social Welfare, 19*(4), 463–470.

Gray, M., Coates, J., & Hetherington, T. (eds) (2013). *Environmental social work.* London: Routledge.

Gray, M., Stepney, P., & Webb, S.A. (2012). Critical social work. In P. Stepney & D. Ford (eds), *Social work models, methods and theories: A framework for practice* (2nd edn). Lyme Regis: Russell House Publishing. 255–269.

Gray, M., & Webb, S.A. (2009). The return of the political in social work. *International Journal of Social Welfare, 18*(1), 111–115.

Gray, M., & Webb, S.A. (eds) (2013). *Social work theories and methods* (2nd edn). London: Sage.

Harman, G. (2005). Some preconditions of universal philosophical dialogue. *Dialogue and Universalism, 1–2,* 164–180.

Harris, J. (2003). *The social work business.* London: Routledge.

Harvey, D. (1989). *The condition of postmodernity: An enquiry into the origins of cultural change.* Oxford: Blackwell.

Harvey, D. (2011). *The enigma of capital and the crises of capitalism* (2nd edn). Oxford: Oxford University Press.

Honneth, A. (2007). *The struggle for recognition: The moral grammar of social conflicts.* London: Polity Press.

Houston, S. (2008). Transcending ethno-religious identities in Northern Ireland: Social work's role in the struggle for recognition. *Australian Social Work, 61*(1), 25–41.

Houston, S. (2010). Beyond homo economicus: Recognition, self-realization and social work. *British Journal of Social Work, 40,* 841–857.

Houston, S., & Dolan, P. (2008). Conceptualising child and family support: The contribution of Honneth's critical theory of recognition. *Children and Society, 22*(6), 458–469.

Howe, D, (2009). *A brief introduction to social work theory.* Basingstoke: Palgrave Macmillan.

Ife, J. (1997). *Rethinking social work: Towards critical practice.* Melbourne: Longman.

Ife, J. (2001). *Human rights and social work: Towards rights-based practice.* Cambridge: Cambridge University Press.

Invisible Committee, The (2008). *The coming insurrection.* London: Semiotexte.

Kemshall, H. (2010). Risk rationalities in contemporary social work policy and practice. *British Journal of Social Work, 40*(4), 1247–1262.

Laclau, E., & Mouffe, C. (2001). *Hegemony and socialist strategy: Towards a radical democratic politics* (2nd edn). London: Verso.

Lingis, A. (2007). *The first person singular.* Chicago: Northwestern University Press.

Lipsky, M. (1983). *Street-level bureaucracy: Dilemmas of the individual in public services.* New York: Russell Sage Foundation.

Marston, G., & McDonald, C. (2012). Getting beyond 'heroic agency' in conceptualising social workers as policy actors in the twenty-first century. *British Journal of Social Work, 42*(6), 1022–1038.

McLaughlin, K. (2005). From ridicule to institutionalization: Anti-oppression, the state and social work. *Critical Social Policy, 25*(3), 283–305.

Mendes, P. (2010). Retrenching or renovating the Australian welfare state: The paradox of the Howard government's neo-liberalism. *International Journal of Social Welfare, 18*(1), 102–110.

Noys, B. (ed.) (2011). *Communization and its discontents: Contestation, critique, and contemporary struggles.* Retrieved 10 January 2013 from http://www.minor compositions.info/wp-content/uploads/2011/11/CommunizationDiscontents-web.pdf.

Pearson, G. (1975). *The deviant imagination: Psychiatry, social work and social change.* London: Macmillan.

Rossiter, A. (2000). The professional is political: An interpretation of the problem of the past in solution-focused therapy. *American Journal of Orthopsychiatry, 70*(2), 150–161.

Schram, S. (2012). Welfare professionals and street-level bureaucracy. In M. Gray, J. Midgley, & S.A. Webb (eds), *Sage Handbook of Social Work.* London: Sage. 67–80.

Smith, R. (2012). Castells, power and social work. *British Journal of Social Work, 42*(2), 283–299.

Standing, G. (2011). *The precariat: The new dangerous class.* New York: Bloomsbury Academic.

van Der Pijl, K, (2006). A Lockean Europe. *New Left Review, 37,* 9–38.

Webb, S.A. (2009). Against difference and diversity in social work: The case of human rights. *International Journal of Social Welfare, 18,* 307–316.

Webb, S.A. (2010). (Re)Assembling the Left: The politics of redistribution and recognition in social work. *British Journal of Social Work, 40*(8), 2364–2379.

Wright, E.O. (2012). Transforming capitalism through real utopias. *American Sociological Review,* Published online before print 26 December 2012. doi:10.1177/0003122412468882.

Žižek, S. (1999). Carl Schmitt in the age of post-politics. In C. Mouffe (ed.), *The challenge of Carl Schmitt.* London: Verso. 18–37.

2

A History of Critical and Radical Social Work

Bob Pease

Many books on radical and critical social work begin with a historical account of progressive practice in the early settlement movement of the Victorian era. Most, however, focus on the 1970s and early 1980s, when radical social work was at the forefront of debates on the future of the profession and its place in modern society. Contemporary forms of critical social work face challenges reminiscent of these earlier debates, with ongoing concerns about the applicability of social change theories for direct practice in social work. This chapter offers a thematic engagement with the origins of critical social work rather than a strict historically linear account of its development, for which there are already many published works available in North America (Reisch & Andrews, 2001), the UK (Lavalette, 2011; McLaughlin, 2008) and Australia (McDonald, 2007; Mendes, 2009; Pease, 2009a).

Critics have raised questions about whether critical social work can function at all within the institutional context of the capitalist state: to what extent does translating critical approaches to social work into the mainstream dilute and fragment their radical potential? How much should social work focus on community development and collectivist-based activism as opposed to working with individuals and families? Is radical social work compatible with professionalism, or not? How might the contradictions between constructivist and normative approaches to knowledge in critical social work be addressed? Those who challenge critical social workers' political activism in the twenty-first century echo the critics of radical social work in the 1970s who argued that political action had no place in professional social work practice (Lavalette, 2011). Linking structural and sociocultural analyses to the lived experiences of individuals has been a historical tension that has plagued social work since its inception. In the 1970s, class

21

analysis was critiqued for subsuming gender, race and sexuality issues. Forty years later, in response to intersectional approaches to oppression, there are calls to restore primacy to analyses of structural class-based forms of oppression (see Chapter 9).

Lavalette (2011) argues that social workers today are more confident in responding to these issues than they were in the 1970s. This chapter explores the attempts to move beyond these historical debates in the context of new challenges posed by neoliberalism, globalization and the politics of redistribution and recognition. It asks whether a framework for critical social work in the twenty-first century, capable of addressing the limitations of these debates of the past, can be constructed.

Reflections on the Marxist Heritage of Critical Social Work

The main theoretical influences on radical social work in the 1970s were Marxism and neo-Marxism. Drawing on writers such as Antonio Gramsci, Louis Althusser and Nicos Poulantzas, the focus was on the class-based nature of capitalist society and social work's controlling functions within the capitalist state (Lavalette, 2011; McLaughlin, 2008). McLaughlin (2008) traces the debates of that period between the structuralist Marxists, who were pessimistic about progressive change within the state, through to the reformists, who defended progressive welfare reforms and working within rather than against the state. Much of this debate centred on the state's potential to bring about progressive change. There were also challenges to Marxism by feminist, anti-racist and radical therapy movements (Lavalette, 2011; Weinstein, 2011). Influential texts at this time included, in chronological order, Bailey and Brake (1975), Corrigan and Leonard (1978), Galper (1975), Pritchard and Taylor (1978) and Galper (1980).

While it has only ever had a minority presence in social work generally, a number of commentators have acknowledged the progressive impact of radical social work on social work today. Clearly, one of its progressive legacies is its attention to critical social theory in understanding the issues that social workers have to deal with (Williams, 2011) and the significance of social context in influencing human behaviour (Mendes, 2009). Its structural analyses of the problems facing citizen users has influenced mainstream theories and models of practice and shaped the development of empowerment-focused, anti-oppressive and anti-discriminatory approaches in the UK (Jones, 2011; Lavalette & Ferguson, 2007; Thompson, 2010; Weinstein, 2011). Ferguson and Woodward (2009) argue convincingly that these developments would not have been possible without the radical structural analyses of Marxist social work in the 1970s.

To what extent, then, have radical and conventional forms of social work converged? Is radical practice now just a feature of mainstream practice? McDonald (2007) believes so, arguing that more recently, critical social work practice guidelines are no different from 'good practice' in mainstream professional social work. Many aspects of radical social work, including its emphasis on empowerment, human rights and social justice, have become integrated into the language, if not the practice of mainstream social work (Langan, 2002). In Australia, ecological systems theory and the 'multi-dimensional approach', which acknowledge the 'bio-psycho-social-spiritual' dimensions of a person's life, have incorporated elements of the strengths perspective, empowerment approach, narrative therapy and solution-focused practice (Harms, 2007). Wood and Tully (2006) regard these approaches as consistent with their structural approach, and Ferguson (2008) sees them as consistent with his notion of critical best practice (see Chapter 7).

However, radical critiques of these approaches have not been addressed adequately by writers promoting their progressive use. For example, Margolin (1997) argues that, while social work espouses an understanding of structural causes of social problems, it continues to focus on interventions with individuals. Baines (2007) says empowerment, as a form of social justice-oriented practice, was appropriated and reshaped as individual self-promotion and co-opted into the neoliberal agenda of self-interested citizens. Gray (2011) makes a similar observation about the strengths perspective. Consequently, discourses of empowerment, strengths and social justice serve to legitimize normative mainstream approaches, while providing a radical veneer to conservative practice. Important as these developments are, the emergence of anti-oppressive and anti-discriminatory practice has failed to do justice to this radical heritage (Williams, 2011) and focuses more on changing the language, behaviour and attitudes of individuals than the material conditions of their lives (Ferguson & Woodward, 2009). Reisch (2005) argues that empowerment and strength-based approaches to social work do not constitute forms of radical practice, because whatever progressive meanings they once might have had have been assimilated in the contemporary neoliberal environment. As Simpkin (1983) noted, bringing critical approaches into mainstream social work runs the risk of diluting and fragmenting their radical potential. To what extent has this occurred?

The Shifting Language of Politically Progressive Social Work

The terminology used to describe politically progressive forms of social work practice has varying meanings within different national borders (Pease, 2009b). While critical and structural social work were most commonly used in North America and Australia from the 1980s onwards, they meant different things. Structural social work in the USA (Middleman & Goldberg, 1974; Middleman & Goldberg Wood, 1993; Wood & Tully, 2006) was different to that in Canada, which was more explicitly informed by critical social theory (Moreau, 1979; Mullaly, 2007). Structurally grounded critical social work in Australia (Allan, Briskman, & Pease, 2009; Allan, Pease, & Briskman, 2003), too, was not synonymous with forms of critical practice in the UK based on critical reflection (Adams, Dominelli, & Payne, 2009).

More recently, Gray and Webb (2013) highlighted these distinctions in their idea of broad and narrow meanings of critical social work. In its broad meaning, 'critical social work' is concerned with particular models of practice, including critical best practice, critical constructive approach, strength-based approaches, advocacy and empowerment. Its narrow definition as 'Critical social work' refers to the range of progressive agendas informing critical social work, including Marxism, feminism, critical social theory and anti-racism. The inclination here is to invert this approach and to refer to the broad definition as an umbrella term for encompassing a variety of different progressive approaches – in the sense that Mullaly (2007) uses the term – and a narrow definition to designate particular conceptual frameworks for Critical social work practice, such as those advocated by Healy (2000) and Fook (2002).

Iain Ferguson (2008) says that the main distinction between critical and radical social work is that the former incorporates postmodern theories, and the latter, Marxist approaches. Payne (2005) similarly argues that critical social work departed significantly from radical social work when it embraced the postmodern agenda. Dalrymple and Burke (2006), however, note the influence of both postmodernist and modernist approaches on critical social work. Likewise Allan (2009) believes models of social justice-informed practice endeavour to move beyond the limitations of postmodernist and modernist approaches on their own. Allan et al. (2003, 2009) avoided the adoption of a particular model of critical social work and encouraged contributors to explore a wide range of critical theory-informed approaches.

These distinctions aside, Coleman (2011) believes radical social work has now become widely respectable within social work, while Wagner (2009) observes that self-defined radical social workers are rarely concerned with revolutionary change but use the radical agenda to denote support for liberal and progressive politics. For Wagner (2009), radical social work is a form of conceit since it fails to recognize the structural constraints on practice or the 'class elitism' that informs their thinking. The terms critical and radical social work are often used interchangeably because, in contrast to what Payne (2005) and Iain Ferguson (2008) suggest, a change in language does not necessarily signify a departure from structuralist Marxist-informed approaches.

Revisiting the Postmodern–Marxist Divide: Working the Contradictions

From the beginning, postmodern ideas were controversial in critical social work since they could be used to: (1) support conservative policies and practices (I. Ferguson, 2008; Ife, 1997; Lundy, 2004; McBeath & Webb, 1991); (2) obscure the material reality of oppression (Mullaly, 2007) and undermine the commitment to social justice and human rights by rejecting metanarratives (Ife, 1997). Iain Ferguson (2008) criticizes postmodernism for its anti-realism and moral relativism, but Healy (2000) and Fook (2002) believe it is possible to develop a 'critical postmodernism' that avoids the critique of relativism. Lundy (2004) comments that, if all accounts were equal, as post-modernists suggest they are, then reactionary theories and views would also have to be validated. Leonard (1997) maintains that postmodernism has no critical intellectual base on its own and has to be linked to Marxism and feminism to be able to offer anything worthwhile to an emancipatory project.

Webb (2010), however, argues that all postmodern approaches are inconsistent with emancipatory models of social work concerned with social justice. Ferguson and Lavalette (1999) also challenge the view that postmodern themes can be incorporated with Marxist perspectives to develop an emancipatory social work. In their view, postmodernism, in any of its forms, has nothing to offer critical social work practice because of its rejection of universalist and materialist perspectives on exploitation that lead to a shift away from structurally determined oppression towards free-flowing diverse identities. McBeath and Webb (2005) also maintain that postmodern ideas in critical social work do not live up to their claimed radical potential, and critical social work has been weakened by its engagement with Foucault and postmodern ideas. Gray and Webb (2013) further argue that Foucault and Marxism do not sit comfortably together because they are based on incompatible theoretical traditions.

Attempts by Fook (2002), Morley (2004) and Stepney (2006), among others, who advocate combining a structural analysis with critical postmodernism in framing a critical social work practice, can be criticized for failing to address conceptual inconsistencies and epistemological contradictions. However, this does not mean that all attempts to use Marxist and Foucauldian ideas are fraught. The key issue is whether critical theory is subordinated under postmodernism, or vice versa. The latter is argued here in the form of a postmodern critical theory (Pease, 2002), as distinct from the critical postmodernism advocated by Healy (2000), Fook (2002) and Morley (2004).

Numerous writers have demonstrated the usefulness of Foucault in articulating a radical and progressive vision of social work practice (Chambon,

Irving, & Epstein, 1999; Gilbert & Powell, 2010; Irving, 2009; Margolin, 1997). These writers cannot be dismissed simply as accepting postmodernism uncritically as some structuralist writers suggest (I. Ferguson, 2008; Webb, 2009). They demonstrate the ways in which dominant discourses and regimes of power/knowledge provide insight into relations at the micro level of practice.

Marxist and neo-Marxist analyses continue to be useful for understanding the impact of economic managerialism and neoliberalism on social work. Although, in the past, Marxist frameworks have been criticized for oversimplifying complex social phenomena and multiple systems of oppression into matters solely concerned with class and the economy, it is also true that some post-Marxist, queer, feminist and poststructural approaches ignore class altogether (Grosz, 1994; Parton & O'Byrne, 2000; Witkin & Saleebey, 2007). Marxism has important contributions to make to the resurgence of critical social work, and this does not have to be at the expense of other critical forms of knowledge. The real value of Marxism in the contemporary context might have less to do with resurrecting Marx's historical materialism and more to do with the richness of the postulates of Marxism as a method of diagnosis and strategy of intervention. This involves focusing on historical specificity and empirical investigations of concrete circumstances of oppression (Hunt, 2004). Thus, Marxist-informed questions about the way in which class and economic relations might be impacting on social and political outcomes are more useful than *a priori* assumptions about the primacy of class-based determinacy. Such an approach leaves open the possibility that, in specific historical contexts, a variety of forms of social relations might also be significant.

Most new developments – whether conceptual or programmatic – have gains and losses (Price & Simpson, 2007), and social work has contradictory functions, some of which are progressive and others which are regressive (Lavalette & Ioakimidis, 2011). Social workers are faced with the contradiction of being commissioned to work with individuals who are oppressed, while at the same time being employed by the state to regulate these very same people, which often compounds their oppression (Nichols & Cooper, 2011). While it is not uncommon to regard social work as being at the apex of contradictions, it is less common, however, to understand this conflict in terms of Marxist sociology. Price and Simpson (2007) argue that, as social workers are constantly dealing with tensions and contradictions, many of which reflect the wider society in which social work is located, Marxism is useful in understanding the basis of these social forces and providing a powerful methodological tool to analyse these contradictions as dynamic. Such an analysis also provides guidance about how to intervene to bring about progressive change (Pease, 1991).

Critical Social Work at the Micro Level of Direct Practice

How do the strategies associated with structural change relate to the immediate needs of citizen service users with whom social workers engage in their day-to-day practice? To what extent can the progressive agendas of critical theorists be related to the daily experiences of social workers? A number of social work writers have raised concerns about the applicability of social-change agendas and critical social work strategies for direct practice (Healy, 2005; Hick & Pozzuto, 2005; Payne, 2005). With its emphasis on collective social action over the immediate needs of individual service users and focus on structural transformation while ignoring the emotional distress of individuals (Mendes, 2010), radical social work is likely to be dismissed by some as being too far removed from the realities of front-line practice. Harry Ferguson (2008) has introduced the notion of 'critical best practice' because, in his view, radical social work has not moved beyond the level of critique (see Chapter 7).

Critical sociological analyses focused on the oppressive material conditions of people's lives – the structural dimension – run the risk of ignoring their direct, individual experiences of and responses to these conditions – the psychological dimension. While some forms of radical social work rejected individual casework, since the 1970s many have drawn upon radical and critical psychologies to engage in progressive forms of counselling and support (Dowrick, 1983; Frost, 2008; Lundy, 2004; Moreau, 1979; Pease, 2003). Clearly, some are concerned that any acknowledgement of the subjective – personal – experiences of oppressed people might lead to the privileging of the psychological over the structural dimension (Frost, 2008). However, some critical psychological approaches, such as feminist and radical therapies (Burstow, 1992; Kearney, 1996; Parker, 2007; Proctor et al., 2006), can sit comfortably alongside structural social work.

Social work has always defined its focus as being the individual within a social context. However, linking structural and sociocultural analyses to the lived experiences of individuals has been challenging and has plagued social work since its inception. Some critics have charged social work with focusing on individuals in isolation from the wider social context of their lives (Price & Simpson, 2007). The struggle has been how to address the individual without succumbing to the pathology of liberal individualism (Nichols & Cooper, 2011). Has social work been able to move beyond individualistic approaches to practice? A tension is evident when social work courses teach critical approaches to social policy and community development, while at the same time relying uncritically upon cognitive-behavioural and psychodynamic psychologies to inform work with individuals and families. This split between radical social policy and community development and normative individual and family work has been a constant tension within social work education.

Some politically progressive social work educators have defended behavioural and psychodynamic therapies as consistent with a social justice approach (Wakefield, 2005). Similarly, some regard strength-based, solution-focused and ecological models as consistent with critical social work (Costello, 2009; H. Ferguson, 2008; Wood & Tully, 2006). But, if social work with individuals is to be consistent with critical theory and its focus on the socially constituted and relational subjectivity of the individual, it needs to overcome its reliance upon liberal individualism (Allen, 2007; Nichols & Cooper, 2011). Minimally, social workers can avoid pathologizing service users and holding them responsible for problems shaped by structural and material conditions.

One of the key contributions of radical social work in the 1970s and 1980s was to challenge the pathologizing of individuals through redefining individual problems as social and political problems – personal problems as public issues. This meant critiquing the various forms of personality theory used by social workers at the time in direct interventions. Langan (2011) argues that, if we were to revive the radical tradition, we would need to challenge the construction of the autonomous subject in contemporary social work. This would mean critiquing the rise of positive psychology and perspectives on the individual that continue to ignore the determining function of social and economic structures.

Critical social work thus needs to address subjectivity head-on (see Webb, 2013). Almost thirty years ago, in *Personality and Ideology*, Leonard (1984) made a valuable contribution to understanding the individual within radical social work. He saw the disjuncture between social work's understandings of the social order and of the individual as one of the major barriers to a critical social work practice with individuals and families. Thirteen years later, he argued that a critical social work practice had to be informed by a critical psychology that had yet to be fully developed (Leonard, 1997). Leonard's work has been extended by attempts within the critical tradition to theorize the relationship between self and society with a particular emphasis on challenging oppression and domination (Pease, 2003).

More recently, Frost and Hoggett (2008) talked about the need for a post-liberal conception of subjectivity. A liberal subject is premised upon individual autonomy, agency and rationality, whereas a post-liberal subject emphasizes relationality. Put differently, we are social beings. Drawing upon Bourdieu's concept of social suffering, they emphasize the importance of focusing on people's subjective – personal – experience of oppression, poverty and domination. In their view, it is important to address the psychic effects of social injustice. If critical social work were to have a future, it would need to provide guidance on how to address the suffering of individuals in the context of political processes at the societal level (Beresford, 2011).

Redistribution and Recognition in Critical Social Work

A number of writers have identified the usefulness of the recent redistribution/recognition debates of Fraser and Honneth (2003) to progressive forms of social work practice (Garrett, 2010; Gray & Boddy, 2010; Houston, 2008, 2010; Houston & Dolan, 2008; McDonald & Merrill, 2002; Webb, 2009, 2010). One of the key points of disagreement between Fraser and Honneth (2003) is in relation to whether or not the injustices associated with misrecognition are primarily psychological. Fraser (in Fraser & Honneth, 2003) prefers to talk about the wounds of misrecognition as a form of status inequality, i.e. they result in people being treated unequally.

From Fraser we learn that a social justice-informed approach to social work must acknowledge both cultural and economic influences and address economic and cultural injustices. This means challenging inequality and injustice. From Honneth we learn that a social justice-informed approach must address issues of diversity and difference – and all forms of discriminatory 'misrecognition'. But Webb (2009) believes struggles for recognition – acceptance of diversity and difference – undermine struggles for equality – sameness. In his view, struggles for external recognition do not constitute a progressive form of politics, and postmodern ideas about diversity and difference are not helpful in responding to this dual focus (Webb, 2010). Garrett (2010) also believes that the politics of recognition gives too much attention to the experience of suffering under misrecognition, and diverts attention away from those engaged in the processes of misrecognition – those supporting discriminatory practices. It seems that, for Webb (2010) and Garrett (2010), too much emphasis is given in postmodern approaches to cultural recognition and affirmations of difference.

Essentially, this is a debate about the source of injustice and inequality, whether it accrues from people's cultural and group identity or from their material and social conditions. Are people poor because they belong to a minority group or because they lack access to essential social and economic resources? Clearly, both issues are important because minority groups in society tend to bear the brunt of discrimination, and poor people are unequal because they lack access to resources. The essential question is how much attention should be given to cultural difference and individual and group identity in the context of material inequalities. For some Marxists, any attention to culture and difference is too much (Webb, 2009, 2010).

Again, this comes back to the historical debate about the value of cultural struggles over identity versus economic struggles over the distribution of resources. This is reminiscent of debates in the 1970s between critical theorists concerned about consciousness and ideology and structuralist Marxists focused on changing material conditions. If critical social work were to move forward, it would have to avoid dichotomizing these positions and establish an integrated model of social justice.

The Changing Political Context of Critical Social Work: The State and Neoliberalism

Social work in many contexts is conducted primarily within state-based agencies charged with maintaining social order. However, the contemporary sociopolitical environment in which social work operates has changed dramatically in many Western countries since the 1970s and 1980s. Managerialism and market-driven forces have transformed the labour process in social work, especially in the UK and Australia (Lavalette, 2011), eroded the one-on-one time that social workers spend with service users (Weinstein, 2011), and imposed huge constraints on the possibilities for radical practice in the state sector (Ferguson & Woodward, 2009). In this tighter regulatory framework, the social work role has been transformed into one of resource management and risk assessment (Stepney, 2006). While the contradictions between social work's anti-oppressive and control functions is nothing new (Dalrymple & Burke, 2006), the problematization of institutions of the state in much contemporary social work writing is a new concern for Ferguson and Lavalette (1999). Many social work writers in Australia and the UK now question whether social workers can engage in critical social work at all within statutory agencies (Beresford, 2011; Ferguson & Woodward, 2009; McDonald, 2007).

The notion of 'room to move' within state-employing organizations implied an expectation that radical social workers in the 1970s would bring critical analyses to bear on the problems facing service users. This latitude has been curtailed in the neoliberal context of greater regulation and control of social workers discussed above. Just as some radical critics in the 1970s argued, Wagner (2009) believes social workers cannot break out of the constraints imposed on their practice within the state to enact any form of significant social change. So while they might have radical analyses in their heads, their doing of individual work with service users cannot lead to any form of radical practice. McDonald (2007) also argues that there are no longer spaces within the state for any forms of critical or radical practice (see the discussion about deviant social work and street-level bureaucracy in Chapter 1 as a counter-argument).

Statutory social work has always posed a challenge to critical social practice. Millar (2008) notes the contradiction between conceptions of anti-oppressive practice in the UK, which emphasize the importance of addressing structural issues, and the failure to identify the structural constraints imposed by the state in developing anti-oppressive interventions. In the UK, McLaughlin (2005) observes that anti-oppressive social work practice has been coopted by the state as the now benign welfare provider.

The control exerted by the state must be recognized but, at the same time, notwithstanding the constraints imposed on social workers, there remain some spaces for resistance and engagement that do not simply reproduce the state's power. What is most important here is that social workers reject the notion of the state and the welfare apparatus within it – now extended into society through privatization – as neutral or benign. It is essential that critical social work education develop analyses to interrogate the power of the state and its extension into the community and develop strategies to enable social workers to find spaces in which to challenge that power. Otherwise, it will be subjected to critique for its lack of reflexivity in analysing the context in which it is being practised (see Chapter 5).

The debate in the 1980s about the limitations and potential to work within and against the state (London to Edinburgh Weekend Return Group, 1980) has been neglected in recent years. There was general agreement among radical social workers that the state was a source of oppression, but disagreement about the potential to develop radical practices within it. One of the important legacies of the Marxist approach was the capacity to think dialectically and to develop practices that worked with the contradictions within the state and social work itself (Corrigan & Leonard, 1978). These understandings need to be adapted to the changing context of the neoliberal state, community organizations and social work.

The rise of neoliberalism around the world in the 1990s and the twenty-first century is one of the major changes penetrating and transforming social work (Ferguson & Woodward, 2009; Wallace & Pease, 2011). With its emphasis on free-market economics, the privatization of government services, free trade, user-pays services and new public management, neoliberalism has had a significant impact on human service provision. State welfare services have been restructured to allow for greater privatization, consumer choice, small government, big society, market values and individualism (Jordan, 2010).

Neoliberalism has created significant obstacles for critical social work practice in the twenty-first century. Neoliberal ideas have penetrated the psyche of social workers, often unconsciously, since one of the ways in which it works is by playing on the notion of choice, especially the idea that consumers want and must be able to choose from a range of service options

(Davies, Gottsche, & Bansel, 2006). To develop a critical practice, social workers would need to engage in a systematic struggle against neoliberalism and the increasing gap between the rich and poor developing under its watch. Social work education, too, has not escaped the liberal onslaught towards narrow technicist competency-based models focusing on efficiency and outcomes, which although pre-dating neoliberalism (Gambrill, 1983), gained a new ascendancy at this time. Singh and Cowden (2009) argue that social work educators' failure to challenge anti-intellectualism has allowed neoliberalism to gain a hold. Part of the process of challenging neoliberalism is the development of critical theoretical frameworks that sensitize social workers to the impact of neoliberal ideas on their own thinking about and education for practice.

Moving beyond Evidence-based Practice and Professional Elitism

McDonald (2007) has argued that the rise of evidence-based practice indicated a move away from critical and radical social work. The socially constructed nature of knowledge – articulated in the social sciences – is favoured in social work (Fraser et al., 1991; Gottschalk & Witkin, 1991; Kondrat, 1992; Peile, 1988). While social workers have long resisted positivism, science and rationality, some have embraced scientific and evidence-based practice (Gray, Plath, & Webb, 2009; Trinder, 2000). The debates over what constitutes evidence are located in wider divisions between objectivists (positivists) and subjectivists (interpretivists or social constructionists) about the nature of human behaviour and social reality. Social constructivists and postmodernists have emphasized the importance of seeing science and knowledge as socially constructed. However, from a critical social work perspective, if there were no objective reality, how could social workers develop the foundations for emancipatory projects?

Evidence-based practice has been subjected to significant criticisms by critical social work writers (McDonald, 2006; Trinder, 2000; Webb, 2001; Witkin, 1996). However, its critics often fail to develop alternatives or emphasize qualitative, interpretivist and critically reflective approaches as the way forward (Avis, 2006; Feltman, 2005; Plath, 2006). Critical social work is based on an alternative philosophy of science paradigm which challenges the epistemological privileging of positivism or objectivism and the primacy of empirical facts (Houston, 2001; Pease 2009b). It is proposed here that critical social workers develop the foundation for 'critical knowledge-informed practice' to encompass radical sociological thought, ethnographic qualitative research, tacit knowledge, critically reflective practice, parity of participation and citizen-based knowledge. Social workers must challenge the interests served by epistemological empire building, such as that of evidence-based practice, which is the form of science most suited to reproducing capitalism. Only a valuing of knowledge from diverse sources, driven by a commitment to social transformation, would enable social work to fulfil its emancipatory objectives (Pease, 2009b).

The expansion of evidence-based social work restricts social workers to forms of research valued in terms of the linear hierarchy of facts and, by implication, constrains them from exploring alternative forms of knowledge generation (Ferguson & Woodward, 2009; Pease, 2009b). At the same time, it promotes a new form of professionalism in social work 'from authority to accountability' (Gambrill, 1999, 2001; Sommerfeld & Herzog, 2005) that Reisch (2005) believes has suppressed radical and critical forms of social work practice. Evidence-based practice naively attempts to brand itself as politically neutral.

Ferguson and Woodward (2009) believe that social work is worth fighting for, but do not interrogate whether the contemporary form of professionalism within social work is worth defending, or whether the tolerant, liberally compliant professional social worker can cohere with a militant political stance of radical social work. The debate over professionalism in social work, which began with Flexner's famous address in 1915 and, according to Reisch (2005), continued in the 1970s, when many social workers argued professionalism was incompatible with radical social work practice, needs to be revisited in the twenty-first century. From a radical social work perspective, the status inequality between professionals and service users perpetuates oppression. Joyce, Corrigan and Hayes (1988) report that radical social workers advocated unionization as an alternative to professionalization because they saw social workers as members of the new working class. However, others, like Specht and Courtney (1994), maintained that radical forms of practice were consistent with professionalism.

In their account of the history of radical social work in the USA, Reisch and Andrews (2001) questioned whether social work had ever been – or could ever be – a radical profession. Many of the critics of radical social work in the 1970s argued that political action had no place in professional social work practice (Brewer & Lait, 1980; Halmos, 1978). Others saw political action as an ethical imperative (Bailey & Brake, 1975; Galper, 1975, 1980), but some saw the organizational bias of social work – with a code of ethics emphasizing loyalty to the employing organization – as a limit on radical practice (Margolin, 1997). If radical and critical practice conflicts with professionalism, then it can only be realized fully outside of professional roles and organizations. Thus, it is necessary to address some forms of critical engagement for social transformation within the limitations and potential of professional social work.

Rethinking Oppression in Critical Social Work

The analysis of multiple oppressions in critical and anti-oppressive practice has its forerunner in the early formulations of structural social work in Canada, an approach which arose as a result of the dominance of class analysis. Moreau (1979) challenged the hierarchy of oppressions – class, gender and race – arguing that all forms of oppression were equal and none should be given primacy. However, with the rise of anti-oppressive and anti-discriminatory practice, which brought race, gender, sexuality, disability and age to the fore, class was often ignored. While anti-oppressive social work increased awareness of multiple forms of oppression, the focus on identity and difference has been critiqued for failing to acknowledge the continuing importance of class (Ferguson, 2011). To the extent that class is recognized as a factor in oppression, the focus tends to be on classism as a form of prejudice rather than class embodied in the structure of unequal capitalist social relations (Ferguson & Woodward, 2009).

Marxists reject the intersectional approach, which holds that compound forms of oppression intersect to cause disadvantage, because they see class as the central cause of all forms of oppression (I. Ferguson, 2008; Lavalette & Mooney, 2000; Thompson, 2009). De Montigny (2011) argues that the concept of oppression itself fails to do justice to social relations, noting that the radical social workers of the 1970s did not focus on oppression as such, but on transforming social relations. The problem with the concept of oppression, he argues, is that it comes to be understood as forms of discrimination, such as racism, sexism, heterosexism and classism, which are merely some of the effects of social relations. Ferguson and Lavalette (1999), for example, take issue with the analysis that locates class as being no more significant than other forms of oppression, and they challenge the view that all oppressions are equal. They believe the power within capitalist societies is distinctly different from the kind of power behind working-class men who abuse women or able-bodied people who abuse disabled people. The key issue, however, is whether analyses of gender, race, sexuality and disability should be subsumed under class analysis, as some Marxists have argued.

One debate is about the extent to which oppression is systematic and structural as opposed to interpersonal. Ferguson and Lavalette (1999) maintain that the implication that we all oppress one another in different ways ignores oppressive structures and the state as sources of oppression. Are some forms of oppression based simply on interpersonal prejudice? For example, some have argued that age and disability discrimination are not structural and hence are less important than class and race (Ferguson & Woodward, 2009). Such distinctions generate heated debates because they sometimes demote these forms of oppression as being less significant. In challenging the notion of a hierarchy of oppressions, specific groups are concerned that their experiences and analyses of oppression would not get adequate recognition. Furthermore, many marginalized groups are concerned that their oppression would be ignored completely in the multiple oppressions model (Barnoff & Moffatt 2007). Anti-racist theorists, for example, challenge the intersectional approach for diluting the concept of race (Walter Taylor, & Habibis, 2011). Thus, some Marxists, radical feminists and anti-race theorists argue that the hierarchy of oppressions model should be retained (Carastathis, 2008; I. Ferguson 2008; Williams, 1999). They merely disagree on whether the primary cause of all oppressions is class, gender or race.

Fellows and Razack (1998) talk about the 'race to innocence' in which particular oppressed groups emphasize their oppressed status and refuse to recognize their privilege in relation to other oppressed groups. The challenge is to be able to recognize the specific experiences of particular forms of oppression without giving primacy to their particularity. An intersectional approach to oppression does not need to maintain that all oppressions are equal in every context. Furthermore, the specific dynamics of particular forms of oppression do not need to be denied in an intersectional model. Some forms of oppression are likely to be more significant for some groups in particular times and circumstances (Barnoff & Moffatt, 2007). While many advocates of intersectional analyses argue that primacy should not be given to any one system of domination, the reality is that some systems of domination, such as capitalism, are more politically significant than others. Perry's (2001) analysis of how the interlocking systems of domination interact within specific contexts provides useful insights into the impact of different forms of domination, oppression and injustice.

Addressing Privilege and Situating Ourselves

More attention is given in critical social work to the processes that reproduce oppression than those that perpetuate dominance. Thus, the struggle for social justice is often conceived in terms of empowering service users who may be oppressed by class, race, gender and sexuality. Little attention is given to the ways in which the positioning of the professional worker may embody class, race, gender and sexual privilege. Social workers thus need to be aware of how their personal power and privilege is maintained or challenged in their encounters with service users and other workers (Rossiter, 2000).

A number of writers have drawn attention to the need for critical social work to address privilege as the flipside of oppression (Barnoff & Moffatt, 2007; Carniol, 2005; Pease, 2006, 2010). Carniol (2005) discusses the importance of social workers analysing their social location as a precursor to analysing that of others. He emphasizes the importance of social workers using their critical consciousness to deepen their awareness of their own privilege as well as their oppressive circumstances. Such awareness is an important first step if social workers are to become involved in undoing those privileges.

In recent years, whiteness as a concept has been introduced into critical social work (Jeyasingham, 2011; Nyland, 2006; Walter et al., 2011; Young, 2004). McDonald (2007), for example, challenges the colonialism and whiteness of the professional project in social work. Drawing upon Ife (2001) and Briskman (2003), she challenges the assumed superiority of colonialist practice and advocates indigenous perspectives. Walter et al. (2011) criticize anti-oppressive theory for being located within a Western epistemology and encourage the development of indigenous epistemologies as an alternative knowledge source for critical social work practice.

Although the first challenge to professional imperialism came from Midgley (1983) in relation to the wholesale importation of Western social work models into Africa and Asia, more recent objections have come from indigenous and anti-colonialist scholars who question the widely held belief that social work is applicable to all societies (Gray, Coates, & Yellow Bird, 2008). Despite these objections, Midgley (in Gray et al., 2008) argues that professional imperialism in social work remains a challenge. Gray et al. (2008) argue that social work is a Western construction and Rossiter (2011) maintains that the very idea of social work is premised on a white, male, middle-class, heterosexual subject. However, the normativity of social work is rarely acknowledged, let alone addressed from a political perspective. Critical social work must engage with the profession's normative basis and Western bias. This entails confronting an uncomfortable ambivalence about identifying with social work itself. Generally, social workers are not conflicted about professionalism or expertise. Politically aware social workers, however, are aware that neutrality in social work is impossible.

Conclusion

Ferguson and Woodward (2009) believe it is important to rediscover 'the radical kernel' that inspired social workers in the UK in the 1970s and 1980s. Looking back to radical social work's past provides the basis of inspiration through the example of those who extended the boundaries of its political reach, necessity and relevance. It is inspiring to recall the courage of those who spoke out and challenged structural inequalities and the individualizing and pathologizing of people's problems. At the same time, in exploring how to move forward in the present, many of the debates and dilemmas with which radical social workers grappled 40 years ago seem to be resurfacing. As Williams (2011) suggests, it was too much to expect that a radical caucus within social work and the local state could bring about significant structural change in welfare. Given the massive constraints on social work as a profession, small gains were all that could be expected. While these incremental changes may not live up to some of the visions of the radical social work movement, they nevertheless provide the basis for local practices of resistance (see Chapter 1). Perhaps, as the book's editors suggest, we are, indeed, entering a new phase that will impact decisively on social work and in which a 'New Social Work Left' can emerge. This would focus primarily on the invention of new political forms to guide radical emancipatory projects, as well as develop strategies of resistance to the impact of neoliberalism. As the social philosopher André Gorz (1973) said in another context, small non-reformist reforms can unmask the sources of social inequality. If critical social work can avoid being part of the process of capitalist oppression and privilege, then it can continue to make strong claims for political relevance in the twenty-first century.

References

Adams, R., L. Dominelli, & M. Payne (eds) (2009). *Social work: Themes, issues and critical debates* (2nd edn). Basingstoke: Palgrave Macmillan. 209–217.

Allan, J. (2009). Theorising new developments in critical social work. In J. Allan, L. Briskman, & B. Pease (eds), *Critical social work: Theories and practices for a socially just world*. Sydney, NSW: Allen & Unwin. 30–44.

Allan, J., Briskman, L., & Pease, B. (eds) (2009). *Critical social work: Theories and practices for a socially just world*. Sydney, NSW: Allen & Unwin.

Allan, J., Pease, B., & Briskman, L. (eds) (2003). *Critical social work*. Sydney, NSW: Allen & Unwin.

Allen, A. (2007). *The politics of our selves: Power, autonomy, and gender in contemporary critical theory (new directions in critical theory)*. New York: Columbia University Press.

Avis, M. (2006). Evidence for practice, epistemology and critical reflection. *Nursing Philosophy, 7*, 216–224.

Bailey, R., & Brake, M. (eds) (1975). *Radical social work*. London: Edward Arnold.

Baines, D. (2007). Anti-oppressive social work practice: Fighting for space, fighting for change. In D. Baines (ed.), *Doing anti-oppressive practice: Building transformative politicized social work*. Halifax, NS: Fernwood Press. 1–30.

Barnoff, L., & Moffatt, K. (2007). Contradictory tensions in anti-oppressive practice in feminist social services. *Affilia: Journal of Women and Social Work, 22*(1), 56–70.

Beresford, P. (2011). Radical social work and service users: A crucial connection. In M. Lavalette (ed.), *Radical social work today: Social work at the crossroads*. University of Bristol: Policy Press. 95–114.

Brewer, C., & Lait, J. (1980). *Can social work survive?* London: Temple Smith.

Briskman, L. (2003). Indigenous Australians: Towards postcolonial social work. In J.

Allan, Pease, B., & Briskman, L. (eds), *Critical social work: An introduction to theories and practices*. Sydney, NSW: Allen & Unwin. 92–106.

Burstow, B. (1992). *Radical feminist therapy: Working in the context of violence*. Newbury Park, CA: Sage.

Carastathis, A. (2008). The invisibility of privilege: A critique of intersectional models of identity. *La Review du Creum*, *3*(2), 23–38.

Carniol, B. (2005). *Case critical: Social services and social justice in Canada* (5th edn). Toronto, ON: Between the Lines.

Chambon, A., Irving, A., & Epstein, L. (eds) (1999). *Reading Foucault for social work*. New York: Columbia University Press.

Coleman, S. (2011). The radical burden. *Journal of Progressive Human Services*, *22*, 3–7.

Corrigan, P., & Leonard, P. (1978). *Social work practice under capitalism: A Marxist approach*. London: Macmillan.

Costello, S. (2009). Reconstructing social work practices with families. In J. Allan, Pease, B., & Briskman, L. (eds), *Critical social work: An introduction to theories and practices*. Sydney, NSW: Allen & Unwin. 139–154.

Dalrymple, J., & Burke, B. (2006). *Anti-oppressive practice: Social care and the law* (2nd edn). Maidenhead, Berkshire: Open University Press.

Davies, B., Gottsche, M., & Bansel, P. (2006). The rise and fall of the neo-liberal university. *European Journal of Education*, *41*(2), 305–319.

de Montigny, G. (2011). Beyond anti-oppressive practice: Investigating reflexive social relations. *Journal of Progressive Human Services*, *22*, 8–30.

Dowrick, C. (1983). Strange meeting: Marxism, psychoanalysis and social work. *British Journal of Social Work*, *13*, 1–18.

Fellows, M., & Razack, R. (1998). The race to innocence: Confronting hierarchical relations among women. *Journal of Gender, Race and Justice*, *1*, 335–352.

Feltman, C. (2005). Evidence-based psychotherapy and counselling in the UK: Critique and alternatives. *Journal of Contemporary Psychotherapy*, *35*(1), 131–143.

Ferguson, H. (2008). The theory and practice of critical best practice in social work. In. K. Jones, Cooper, B., & Ferguson, H. (eds), *Best practice in social work: Critical perspectives*. Basingstoke: Palgrave Macmillan. 15–37.

Ferguson, I. (2008). *Reclaiming social work: Challenging neoliberalism and promoting social justice*. London: Sage.

Ferguson, I. (2011). Why class (still) matters. In M. Lavalette (ed.), *Radical social work today: Social work at the crossroads*. Bristol: University of Bristol and Policy Press. 115–134.

Ferguson, I., & Lavalette, M. (1999). Social work, postmodernism and Marxism. *European Journal of Social Work*, *2*(1), 27–40.

Ferguson, I., & Woodward, R. (2009). *Radical social work in practice: Making a difference*. Bristol: Policy Press.

Fook, J. (2002). *Social work: Critical theory and practice*. London: Sage.

Fraser, M., Taylor, M., Jackson, R., & O'Jack, J. (1991). Social work and science: Many ways of knowing? *Social Work Research and Abstracts*, *27*(4), 5–15.

Fraser, N., & Honneth, A. (2003). *Redistribution or recognition? A political-philosophical exchange*. London: Verso.

Frost, L. (2008). Why teach social work students psychosocial studies? *Social Work Education*, *27*(3), 243–261.

Frost, L., & Hoggett, P. (2008). Human agency and social suffering. *Critical Social Policy*, *28*(4), 438–460.

Galper, J. (1975). *The politics of social services*. Englewood Cliffs, NJ: Prentice-Hall.

Galper, J. (1980). *Social work practice: A radical approach*. Englewood Cliffs, NJ: Prentice Hall.

Gambrill, E.D. (1983). *Casework: A competency-based approach*. Englewood Cliffs, NJ: Prentice-Hall.

Gambrill, E.D. (1999). Evidence-based practice: An alternative to authority-based practice, *Families in Society: The Journal of Contemporary Human Services*, *80*(4), 341–350.

Gambrill, E.D. (2001). Social work: An authority-based profession. *Research on Social Work Practice*, *11*(2), 166–175.

Garrett, P.M. (2010). Recognizing the limitations of the political theory of recognition: Axel Honneth, Nancy Fraser and social work. *British Journal of Social Work*, *40*, 1517–1533.

Gilbert, T., & Powell, J. (2010). Power in social work in the United Kingdom: A Foucauldian excursion. *Journal of Social Work*, *10*(1), 3–22.

Gorz, A. (1973). *Socialism and revolution*. New York: Basic Books.

Gottschalk, S., & Witkin, S. (1991). Rationality in social work: A critical examination. *Journal of Sociology and Social Welfare*, *18*(4), 121–136.

Gray, M. (2011). Back to basics: A critique of the strengths perspective in social work. *Families in Society: The Journal of Contemporary Social Services*, *92*(1), 5–11.

Gray, M., & Boddy, J. (2010). Making sense of the waves: Wipeout or still riding high? *Affilia: Journal of Women and Social Work*, *25*(4), 368–389.

Gray, M., Coates, J., & Yellow Bird, M. (eds) (2008). *Indigenous social work around the world: Towards culturally relevant education and practice*. Aldershot, Hants: Ashgate.

Gray, M., Plath, D., & Webb, S.A. (2009). *Evidence-based social work: A critical stance*. London: Routledge.

Gray, M., & Webb, S.A. (2013). Critical social work. In M. Gray & S.A. Webb (eds), *Social work theories and methods* (2nd edn). London: Sage. 99–109.

Grosz, E. (1994). *Volatile bodies: Towards a corporeal feminism*. Sydney, NSW: Allen & Unwin.

Halmos, P. (1978). *The personal and the political: Social work and political action*. London: Hutchinson.

Harms, L. (2007). *Working with people: Communication skills for reflective practice*. Melbourne, VIC: Oxford University Press.

Healy, K. (2000). *Social work practices: Contemporary perspectives on change*. London: Sage.

Healy, K. (2005). *Social work theories in context: Creating frameworks for practice*. Basingstoke: Palgrave Macmillan.

Hick, S., & Pozzuto, R. (2005). Introduction: Towards 'becoming' a critical social worker. In S. Hick, J. Fook, & R. Pozzuto (eds), *Social work: A critical turn*. Toronto, ON: Thompson. ix–xviii.

Houston, S. (2001). Beyond social constructionism: Critical realism and social work. *British Journal of Social Work*, *31*, 845–861.

Houston, S. (2008). Communication, recognition and social work: Aligning the ethical theories of Habermas and Honneth. *British Journal of Social Work*, *39*(7), 1274–1290.

Houston, S. (2010). Beyond homo economicus: Recognition and social work. *British Journal of Social Work*, *41*, 841–469.

Houston, S., & Dolan, P. (2008). Conceptualising family support: Honneth's theory or recognition. *Children & Society, 22*(6), 458–469.

Hunt, A. (2004). Getting Marx and Foucault into bed together. *Journal of Law and Society, 31*(4), 592–609.

Ife, J. (1997). *Rethinking social work: Towards critical practice.* Melbourne: Longman.

Ife, J. (2001). *Human rights and social work: Towards rights-based practice.* Cambridge: Cambridge University Press.

Irving, A. (2009). Michel Foucault. In M. Gray & S.A. Webb (eds), *Social work theories and methods.* London: Sage. 43–52.

Jeyasingham, D. (2011). White noise: A critical evaluation of social work education's engagement with whiteness studies. *British Journal of Social Work*, Advance Access, 1–18. First published online 7 August, 2011doi:10.1093/bjsw/bcr110.

Jones, C. (2011). The best and worst of times: Reflections on the impact of radicalism on British social work education in the 1970s. In M. Lavalette (ed.), *Radical social work today: Social work at the crossroads.* Bristol: Policy Press. 27–44.

Jordan, B. (2010). *Why the third way failed: Economics, morality and the origins of the 'Big Society'.* Bristol: Policy Press.

Joyce, P., Corrigan, P., & Hayes, M. (1988). *Striking out: Trade unionism and social work.* Basingstoke: Macmillan.

Kearney, A. (1996). *Counselling, class and politics: Undeclared influences in therapy.* Ross-on-Wye, Herefordshire: PCCS Books.

Kondrat, M. (1992). Reclaiming the practical: Formal and substantive rationality in social work practice. *Social Service Review, 66*(2), 237–255.

Langan, M. (2002). The legacy of radical social work. In R. Adams, L. Dominelli, & M. Payne (eds), *Social work: Themes, issues and critical debates* (2nd edn). Basingstoke: Palgrave Macmillan. 209–217.

Langan, M. (2011). Rediscovering radicalism and humanity in social work. In M. Lavalette (ed.), *Radical social work today: Social work at the crossroads.* Bristol: Policy Press. 153–164.

Lavalette, M. (2011). Introduction. In M. Lavalette (ed.), *Radical social work today: Social work at the crossroads.* University of Bristol: Policy Press. 1–10.

Lavalette, M., & Ferguson, I. (eds) (2007). *International social work and the radical tradition.* Birmingham: Venture Press.

Lavalette, M., & Ioakimidis, V. (2011). International social work or social work internationalism? Radical social work in global perspective. In M. Lavalette (ed.), *Radical social work today: Social work at the crossroads.* University of Bristol: Policy Press. 135–152.

Lavalette, M., & Mooney, G. (2000). Introduction: Class struggle and social policy. In M. Lavalette & G. Mooney (eds), *Class struggle and social welfare.* London: Routledge. 1–12.

Leonard, P. (1984). *Personality and ideology: Towards a materialist theory of the individual.* London: Macmillan.

Leonard, P. (1997). *Postmodern welfare: Reconstructing an emancipatory project.* London: Sage.

London to Edinburgh Weekend Return Group. (1980). *In and against the state.* London: Pluto.

Lundy, C. (2004). *Social work and social justice: A structural approach to practice.* Peterborough, ON: Broadview Press.

Margolin, L. (1997). *Under the cover of kindness: The invention of social work.* Charlottesville: University Press of Virginia.

McBeath, G., & Webb, S.A. (1991) Social work, modernity and postmodernity. *Sociological Review, 39*(4), 210–221.

McBeath, G., & Webb, S.A. (2005). Post critical social work analytics. In S. Hick, J, Fook, & R. Pozzuto (eds), *Social work: A critical turn.* Toronto, ON: Thompson. 167–186.

McDonald, C. (2006). *Challenging social work: The context of practice.* Basingstoke: Palgrave Macmillan.

McDonald, C. (2007). Wizards of Oz? The radical tradition in Australian social work (and what we can learn from Aotearoa New Zealand). In M. Lavalette & I. Ferguson (eds), *International social work and the radical tradition.* Birmingham: Venture Press. 33–49.

McDonald, C., & Merrill, D. (2002). It shouldn't have to be a trade: Recognition and redistribution in care work advocacy. *Hypatia, 17*(2), 68–83.

McLaughlin, K. (2005). From ridicule to institutionalization: Anti-oppression, the state and social work. *Critical Social Policy, 25*(3), 283–305.

McLaughlin, K. (2008.) *Social work, politics and society: From radicalism to orthodoxy.* Bristol: Policy Press.

Mendes, P. (2009). Tracing the origins of critical social work. In J. Allan, L. Briskman, & B. Pease (eds), *Critical social work: Theories and practices for a socially just world.* Sydney, NSW: Allen & Unwin. 17–29.

Mendes, P. (2010). Retrenching or renovating the Australian welfare state: The paradox of the Howard government's neo-liberalism. *International Journal of Social Welfare,* 18(1), 102–110.

Middleman, R., & Goldberg, G. (1974). *Social service delivery: A structural approach to social work practice.* New York: Columbia University Press.

Middleman, R., & Goldberg Wood, G. (1993). So much for the bell curve: Constructionism, power/conflict, and the structural approach to direct practice in social work. *Journal of Teaching in Social Work, 8*(1/2), 129–146.

Midgley, J. (1983). *Professional imperialism in the third world.* London: Heinemann.

Midgley, J. (2008). Promoting reciprocal international social work exchanges: Professional imperialism revisited. In M. Gray, J. Coates, & M. Yellow Bird (eds), *Indigenous social work around the world: Towards culturally relevant education and practice.* Aldershot, Hants: Ashgate. 31–45.

Millar, M. (2008). Anti-oppressiveness: Critical comments on a discourse and its context. *British Journal of Social Work, 38,* 362–375.

Moreau, M. (1979). A structural approach to social work practice. *Canadian Journal of Social Work Education, 5*(1), 78–94.

Morley, C. (2004). Critical reflection in social work: A response to globalisation? *International Journal of Social Welfare, 13,* 297–303.

Mullaly, B. (2007). *The new structural social work.* Don Mills, ON: Oxford University Press.

Nichols, L., & Cooper, L. (2011). Individualism and its discontents in social work: Proposing a counternarrative for a new vision of social work theory and practice. *Journal of Progressive Human Services, 22,* 84–100.

Nyland, D. (2006). Critical multiculturalism, whiteness and social work: Towards a more radical view of cultural competence. *Journal of Progressive Human Services, 17*(2), 27–41.

Parker, I. (2007). *Revolution in psychology: Alienation to emancipation*. London: Pluto Press.

Parton, N., & O'Byrne, P. (2000). *Constructive social work: Towards a new practice.* Basingstoke: Palagrave Macmillan.

Payne, M. (2005). *Modern social work theory* (3rd edn). Basingstoke: Palgrave Macmillan.

Pease, B. (1991). Dialectical models versus ecological models in social work practice. Proceedings of the *11th Asia Pacific Regional Seminar on Social Work*. Hong Kong: International Federation of Social Workers.

Pease, B. (2002). Rethinking empowerment: A postmodern reappraisal for emancipatory practice. *British Journal of Social Work, 32*(1), 135–147.

Pease, B. (2003). Rethinking the relationship between the self and society. In J. Allan, B. Pease, & L. Briskman (eds), *Critical social work: An introduction to theories and practices.* Sydney, NSW: Allen & Unwin. 187–201.

Pease, B. (2006). Encouraging critical reflections on privilege in social work and the human services. *Practice Reflexions, 1*(1), 15–26.

Pease, B. (2009a). From radical to critical social work: Progressive transformation or mainstream incorporation? In R. Adams, L. Dominelli, & M. Payne (eds), *Critical practice in social work* (2nd edn). Basingstoke: Palgrave Macmillan. 189–198.

Pease, B. (2009b). From evidence-based practice to critical knowledge in post-positivist social work. In J. Allan, L. Briskman, & B. Pease (eds), *Critical social work: Theories and practices for a socially just world*. Sydney, NSW: Allen & Unwin. 45–67.

Pease, B. (2010). *Undoing privilege: Unearned advantage in a divided world.* London: Zed Books.

Peile, C. (1988). Research paradigms in social work: From stalemate to creative synthesis. *Social Service Review, 62*(1), 1–19.

Perry, B. (2001). *In the name of hate: Understanding hate crimes*. New York: Routledge.

Plath, D. (2006). Evidence-based practice: Current issues and future directions. *Australian Social Work, 59*(1), 56–72.

Price, V., & Simpson, G. (2007). *Transforming society: Social work and sociology*. Bristol: Policy Press.

Pritchard, C., & Taylor, R. (1978). *Social work: Reform or revolution?* London: Routledge & Kegan Paul.

Proctor, G., Cooper, M., Sanders, P., & Malcolm, B. (2006). *Politicizing the person-centred approach: An agenda for social change*. Ross-on-Wye, Herefordshire: PCCS Books.

Reisch, M. (2005). American exceptionalism and critical social work: A retrospective and prospective analysis. In I. Ferguson, M. Lavalette, & E. Whitmore (eds), *Globalisation, global justice and social work*. London: Routledge. 157–172.

Reisch, M., & Andrews, J. (2001). *The road not taken: A history of radical social work in the United States*. Philadelphia, PA: Brunner-Routledge

Rossiter, A. (2000). The professional is political: An interpretation of the problem of the past in solution-focused therapy. *American Journal of Orthopsychiatry, 70*(2), 150–161.

Rossiter, A. (2011). Unsettled social work: The challenge of Levinas' ethics. *British Journal of Social Work, 41*, 980–995.

Simpkin, M. (1983). *Trapped within welfare: Surviving social work* (2nd edn). London: Macmillan.

Singh, G., & Cowden, S. (2009). The social worker as intellectual. *European Journal of Social Work, 12*(4), 479–493.

Sommerfeld, P., & Herzog, P. (eds) (2005). *Evidence based social work: Towards a new professionalism*. Berne: Peter Lang.

Specht, H., & Courtney, M. (1994). Unfaithful angels: How social work abandoned its mission. New York: The Free Press.

Stepney, P. (2006). Mission impossible? Critical practice in social work. *British Journal of Social Work, 36,* 1289–1307.

Thompson, A. (2009). Radical social work in contemporary times. *Journal of Progressive Human Services, 20,* 110–111.

Thompson N. (2010). *Theorizing social work practice.* Basingstoke: Palgrave Macmillan.

Trinder, L. (2000). A critical appraisal of evidence-based practice. In L. Trinder & S. Reynolds (eds), *Evidence-based practice: A critical appraisal.* Oxford: Blackwell Science. 212–241.

Wagner, D. (2009). Radical social work as conceit. *Journal of Progressive Human Services, 20,* 104–106.

Wakefield, J. (2005). Putting Humpty together again: Treatment of mental disorder and pursuit of justice as parts of social work's mission. In. S. Kirk (ed.), *Mental disorders in the social environment.* New York: Columbia University Press. 293–309.

Wallace, J., & Pease, B. (2011). Neoliberalism and Australian social work: Accommodation or resistance? *Journal of Social Work, 11*(2), 132–142.

Walter, M., Taylor, S., & Habibis, D. (2011). How white is social work in Australia? *Australian Social Work, 64*(1), 6–19.

Webb, S.A. (2001). Considerations on the validity of evidence based practice in social work. *British Journal of Social Work, 31*(1), 57–59.

Webb, S.A. (2009). Against difference and diversity in social work: The case of human rights. *International Journal of Social Welfare, 18,* 307–316.

Webb, S.A. (2010). (Re)assembling the Left: The politics of redistribution and recognition in social work. *British Journal of Social Work, 40*(8), 2364–2379.

Webb, S.A. (2013). The subject of social work: Towards a new perspective on discrimination. In C. Cocker & T. Hafford Letchfield (eds), *Rethinking anti-discriminatory practice, diversity and equality in social work.* Basingstoke: Palgrave Macmillan.

Weinstein, J. (2011). Case Con and radical social work in the 1970s: The impatient revolutionaries. In M. Lavalette (ed.), *Radical social work today: Social work at the crossroads.* Bristol: Policy Press. 11–26.

Williams, C. (1999). Connecting anti-racist and anti-oppressive theory and practice: Retrenchment or reappraisal? *British Journal of Social Work, 29,* 211–230.

Williams, C. (2011). The jester's joke. In M. Lavalette (ed.), *Radical social work today: Social work at the crossroads.* Bristol: Policy Press. 59–78.

Witkin, S. (1996). If empirical practice is the answer, what is the question? *Social Work Research, 20*(2), 69–75.

Witkin, S., & Saleebey, D. (eds) (2007). *Social work dialogues: Transforming the canon in inquiry, practice and education.* Alexandria, VA: Council on Social Work Education.

Wood, G., & Tully, C. (2006). *The structural approach to direct practice in social work: A social constructionist perspective* (3rd edn). New York: Columbia University Press.

Young, S. (2004). Social work theory and practice: The invisibility of whiteness. In A. Moreton-Robinson (ed.), *Whitening race: Essays in social and cultural criticism.* Canberra, ACT: Aboriginal Studies Press. 104–118.

3

Mapping the Theoretical and Political Terrain of Social Work

Paul Michael Garrett

I mean it's almost like you need less and less bright people doing social work because actually what you don't want them to do is to kind of really think too much about the wider issues, the wider aspects of what they're doing, what you want them to do really is to do what they're told. (Joe, a social work team manager who works with disabled children and their families, in Thomas & Davies, 2005, p. 724)

Possibly, Joe's remarks on how a concern with the 'wider issues, the wider aspects' of social work resonate with other recent comments by contemporary writers on how their personal attempts to develop more sociologically informed, radical ways of thinking and working have resulted in pressures within the workplace. Rogowski (2010), for example, has exposed the less than positive response of his local office to his attendance at a conference on the future direction of social work. In a less overtly political manner, another respected author of textbooks for students remarks that, when he began his career, he was 'discouraged from asking questions or developing' his knowledge base:

I was simply urged to 'get on with the job', without any real clarity about what the job actually was or how to go about it. It was largely a case of copying what other staff did and doing the best I could without any real depth of understanding. (Thompson, 2010, p. xi)

These accounts are troubling in that they reveal how an anti-theorizing culture is prevalent in many social work workplaces.

Initially, this chapter stresses the importance of critical theory within social work and draws attention to the opposition to a theoretically informed practice. Next, the aim is to identify what can be regarded as the four competing theoretical perspectives dominating thinking about social work and related spheres. It then argues that a critical feminist orientation is significant and should inform social work. In the second half of the chapter, reference is made to some key thinkers whose interventions remain important for contemporary times in which neoliberalism remains dominant, but contested. This brief discussion is not, of course, exhaustive.

Making the Case for Critical Theory within Social Work

Theory represents an attempt 'to explain a phenomenon ... by providing a structured set of concepts that help us to understand the subject matter concerned' (Thompson, 2010, p. 4). This broad definition can encompass theoretical models of social work intervention, such as 'crisis' and 'task-centred' intervention (Coulshed, 1988). They are theoretical models of how to *do* social work. Yet, theory can also include theoretical perspectives on social work or ways of thinking about the nature of social work and its relationship to the 'wider issue' mentioned by Joe at the outset. Bringing to the fore more encompassing reflections on how society is socially and economically organized, this latter dimension leads to the terrain of critical social theory. Indeed, Part II of the book takes this exploration forward by examining approaches to critical practice.

Callinicos (1999) believes that social theory is 'indispensable to engaging with the present' (p. 9):

> [Social theory] seeks to understand society as a whole; distinguishes between and makes generalizations about different kinds of society; is concerned in particular to analyze modernity, the social life, the forms of social life which have come to prevail first in the West and increasingly in the rest of the world over the past couple of centuries. (Callinicos, 1999, p. 2)

Classical modernist social theory was, developed by a triumvirate of leading thinkers: Karl Marx (1818–83), Max Weber (1864–1920) and Émile Durkheim (1858–1917). The specific focus of this chapter is on critical theory, and the 'political' dimension to such theory troubles many within the social work academy, and beyond, who are discomforted with any destabilization of mainstream, officially endorsed understandings. Yet, as Erich Fromm (in Back, 2007) pointed out, 'Critical thinking is a quality, it's an approach to the world, to everything; it's by no means critical in the sense of hostile, negative, nihilistic, but on the contrary critical thought stands in the service of life' (p. 8).

According to Calhoun (2003), critical theory should be understood as 'the project of social theory that undertakes simultaneously critique of received categories, critique of theoretical practice, and critical substantive analysis of social life in terms of the possible, not just the actual' (p. 63). This can also be related to the comments of Herbert Marcuse on what he dubbed 'negative thinking'. In contrast to uncritical thinking, which 'derives its beliefs, norms and values from the existing thought and social practices', negative or critical thinking 'negates existing forms of thought and reality from the perspective of higher possibilities' (Kellner, 2002, pp. xiv–xv). Perhaps this recognition that there are 'higher possibilities' also operates at the level of feelings and emotions and in how people can intuit a different reality, a different ordering and arrangements of things. It also draws attention to context by highlighting what is present in particular actions at particular places at different historical junctions.

Responding to the 'anti-theory' position

The aspiration to incorporate an awareness of the possibilities provided by critical social theory has frequently met with resistance from those seeking to define and delimit what might be regarded as 'social work'. Furthermore, Mullaly (1997) argues that many

> social workers either turn cold or rebel at the mere mention of theory. Theory is viewed as esoteric, abstract, and something people discuss in universities. Practice on the other hand, is seen as common sense, concrete, and occurring in the real world. Social work is viewed by many as essentially a pragmatic profession that carries out practical tasks. Theory has little direct relevance and actually obscures the truth (i.e. practical) nature of social work. Spontaneity and personal qualities of the social worker are more important than theory. (p. 99)

Allegedly, since '*doing* social work is more important than thinking about it' (Gray & Webb, 2013, p. 6; original emphasis), many social workers may even tend 'to elevate theoretical ignorance to a level of professional virtue' (Mullaly, 1997, pp. 99–100). The notion that social work is ill-served by theoreticians reflects a dominant understanding periodically reinforced by official statements stressing the 'practical' nature of the profession (Gray & Webb, 2013). A representative of the UK government has gone so far as to state that social work could be undertaken on an entirely voluntary basis by 'retired City bankers or ex-insurance brokers' ('Minister calls for more child protection volunteers', *Guardian*, 30 October 2010, p. 21). Although, in the period leading up to the 2010 UK election, the Conservative Party (2007) attempted to win favour with the profession, the assumption underlying the Minister's declaration is that social work – perceived here as a form of loosely organized 'common sense' – could be done on the cheap, by well-intentioned (and evidently financially comfortable) laypeople. Moreover, the reference to the retired wealthy implies not only a blatant class bias, but also an under-standing that life experience is the paramount factor for those discharging the social work role. Here experience 'means something specific – primary experi-ence, unmediated by theory, reflection, speculation, argument, etc. It is thought superior to other forms of life because it is rooted in reality: experience is "real" – speculation and theory are "airy-fairy"' (Hall et al., 1978, p. 152).

Within this experiential paradigm, theorizing has no relevance. Nonetheless, 'all practice is theory based' (Mullaly, 1997, p. 99): it is merely that the theory is often implicit or unspoken. However, as Gray and Webb (2013) assert, every 'social work practice is the bearer and articulation of more or less theory-laden beliefs and concepts. Even those who try to refute the value of theory by claiming that social work is just "good common sense" are, in fact, articulating a distilled version of philosophical theories about common sense' (p. 5). All social work practice is 'based on theorizing' and it remains a 'fallacy' to refer to 'theoryless practice' (Thompson, 2010, p. 5):

> Even where the theoretical understandings cannot be directly articulated by a practitioner, they will still be there. That is practitioners will be making assump-tions about a range of factors (the nature and causes of human behaviour; how society works; the nature and causes of social problems; how best to communicate; how to recognize emotional reactions and so on) and basing these assumptions on concepts, wherever they are derived from. Some sort of conceptual framework (and therefore theory) and is therefore inevitable. (Thompson, 2010, p. 7)

According to Thompson (2010), theory and practice are 'two sides of the same coin. To undertake social work activities is not to choose between theory and practice, but rather to fuse the two – to engage in actions (prac-tice) that are shaped by knowledge and understanding (theory)' (p. xvi).

Clearly, theory cannot be mechanistically 'applied' to practice. Partly rooted in a positivistic understanding of intellectual inquiry, this way of perceiving theory is reflected in how social work curricula tend to map learning for future practitioners. Ideas, such as those of Davies (1981), that social workers are 'maintenance mechanics' are – as well as being deeply ideological – likely to reinforce the notion that theory can be applied to practice in a fairly straight-forward and unproblematic fashion. Indeed, the whole idea of *applying* theory to practice is deeply problematic because it rests on the 'mistaken assumption that there are simple, direct one-to-one links that can be made between theory and practice' (Thompson, 2010, p. xvii). Thompson (2010) elaborates:

practitioners do not simply use a theoretical knowledge base in a direct way... but, rather, go through a more complex process of 'theorizing' practice – that is using a set of concepts to act as a framework or making sense of the situations we encounter in practice and how these relate to the wider context of social work and indeed of society itself. (p. xii)

Social work 'involves dealing with complexity. Its challenges are far too demanding and multi-layered to be amenable to simple, formulaic approaches' (Thompson, 2010, p. xv). Its emphasis, therefore, is on '*integrating* theory and practice' (Thompson, 2010, p. 15; emphasis added). That is to say, 'theory should inform practice, but practice should also inform theory ...What we have is a dialectical relationship' (Thompson, 2010, pp. 15–16).

Dangers exist in simply relying on 'practice wisdom', given that for 'many years the accepted wisdom took little or no account of the significance of discrimination in people's lives, due to the individualistic focus of social work at that time' (Thompson, 2010, p. 5). Furthermore, as Schön (1992) observes, 'systems of intuitive knowing are dynamically conservative, actively defended, actively resistant to change' (p. 610). It is possible to stretch such points a little further and to argue that 'practice wisdom' or unquestioned 'common sense' dominant in particular fields of social work, or within particular establishments, actually facilitated the 'corruption of care' and the installation and acceptance of abusive practices (Wardhaugh & Wilding, 1993). This analysis has particular resonance in Ireland, given the revelations about institutional abuse in locations such as Industrial Schools (Garrett, 2012a, 2013b).

Contemporary Theoretical Perspectives within Social Work

The last decade has seen the publication of a range of books seeking, with differing degrees of success, to illuminate the usefulness of sociology and social theory for social work (see, for example, Cunningham & Cunningham, 2008; Ferguson, 2004; Llewellyn, Agu, & Mercer, 2008; McLaughlin, 2008; Price & Simpson, 2007; Thompson, 2010; Webb, 2006). Beyond these important academic contributions, it could be argued that, since the very definition of social work provided by the International Federation of Social Workers (IFSW) locates the profession within the 'bigger picture', the coupling of social work and social theory should not be controversial. The IFSW maintains:

The social work profession promotes social change, problem solving in human relationships and the empowerment and liberation of people to enhance well

Table 3.1   *Theoretical perspectives underpinning social work*

Perspective	Characteristics
Therapeutic–psychodynamic	It was 'psychoanalysis which gave social work ... [the] scientific patina and vocabulary so critical to its claim for professional recognition' (Jones, 2011, p. 33). Some in social work have attempted to reinstall this perspective at the centre of theory and practice, and there have been calls for a renewed 'emotionally intelligent relationship-based social work and psychodynamic understandings of practice' (Ferguson, 2010, p. 136). An emphasis on 'good authority' (Ferguson, 2011, p. 97) and the sensory and tactile aspects of practice is characteristic of this approach, whose disavowal of collective solutions to social problems is coupled with an implicit nostalgic hankering for the social work of the 1950s and early 1960s.
Socialist–collectivist	Through a socialist-collectivist lens, seeking personal and social fulfilment is impossible given the constraints that capitalism imposes. This perspective stresses the importance of collectivist solutions to personal problems. In the UK, 'radical social work' was promulgated by *Case Con*, the 'revolutionary magazine for social workers' during the period 1970–77 (Weinstein, 2011, p. 11), and Bailey and Brake's (1975) volume (see also Corrigan, 1982; Joyce, Corrigan, & Hayes, 1988). More recently, a revival of radical social work has been articulated by Jones (1983) and Lavalette (2011). Organizationally, the perspective is reflected in the politics of the UK Social Work Action Network (SWAN), which developed out of a 'Social Work Manifesto' initially circulated in 2004.
Individualist–reformist	The reformist tradition does not seek major social reformist change but gradual improvement in conditions. Historically, in the UK, it is connected with Fabianism and, in the 1970s and 1980s, with the constellation of approaches connected to 'anti-oppressive practice' which owe something to developments within social work in the USA. The demand that social workers develop skills in 'intimate child protection practice' can be inserted within this 'individualist-reformist' framework (Ferguson, 2011). This orientation calls for a new emphasis on 'relationship-based' social work which is particularly relevant when practitioners have to move among 'marginalized families' living in what are termed 'poor and disgusting conditions' (Ferguson, 2011, p. 97).
Managerialist–technocratic	Perceives a thoroughly neoliberalized social work as a 'business' which, in its dominant lexicon, aims to provide an 'excellent' and 'quality' range of services to a diverse range of 'customers'. It can be associated with 'charging' for services and with the blurring of the distinctions between social workers and those who are ancillary and have received less training. Harris (2003) provided a criticism of this approach. There also tends to be an emphasis on electronic technologies and for forms of intervention, which are said to – unambiguously – 'work'.

being. Utilizing theories of human behaviour and social systems, social work inter-
venes at the points where people interact with their environments. Principles of
human rights and social justice are fundamental. (IFSW, 2000)

Clearly, this expansive definition of the profession and its key roles and
activities (embracing 'social change', 'liberation', 'human rights' and 'social
justice') strongly suggests that social workers should be acquainted with
social theory. Indeed, in very broad terms, within social work in the UK, it
is possible to outline four conflicting theoretical perspectives on how society is organized or should be organized and the nature of personal and social
change. These perspectives, sometimes implicit rather than openly stated,
are far from static and evolve over time. Although derived from the UK,
these frameworks can be applied to other national and cultural contexts, yet
it is clear that their marginality or predominance may vary accordingly: for
example, within the Republic of Ireland it is difficult to identify – historically – any major current within the profession adhering to a 'socialist-
collectivist perspective'. Unlike the UK, there have been, however,
consistent attempts to hold onto the vestiges of the 'therapeutic perspective'
(and especially the importance of counselling) as this came under threat
from an ascendant 'managerialist-technocratic perspective' (see Table 3.1).

All four of these perspectives, far from being internally unified and homogeneous, appear to form alternatives, which compete within the field of
social work, to gain supremacy and to exclude the competitors. Although
there may be affinities and points of overlap, resulting in hybrid theoretical
formations, they are, on the whole, identifiably different. Each of the four
theoretical approaches has, in some ways, been challenged by anti-racist,
postcolonial, postmodernist and feminist approaches. Nonetheless, they
appear resilient and apt to be expansionist: for example, attempts have been
made to implant a neoliberal 'managerialist-technocratic perspective'
among the emerging social work professions in the former Eastern bloc. This
has resulted in professional and cultural tensions, particularly in areas of
Eastern Europe, such Croatia, which have their own rich indigenous social
work history.

Feminist Thinking as Critical Thinking

Jan Fook, a supporter of the now exhausted postmodernist perspective
(Matthewman & Hoey, 2006), has written of her experience of postgraduate
study, that she entered

> a world in which it seemed that male academic theorising sociologists tried to
> teach female practising social workers better social work by 'converting' them to a

world of theory (e.g. Althusser), which incidentally seemed to be owned by male academic sociologists. Since I was neither male nor a sociologist, but at that time an academic and social worker I found the dichotomy inadequate as a representation of my own experience and identity. (Fook, in Pease & Fook, 1999, p. 5)

Her experience of the teaching of theory may say a good deal about the particular milieu in which she undertook her postgraduate work. It appears to have been dominated by men who felt they 'owned theory', who were constrained by their intellectual allegiance to a particularly arid form of structural Marxism, and who – because of their apparent elitism – made no effort to link theory to practice.

Fook's comments remain significant, however, because they emphasize the need to infuse contemporary critical theory with a feminist sensibility. This is vital because of how gender is central to the project of neoliberalization. For example, in spring 2011, the Minister for Universities and Science for the Conservative–Liberal Democrat administration in the UK blamed educated working women for the lack of jobs available for working-class men ('Minister blames feminism over lack of jobs for working men', *Guardian*, 2 April, p. 6). For the minister, David Willetts, feminism was probably the 'single biggest factor' for the lack of social mobility.

Ebert (1996) more reasonably argued that the 'dominant' feminist paradigm – which she referred to as 'ludic feminism' – had by then 'largely abandoned the problems of labour and exploitation and ignored their relationship to gender, sexuality, difference, desire, and subjectivity' (p. ix). At a 'time when two-thirds of all labour in the world is done by women' (p. ix), Ebert (1996) maintained that leading feminist theorists, often situated in the more prestigious universities, had 'abandoned' bread-and-butter issues impacting on women's daily lives. Whereas these comments are, to some extent, accurate, the assertion that we are now in a 'post-feminist' era is far less tenable, given the increasing 'feminisation of the proletariat' (Harvey, 2010, p. 15; see also Bunting, 2011). Women now form 'the backbone of the global workforce' (Harvey, 2010, p. 59) and are presently hit harder by public-sector cuts in the UK labour market than men. Luann Good Goodrich (2010) refers to the stark

gendered and racialized inequalities in the global economy and local labor markets, along with the commodification and devaluing of social roles, reproduction labour, and citizenship for women in general and poor, lone women in particular. Globalizing processes have produced a gendered and racialized global labor force that is deeply divided ... Specifically, more women are participating in global labor forces than ever before, yet associated social and economic gains are ambiguous at best, as a disproportionately high number of employed women are working jobs that are insecure, low-wage, without benefits, and part-time. (p. 109)

A former president of the International Association of Schools of Social Work (IASSW) has remarked:

> The media in Western countries has confidently asserted that feminism is passé by claiming that we have entered the post-feminist era. To women like me, this is a strange paradox. For as women experience the feminisation of poverty, increased levels of sexual violence, the loss of welfare state benefits which women have accessed in the recent past, the threatened loss of livelihood and statehood, I marvel at the idea that feminist claims have been realised and need consume the energies of women and girls no longer. (Dominelli, 2002, p. 1)

Given the plurality of perspectives housed beneath the label 'feminism', it is more accurate to refer to feminism(s). However, feminist social work:

> arose out of feminist social action being carried out by women working with women in their communities. Their aim has been to improve women's well-being by linking their personal predicaments and often private sorrows with their social position and status in society. (Dominelli, 2002, p. 6)

Importantly, feminist social work was manifestly rooted in critical thinking and responsive to the everyday concerns of women using and women providing social work services (see also Thomas & Davies, 2005). Cree (2010) has maintained that the assessment of the impact of feminism on mainstream social work ranges from potentially optimistic to the deeply pessimistic. A number of achievements are, however, identifiable. For example, by 'placing gender on the social work map, feminist social workers have challenged the gender neutrality regarding this social division usually upheld in traditional professional social work theories and practice' (Dominelli, 2002, p. 8). Feminist social workers have 'problematised practitioner responses to women's needs' (Dominelli, 2002, p. 9), for example, 'mother blaming', the focus on 'dangerous' mothers and the related the failure to engage with fathers (see Milner, 1993 for an early example). Feminist social workers and academics have also made important contributions to research and endeavoured to reform language practices within social work.

The Neoliberal Landscape

Returning to Joe's comments, which served as a preamble to the chapter, in order to comprehend contemporary social work practice it is vital to try to reach some theoretical understanding of the 'wider issues'. Central here are patterns of neoliberalization and what has been termed the 'conservative revolution' (Bourdieu, 2001, p. 35). Although neoliberalism is frequently left undefined (Boas & Gans-Morse, 2009), seven interconnected components are significant: the relationship between neoliberalism and the 'embedded liberalism' it seeks to supplant or displace; the role of the state within neoliberalism; the gap dividing actually existing neoliberalism and its theory and rhetoric; the concept of 'accumulation by dispossession' and neoliberalism's redistribution in favour of the rich; the centrality of insecurity, precariousness or precarity; the renewed and retrogressive faith in incarceration and, more broadly, what has been termed the 'new punitiveness'; and neoliberalism's need for pragmatism to adapt to different national settings (see also Garrett, 2009, 2012a). At the time of writing, it appears capital is wearying of democracy and that the liquidation of elected governments may form part of an emerging repertoire of options within the European Union (EU). This post-democratic turn is most clearly apparent in Italy, with the installation of the Mario Monti administration and his team of unelected technocrat ministers in November 2011. The Greek government of Lucas Papademos is also formed of technocrats. In both instances, the foundational aim appears to be to construct forms of rule which are 'post-political', with nation-states administered like corporations. In a related development, as the Republic of Ireland approaches the centenary commensuration of independence in 2016, national sovereignty has been surrendered to the International Monetary Fund and European Central Bank.

Furthermore, it remains apparent that the neoliberal project, which many thought had come to a conclusion with the 'crash' has, in fact, been emboldened. The publication of a range of statistics, in late 2011, illuminated how the economic crisis is now being used to *reinforce* economic cleavages and deepen class inequalities (see also Klein, 2007). For example, figures released by the US government on children (ages 0–17) reveal that, in 2009, 21 per cent (15.5 million) lived in poverty. This marked an increase up from 16 per cent in 2000 and 2001. In 2009, 36 per cent of black children, 33 per cent of Hispanic children, and 12 per cent of white, non-Hispanic children lived in poverty. These are increases from 35 per cent, 29 per cent and 10 per cent, respectively, in 2007. Significantly, the percentage of children who lived in families with very high incomes (600 per cent or more of the poverty threshold) nearly doubled, from 7 per cent in 1991 to 13 per cent in 2009 (ChildStats.gov, 2011). Across the globe it is also clear that a redistribution to the rich is taking place during a period of so-called 'austerity', when in the duplicitous words of the UK prime minister, we are allegedly 'all in this together'. Merrill Lynch has reported that the world's 'high net worth individuals [HNWIs] expanded in population and wealth in 2010 surpassing 2007 pre-crisis levels in nearly every region'. Moreover, the 'global population of Ultra-HNWIs grew by 10.2 per cent in 2010 and its wealth by 11.5 per cent' (Merrill Lynch & Capgemini, 2011).

These developments, more specifically the shifts in the distribution of income and wealth, inescapably impact on a range of social work concerns, and this is apparent in the data highlighting how the economic crisis is adversely impacting on mental health. Many governments are now placing an emphasis on notions of 'happiness' and 'well-being' (Ferguson, 2007; see Chapter 12 and 13), yet many of those worst hit by the crisis are experiencing a health emergency. In Greece, for example:

> There are signs that health outcomes have worsened, especially in vulnerable groups. We noted a significant rise in the prevalence of people reporting that their health was 'bad' or 'very bad'. Suicides rose by 17% in 2009 from 2007 and unofficial 2010 data quoted in parliament mention a 25% rise compared with 2009. The Minister of Health reported a 40% rise in the first half of 2011 compared with the same period in 2010. The national suicide helpline reported that 25% of callers faced financial difficulties in 2010 and reports in the media indicate that the inability to repay high levels of personal debt might be a key factor in the increase in suicides. Violence has also risen, and homicide and theft rates nearly doubled between 2007 and 2009. The number of people able to obtain sickness benefits declined between 2007 and 2009. (Kentikelenis et al., 2011, p. 1)

As the authors of this piece in *The Lancet* observe, overall 'the picture of health in Greece is concerning. It reminds us that, in an effort to finance debts, ordinary people are paying the ultimate price' (Kentikelenis et al., 2011, p. 2). Elsewhere, in the EU, there are not dissimilar findings, particularly in those countries where the social state is being subjected to the most severe attacks. In the Republic of Ireland, the cuts in mental health services are taking an insidious form in that staff members who leave or retire are not replaced. It is estimated that approximately 10% of psychiatric nursing staff left the mental health services in 2009' (Mental Health Commission, 2011, p. 10). Similar to Greece:

> Economic adversity and recession specifically has been shown to result in an increase in suicide rates. Studies have also shown that factors in the current economic crisis, such as falling stock prices, increased bankruptcies and housing insecurity (including evictions and the anticipated loss of a home), and higher interest rates are all associated with increased suicide risk. People who are unemployed are two–three times more likely to die by suicide than people in employment. A recent Irish study has shown that during the boom years of the 'Celtic Tiger' male and female rates of suicide and undetermined death were stable during 1996–2006, while suicide among unemployed men increased. Unemployment was associated with a 2–3 fold risk of suicide in men and a 4–6 fold increased risk in women. (Mental Health Commission, 2011, p. 14)

The Mental Health Commission (2011) also reported that by 'mid-2010 one in ten calls to the Samaritans in Ireland were described as "recession-related" and in June 2010 some 50,000 calls were received, up from an average of 35,000 in other months. The suicide rate in Ireland increased from 424 in 2008 to 527 in 2009, an increase of 24%' (pp. 14–15). Related to this development, there has also been a steep rise in the prescribing of some anti-depressive drugs (Mental Health Commission, 2011). Such statistics can only be meaningfully understood if we are willing to draw on critical social theory which encompasses and seeks to interpret the 'bigger picture'.

Critical Theoretical Foundations for a 'New Social Work Left'?

> [W]e do not attempt dogmatically to prefigure the future, but want to find the new world only through criticism of the old ... But if the designing of the future and the proclamation of ready-made solutions for all time is not our affair, then we realize all the more clearly what we have to accomplish in the present – I am speaking of a *ruthless criticism of everything existing*, ruthless in two senses: The criticism must not be afraid of its own conclusions, nor of conflict with the powers that be. (Marx, in Tucker, 1978, p. 13; original emphasis)

Despite the current marginalization of Marxism in social work, it continues to provide a devastating critique of capitalism and remains a vital resource for social workers seeking to understand and develop strategies of resistance to neoliberalization. Marxism has the potential to inject a questioning and critical ambiance into social work theorization and practice. As Wacquant (2004) maintains, the 'primary historical mission of critical thought' is to 'serve as a *solvent of doxa*, to perpetually question the obviousness and the very frames of civic debate so as to give ourselves a chance to think the world, rather than being *thought by* it, to take apart and understand its mechanisms, and thus to reappropriate it intellectually and materially' (p. 101; original emphasis).

Marx provides us with a number of theoretical 'reminders' which might help us to make sense of transformations taking place within the 'world of work' today (see Garrett, 2012a). His critique seems all the more timely given the very scale of the current crisis which, as Callinicos (2010) observes, 'invites, as it did in the case of its predecessor in the 1930s, reflection on the extent to which its causes are systemic, lying in the very nature of the capitalist mode of production' (p. 7). Indeed, we now seemed poised to enter a period of 'eternal austerity' managed, at least in terms of welfare provision if not policing and security, by a 'permanently shrunken state' (Toynbee, 2010, p. 27).

A number of other leftist thinkers can also assist us to theorize the present period. In this sense, the theorization of Antonio Gramsci (1891–1937), which has until recently mostly been ignored within the academic literature of social work, is immensely useful. Perhaps not surprisingly in the context of the present economic crisis, his ideas are gradually beginning to seep into the profession's journals (Garrett, 2013a; MacKinnon, 2009; Singh & Cowden, 2009). Here, a number of authors have focused on some of his key conceptualizations and ideas on, for example Americanism, Fordism and Taylorism; Hegemony; and Common Sense and Intellectuals. Despite the obstacles facing those reading his often difficult work, Gramsci's theoretical formulations continue to be of potential use and can aid our understanding of social work in contemporary times. Furthermore, *thinking* with Gramsci – and bringing him into dialogue with other theorists – might enable social workers to help construct counter hegemonic strategies and a renewed sense of activism.

Attempts have also been made to ascertain whether Pierre Bourdieu's (1930–2002) theorization may have relevance for social workers. Certainly, there are challenges for readers presented by his mammoth contribution. Apart from Bourdieu's dense prose style and the misleading labels frequently attached to him (for example, 'Marxist' or 'Postmodernist'), a further area of difficulty relates to the actual theoretical content of his contribution. Three main flaws in Bourdieu's output relate to his problematic engagement with multiculturalism, 'race' and ethnicity; his occasional overemphasis on the dulled passivity of social actors, particularly the working class; and his views on the nature of the state. Despite the potential drawbacks, his conceptual categories of *habitus*, field and capital – along with the related ideas associated with doxa and symbolic violence – add considerably to social work's repertoire of critical social theory. His more overtly 'political' involvement also contains a number of key 'messages' for social work (Garrett, 2013a; Houston, 2002).

There are also a range of other key thinkers whose work might become more widely known within the social work literature: the co-authored work of Luc Boltanski (1940–) and Ève Chiapello (1965–), Antonio Negri (1933–) and the autonomist Marxists, and Alain Badiou (1937–). All of these authors inhabit a conceptual landscape in which neoliberalism is dominant, but unstable, edgy and fragile. Furthermore, although conceptually challenging, they all potentially signal new directions for social work's engagement with what might be loosely categorized as anti-capitalist social theory. All of these thinkers share a distinct 'leftist' orientation. Boltanski and Chiapello (2005) are in dialogue with key Marxist preoccupations, and although they do not operate within a specifically Gramscian perspective, they 'offer a classic analysis of the mechanics by which hegemony is exercised' (Couldry et al., 2010, p. 110; see also Garrett, 2012a); Badiou's theorization is deeply prob-

Table 3.2   Critical theory and the new politics of social work

Theorists	Themes
Boltanski and Chiapello	Managerialism and contemporary workscapes, the language of 'change' and transformation, hegemony
Negri and the Marxist autonomists	The changing nature of work within capitalism's 'social factory', 'immaterial' labour and 'affective' labour
Badiou	Multiculturalism', 'diversity', 'difference' and, for him, how such ideas are retrogressive in terms of progressive political projects. (Opposition) to the dominance of 'human rights' discourse

lematic, quixotically and arguably Marxist (Garrett, 2012b; Webb, 2009), and Negri's is decidedly Marxist.

A unifying theme connecting a number of the theorists is the project to bring communism in from the cold and create a rupture with the 'squalor of capitalist-parliamentarism' (Badiou, 2003). Hardt and Negri (2000, p. 413) illustrate the twin interests in communism and early Christianity in the attention which they pay to the figure of St Francis. The revolutionary theme is at the heart of Luc Boltanski's (2002) query: what 'has become today of the longing for total revolution? This longing constituted the Left's most characteristic and permanent trait, the ideological centre that it cannot completely deny without breaking with an identity established over two centuries of critique and struggle' (p. 11). Similar claims are present in the work of Badiou (2008, 2010) and Negri, along with his frequent co-writer, Michael Hardt (1960–). As for the habitually controversial Slavoj Žižek (2002), revolution is coupled with an even less popular topic, that of Leninism (see also Budgen, Kouvelakis, & Žižek, 2007). Aside from these broader thematic commonalities, the range of theoretical interests covered by these thinkers is of manifest relevance to key concerns in contemporary social work (see Table 3.2).

Conclusion

This chapter has maintained that there is a need for social workers to develop a critical approach to the profession's governing themes and preoccupations. In this sense, critical social theory is indispensable because it can help us to 'compare, analyse, synthesize, periodize and arrive at a tendential and *structural* account of the concrete situations in which we are historically and geographically immersed' (Brown, 2011, p. 23; original emphasis). Moreover, social work practitioners and academics might ourselves seek to become the 'key thinkers' within the field. In this way, we can aim to interrupt, or disturb, mainstream perceptions and aspire to create new ways of looking at the world and creating more equitable economic and social relationships. In this context, it is vital that attempts are now made to construct a 'new politics' of social work, given the magnitude of the economic crisis.

This chapter has, therefore, suggested that a range of theoretical resources are available which might assist social workers in thinking more theoretically and aid in the construction of a 'new politics' of social work tapered to the times in which we live. While arguing that 'key thinkers' could be created *within* the field of social work, it was also suggested that there were a range of theorists who might aid us in this project. None of this is, however, to imply that 'social work' is a unified field with politically homogenous actors. Despite the values reflected in the various codes of ethics, there are likely to be a range of political views, positions and, aspirations within the profession. Equally important, as Parton (2000) observed a number of years ago:

> [one of] social work's enduring characteristics seems to be its essentially contested and ambiguous nature ... Most crucially, this ambiguity arises from a commitment to individuals and families and their needs on the one hand and its allegiances to and legitimation by the state in the guise of the courts and its 'statutory' responsibilities on the other. (p. 457)

Nonetheless, the challenge is to build new alliances and to participate in actions with others who are intent on resisting this endeavour by the forces of capital to remake and reorder the world. In social work, perhaps this is a strategic opening for the advancement of what the editors call the 'New Social Work Left'?

In this context, aligning the 'New Social Work Left' agenda proposed in this book with the Social Work Action Network (SWAN) now present in England, Wales, Scotland and the Republic of Ireland would be a key strategic move (see Chapter 12). Importantly, if SWAN is allowed to breathe and remain free from the domination of a single political party, it has the potential to create a leftist and progressive space beyond the social work office and the university. Central to the SWAN agenda is the notion that new resources of hope, and political vibrancy, are to be found in the growth of users' movements (such as the disability movement and the mental health users' movement) which have brought innovation and insight to our ways of seeing social and individual problems. This perspective has particular resonance in

Ireland where – in the past – those incarcerated in Industrial Schools and similar institutions, such as the Magdalene laundries, have self-organized and campaigned for public inquiries into how they were treated. Similarly, in recent months it has been people with disabilities who have led opposition against benefit cuts. Such initiatives illuminate the potentiality of self-organized collective movements. The debates they spark can also 'help us think about the shape of an ... engaged social work based around such core "anti-capitalist" values as democracy, solidarity, accountability, participation, justice, equality, liberty and diversity' (Jones et al., 2004). The rest of this book will, therefore, dwell on these themes in developing a new politics for social work.

References

Back, L. (2007). *The art of listening.* Oxford: Berg.

Badiou, A. (2003). *Saint Paul.* Stanford: University of California Press.

Badiou, A. (2008). Communist hypothesis. *New Left Review, 49,* 29–47.

Badiou, A. (2010). *The communist hypothesis.* London: Verso.

Bailey, R., & Brake, M. (1975). (eds), *Radical social work.* London: Edward Arnold.

Boas, T.C., & Gans-Morse, J. (2009). Neoliberalism: From new liberal philosophy to anti-liberal slogan. *Studies in Comparative Economic Development, 44*(2), 137–161.

Boltanski, L. (2002). The Left after May 1968 and the longing for total revolution. *Thesis Eleven, 69,* 1–20.

Boltanski, L., & Chiapello, E. (2005). *The new spirit of capitalism.* London: Verso.

Bourdieu, P. (2001). *Acts of resistance: Against the new myths of our time.* Cambridge: Polity Press.

Brown, N. (2011). Red Years: Althusser's lesson, Rancière's error and the real movement of history. *Radical Philosophy, 170,* 16–25.

Budgen, S., Kouvelakis, S., & Žižek, S. (eds) (2007). *Lenin reloaded.* Durham, NC: Duke University Press.

Bunting, M. (2011). Hectored, humiliated, bullied: Women are bearing the brunt of flexible labour, *Guardian,* 2 May, 23.

Calhoun, C. (2003). Habitus, field and capital: The question of historical specificity. In C. Calhoun, E. LiPuma, & M. Postone (eds), *Bourdieu: Critical perspectives.* Cambridge: Polity Press.

Callinicos, A. (1999). *Social theory.* Cambridge: Polity Press.

Callinicos, A. (2010). *Bonfire of illusions.* Cambridge: Polity Press.

ChildStats.gov (2011). *America's children: Key national indicators of well-being, 2011.* Retrieved 5 December 2011 from http://www.childstats.gov/americaschildren/index3.asp.

Conservative Party. (2007). *No more blame game: The future for children's social workers.* Retrieved 24 October 2011 from http://www.fassit.co.uk/leaflets/No%20More%20Blame%20Game%20-%20The%20Future%20for%20Children's%20Social%20Workers.pdf.

Corrigan, P. (1982). The Marx factor. *Social Work Today*, 26 January, 8–11.

Couldry, N., Gilbert, J., Hesmondhalgh, D., & Nash, K. (2010). The new spirit of capitalism, *Soundings*, *45*, 109–124.

Coulshed, V. (1988). *Social work practice: An introduction*. London: Macmillan.

Cree, V.E. (2010). *Sociology for social workers and probation officers* (2nd edn). Abingdon, Berks: Routledge.

Cunningham. J., & Cunningham, S. (2008). *Sociology and social work*. Exeter, Devon: Learning Matters.

Davies, M. (1981). *The essential social worker*. London: Heinemann.

Dominelli, L. (2002). *Feminist social work theory and practice*. Basingstoke: Palgrave Macmillan.

Ebert, T.L. (1996). *Ludic feminism and after*. Ann Arbor: University of Michigan Press.

Ferguson, H. (2004). *Protecting children in time: Child abuse, child protection and the consequences of modernity*. Basingstoke: Palgrave Macmillan.

Ferguson, H. (2010). Therapeutic journeys: The car as a vehicle for working with children and families and theorizing practice. *Journal of Social Work Practice*, *24*(2), 121–138.

Ferguson, H. (2011). *Child protection practice*. Basingstoke: Palgrave Macmillan.

Ferguson, I. (2007). Neoliberalism, happiness and well-being. *International Socialism*, *117*, 123–143.

Garrett, P.M. (2009). *'Transforming' children's services? Social work, neoliberalism and the 'modern' world*. Maidenhead, Berkshire: McGraw Hill/Open University Press.

Garrett, P.M. (2012a). Adjusting 'our notions of the nature of the State': A political reading of Ireland's child protection crisis. *Capital & Class*, *36 (2)*, 263–281.

Garrett, P.M. (2012b). Reactivating the 'communist hypothesis': Alain Badiou and social work. *European Journal of Social Work*, online access from 12 September, http://www.tandfonline.com/doi/abs/10.1080/13691457.2012.724389.

Garrett, P.M. (2013a). *Social work and social theory*. Bristol: Policy Press.

Garrett, P.M. (2013b). A 'catastrophic, inept, self-serving' church?: Re-examining three reports on child abuse in the Republic of Ireland. *Journal of Progressive Human Services*, *24 (1)*, 1–23.

Good Gingrich, L. (2010). Single mothers, work(fare), and managed precariousness. *Journal of Progressive Human Services*, *21*(2), 107–135.

Gray, M., & Webb, S.A. (eds) (2013). *Social work theories and methods* (2nd edn). London: Sage.

Hall, S., Critcher, C., Jefferson, T., Clarke, J., & Roberts, B. (1978). *Policing the crisis: Mugging, the state and law and order*. Basingstoke: Macmillan Education.

Hardt, M., & Negri, A. (2000). *Empire*. Cambridge, MA: Harvard University Press.

Harris, J. (2003). *The social work business*. London: Routledge.

Harvey, D. (2010). *The enigma of capital and the crises of capitalism*. London: Verso.

Houston, S. (2002). Reflecting on habitus, field and capital: Towards a culturally sensitive social work. *Journal of Social Work*, *2*(2), 149–167.

International Federation of Social Workers (IFSW). (2000). *Definition of social work*. Retrieved 24 October 2011 from http://www.ifsw.org/f38000138.html.

Jones, C. (1983). *State social work and the working class*. London: Macmillan.

Jones, C. (2011). The best and worst of times: Reflections on the impact of radicalism on British social work education in the 1970s. In M. Lavalette (ed.), *Radical social work today: Social work at the crossroads*. Bristol: Policy Press.

Jones, C., Ferguson, I., Lavalette, M., & Penketh, L. (2004). *Social work & social justice: a manifesto for a new engaged practice.* Retrieved 10 December 2012 from http://www.socialworkfuture.org/about-swan/national-organisation/manifesto.

Joyce, P., Corrigan, P., & Hayes, M. (1988). *Striking out: Trade unionism and social work.* Basingstoke: Macmillan.

Kellner, D. (2002). Introduction to the second edition. In H. Marcuse (ed.), *One-dimensional man.* Oxford: Routledge.

Kentikelenis, A., Karanikolos, M., Papanicolas, I., Basu, S., McKee, M., & Stuckler, D. (2011). Health effects of financial crisis: Omens of a Greek tragedy. *The Lancet,* published online 10 October. Retrieved 5 December 2011 from http://www.thelancet.com/journals/lancet/article/PIIS0140-6736(11)61556-0/fulltext.

Klein, N. (2007). *The shock doctrine: The rise of disaster capitalism.* London: Allen Lane.

Lavalette, M. (ed.), (2011). *Radical social work today: Social work at the crossroads.* Bristol: Policy Press.

Llewellyn, A., Agu, L., & Mercer, D. (2008). *Sociology for social workers.* Cambridge: Polity Press.

MacKinnon, S.T. (2009). Social work intellectuals in the twenty-first century: Critical social theory, critical social work and public engagement. *Social Work Education, 28*(5), 512–527.

Matthewman, S., & Hoey, D. (2006). What happened to postmodernism? *Sociology, 40*(3), 529–547.

McLaughlin, K. (2008). *Social work, politics and society.* Bristol: Policy Press.

Mental Health Commission. (2011). *The human cost: An overview of the evidence on economic adversity and mental health and recommendations for action.* Retrieved 5 December 2011 from http://www.mhcirl.ie/News_Events/HCPaper.pdf.

Merrill Lynch & Capgemini (2011). 'Merrill Lynch Global Wealth Management and Capgemini release 15th Annual World Wealth Report', press release, 22 June. Retrieved 5 December 2011 from http://www.capgemini.com/news-and-events/news/merrill-lynch-global-wealth-management-and-capgemini-release-15th-annual-world-wealth-report/.

Milner, J. (1993). A disappearing act: the differing career paths of fathers and mothers in child protection investigations. *Critical Social Policy, 13*(2), 48–64.

Mullaly, B. (1997). *Structural social work.* Toronto, ON: Oxford University Press.

Parton, N. (2000). Some thoughts on the relationship between theory and practice in and for social work. *British Journal of Social Work, 30,* 449–463.

Pease, B., & Fook, J. (1999). Postmodern critical theory and emancipatory social work practice. In B. Pease & J. Fook (eds), *Transforming social work practice.* London: Routledge.

Price, V., & Simpson, G. (2007). *Transforming society? Social work and sociology.* Bristol: Policy Press.

Rogowski, S. (2010). *Social work: The rise and fall of a profession.* Bristol: Policy Press.

Schön, D. A. (1992). The crisis of professional knowledge and the pursuit of an epistemology of practice. *Journal of Interprofessional Care, 6*(1), 49–64.

Singh, G., & Cowden, S. (2009). The social worker as intellectual. *European Journal of Social Work, 12*(4), 1369–1457.

Thomas, R., & Davies, A. (2005). What have the feminists done for us? Feminist theory and organizational resistance. *Organization, 12*(5), 711–740.

Thompson, N. (2010). *Theorizing social work practice*. Basingstoke: Palgrave Macmillan.

Toynbee, P. (2010). Loyal, public service merits more than this cold trashing, *Guardian*, 24 August, 27.

Tucker, R. C. (ed.) (1978). *The Marx–Engels Reader*. London: Norton.

Wacquant, L. (2004). Critical Thought as Solvent of *Doxa*. *Constellations*, *11 (1)*, 97–102.

Wardhaugh, J., & Wilding, P. (1993). Towards an explanation of the corruption of care. *Critical Social Policy*, *13*(1), 4–32.

Webb, S.A. (2006). *Social work in a risk society: Social and political perspectives*. Basingstoke: Palgrave Macmillan.

Webb, S.A. (2009). Against difference and diversity in social work: The case of human rights. *International Journal of Social Welfare*, *18*, 307–316.

Weinstein, J. (2011). *Case Con* and radical social work in the 1970s: The impact of the revolutionaries. In M. Lavalette (ed.), *Radical social work today: Social work at the crossroads*. Bristol: Policy Press.

Žižek, S. (2002). *Revolution at the gates: Selected writings of Lenin from 1917*. London: Verso.

4

Social Work and the Politics of Recognition

Stan Houston

The indomitable presence of 'turbo' capitalism, and its claim to be 'the only and hottest game in town', has been radically undermined by recent events on the world stage. The manifest failures of corporate accounting systems – as exemplified in the Enron and WorldCom scandals – and reckless investments in speculative offshore hedge accounts, along with corporate greed, have shaken neoliberalism to its core. Accumulative, acquisitive and consumptive (over)drives have threatened the normative basis of the existing political economy.

In the USA, permissive borrowing rates for loans and mortgages, combined with reduced asset requirements, eventually showed the folly of increased deregulation, as investments failed to deliver on overly optimistic financial risk-planning and strategizing. Even the French president, Nicholas Sarkozy, uttered with Gallic pique that 'laissez-faire was finished', while Gordon Brown, the former British prime minister, surmised sagaciously that the old world of the Washington consensus was over. Gordon Gekko, the fictional doyen of entrepreneurial avarice, must surely have turned in his grave when surveying the latest crisis tendencies in the global market.

Ironically, governments in Western states have resorted to socialist remedies to deal with the fiscal crisis by recapitalizing established financial houses with huge loans. Moreover, deficits in the balance of payments led some to call for a reinstatement of traditional Keynesian solutions – spending on public works programmes – to stimulate growth. Economic postmortems highlighted the importance of global regulation across national frontiers as an antidote to the very real threat of a great depression coming on the back of failed policies of deregulation, liberalization and privatization. Yet, even so, a one-dimensional culture of pernicious individualism continues unabated in spite of the economic crisis, as does the culture of celebrity, experience of 'bowling alone', and continuing rupture of social solidarity within communities. It has been convincingly shown (Wilkinson & Pickett, 2009) that the increasing gap between the 'haves' and 'have-nots' has deleterious outcomes for both groupings on a range of social, economic and psychological measures. Rates of depression, for instance, are soaring in 'Prozac-infused' Western states.

As a result of the global economic crisis, the threat to investment and resourcing of welfare is at an all-time high. States find it problematic to raise taxation to meet deficits in their balance of payments in order not to offend middle-income voters, so welfare budgets are an easy target. This is despite the change in demographic profiles – ageing populations, dislocated youth within civil society, and heterogeneous family structures. In Britain, in the Blair years, the notable reforms to social welfare, enhancement of parenting programmes and early prevention geared towards the alleviation of child poverty are now being rolled back through the New Right's programme of austere financial retrenchment, despite talk of a commitment to the 'big society'. It is in this context that social work's continuing reliance on a largely individualistic model of intervention in the statutory sector, marked by technocratic and risk-aversive models of delivery, must surely be of particular concern for those committed to the axiom that the 'personal' is the 'political', and vice versa.

For capitalism, what matters is a safety net to restore the public's confidence in the system, in order to gloss over the link between private ills and public issues. Neoliberalism functions to assure and maintain, first, a welfare ideology based on the 'McDonaldization' and commodification of services; secondly, organizational governance through increasing modes of surveillance, pacification and discipline – of professional staff and service users alike; and thirdly, a policy framework featuring, among other things, populist notions of individual life-planning and the personalization of welfare. In all of this, there is a growing tendency to 'psychologize' human problems that have a clear societal basis. Despite the fact that depression may have a biological component, its social origins are not acknowledged sufficiently, and recast as problems of cognition.

It is within this context that a politicized social work should re-examine the contribution of critical social theory, as captured through the early progenitors of the Frankfurt School and their first-, second- and third-wave thinkers. The corpus offers an explanation of economic, political and cultural oppression (through an immanent critique of capitalist society) and charts a programme for emancipation based on the insuperable power of rationality, democratic communication and the essence of personhood itself.

Critical social theory enables the social worker to theorize the imbrication between the 'personal' and the 'political' to generate an informed, yet radicalized *praxis*. Such theorizing embraces an eclectic range of perspectives and ideas, including important psychoanalytic precepts and existential notions. As such, the approach differs from an anti-essentialist and decentred understanding of the person-in-society, one found in poststructuralist and postmodernist schools of thought. Within these schools, the constraints of discourse appear as all-consuming barriers to an agent-led form of emancipatory practice (see Chapter 8).

This chapter examines the work of Axel Honneth (1996, 2004), a modern-day, critical social theorist who has refined and developed his ideas taking account of the heirs to the Frankfurt School (Hegel, Marx and Feuerbach), its founding fathers (Adorno, Horkheimer and Marcuse) and, in particular, Honneth's immediate mentor, Jürgen Habermas. The voice of the Frankfurt School in social work needs to be heard more clearly as it foregrounds the role of human agency, emotion, critical reflection and their connection with emancipatory action in combating nefarious ideologies. Such ideas directly challenge the neoliberal agenda that commodifies relations and negates social connectivity.

Honneth's Theory of Recognition

Honneth's project of work has been to redefine a critical theory of the person in the context of historical social relations in order to posit how emancipatory change might occur. The strong unity of theory and *praxis*, the leitmotif of the Frankfurt School, remains the overriding concern. Rooted in Marx's theory of historical materialism, Honneth redefines the project of critical theory through a consideration of Habermas's linguistic turn to arrive at a theory of inter-subjectivity centred on the notion of 'recognition'. In making this journey, Honneth also leans heavily on the German philosopher, Feuerbach, and his view of the person as a *sensuous* being endowed with corporeality – one engaged purposefully in the social world, shaping it with her actions.

Honneth's project was shaped deeply by Feuerbach's take on philosophical anthropology, whereby, out of our history as a developing species, we attained a sense of reflective identity through social relations with one another and the environment to become morally attuned beings. Our social natures have been anchored in our needs to the point where the rejection of need creates feelings of *disrespect*. Due to the fact needs are omnipresent realities across cultures and historical epochs, they form a moral substratum and hence engender a normative critique of society when they are not met.

Honneth was animated by Feuerbach's critique of transcendentalism, which suggests philosophy should address itself to the inner consciousness of the subject. Instead, Feuerbach argued that human identity formation lay in inter-subjective relations. Furthermore, inter-subjectivity was grounded in embodied subjects interacting with the concrete world. We enter and leave the world through our embodied existence, argued Feuerbach. Upon entering the social world, the subject opens out to it and hence engages in some form of sensuous interchange with others. To be sensuous is to be emotional. When emotions are denigrated, the subject experiences hurt and outrage. It is the intensity of this feeling that led Feuerbach to view human *praxis* as a kind of emancipatory sensualism when denigration is experienced. In other words, the oppressed, propelled by emotional outrage and moral condemnation of their treatment, become politicized in their responses. To struggle through political action for respect is to engage the ethical life.

Marx, according to Honneth, departed from this understanding of oppression by focusing inordinately on labour relations and class action. The more primal sense of inter-subjectivity, articulated by Feuerbach, was present to some degree in his early humanist period of thought, but later lost in his mature work when Marx turned his formidable gaze on economic structures and mechanisms. For Honneth, the early Frankfurt theorists (Adorno and Horkheimer in particular) had also made this mistake. They, too, approached social interaction from the stance of 'labour' relations by making political economy the focus of their empirical work. Despite acknowledging the prescience of much of Habermas's work, including his ideas on inter-subjectivity, social interaction and communication, he too, according to Honneth, fell into a functionalist understanding of social relations with his famous distinction between the 'lifeworld' and 'system'.

Consequently, Honneth's *The Struggle for Recognition* (1996) owed much to the immanent critique of these early German philosophers even though, in an endeavour to reconstruct his own version of critical social theory, he departed from some of their core precepts. However, Hegel's formative influence upon Honneth must also be acknowledged. Hegel was perhaps one of the first thinkers to defend the salience of inter-subjectivity in forming human identity (influencing Feuerbach along the way) and exhort the norm-driven aspects of everyday social interaction. More specifically, Honneth grounded his 'recognition' model in Hegel's early writings at the University of Jena, which became a centre for the development of critical philosophy in the 1790s. Here, the idea of a fundamental unity between people is encountered, one that even precedes their understanding of themselves as separate beings. British object-relations theorist Donald Winnicott (1971), whose thinking we return to later on, captured vividly this idea in his observations of the symbiotic fusion between an infant and her mother. For Hegel, such a foundational sense of inter-being in defining who we are reaches its apogee when we engage fully with one another – when, crucially, we *recognize* one another. But more than that, individuals embrace the ethical life when recognition becomes the hub defining social interaction.

As a corollary, pathological expressions of social life, for Hegel, existed in downplaying the inter-subjective realm as a prime mover in identity formation. For Hegel, atomistic philosophies promoting individualism (one of which is derived from Aristotle) did not capture Johann Fichte's idea that self-consciousness was formed out of a circular, reciprocal reaction from another consciousness. This insight mirrored closely the central premise behind symbolic interactionism, a sociological theory developed by US pragmatist thinker, George Herbert Mead (1967). Borrowing from Mead, Honneth was able to refine his theory of recognition according to Hegelian premises. More specifically, Mead suggested I can evoke in myself the reaction my actions are likely to produce in the person to whom I am talking. For Honneth, Mead had articulated something fundamental to social interaction and moral behaviour: actors' capacity to role-take with others in order to shape their behaviour in ways to maximize success for all concerned. Humans have developed this capacity to carry out an internal dialogue within our heads allowing us to reflect on what others, and society at large, expects of us. For Honneth, role-taking and internal conversations about expectations of our behaviour were formative processes in the recognition of the other.

This early period in Honneth's work, centred on German philosophy and US pragmatism, led to the centrepiece of his programme: an expanded view on the nature of recognition in relation to the formation of the 'self'. Critically, Honneth was interested in how human beings related to themselves to enhance their sense of psychological well-being as a result of how significant others reacted to them. Honneth uses the term 'practical self-relation' to describe this process. As a consequence of positive recognition from others, a strong sense of 'practical self-relation' emerges within the individual. This, in turn, provides integrity and inner freedom.

Formatively, for Honneth, there are three types of recognition producing this ontological well-being within human beings, namely, recognition of the (1) need for love and care; (2) rights as a human being; and (3) strengths, or more precisely, the contribution he or she makes to the community. Table 4.1 sets out these dimensions of recognition and their psychosocial implications.

The attainment of self-confidence comes to the developing individual over the period of the life-course through acts of love and care shown by significant others. Honneth draws on Winnicott's (1971) object-relations theory to provide empirical support for this first major form of recognition. Winnicott challenged Freud's view that human development was mainly an intra-physic affair by arguing that infant development occurred in the context of relationships with objects (that is, people and things). So-called 'good-enough mothering' enabled the child to resolve inner conflicts and move from full dependence to relative interdependence in later life. Of

Table 4.1   Psychosocial implications of Honneth's model of recognition

Forms of recognition	Recognition as love and care	Recognition as acknowledging human rights	Recognition as identifying strengths
Outcomes of recognition	Attainment of of self-confidence	Attainment of self-respect	Attainment of self-esteem
Forms of misrecognition,	Abuse, denigration, criticism and emotional neglect	Denial of rights exclusion and treating the other as an 'object'	Focus on a person's deficits or ignoring his or her worth
Outcome of misrecognition	Lack of self-esteem	Self-disrespect	Lack of worth and dignity among peers

course, the infant might experience misrecognition in the form of parental unavailability, insensitivity, child abuse or undue interference causing inner doubt and insecurity. In this context, the infant's inner working model would be hampered and beset with negative feelings.

The individual also required an acknowledgement of her rights throughout the life-course in order to develop an identity where self-respect prevailed. Rights, for Honneth, should be widely defined. Thus, social, political, economic, civic and liberal rights are necessary (see Chapter 10). Social and individual categories should not pose any barriers to one's access to these rights, regardless of gender, race, culture, nationality, disability, religion and age. Honneth was not just concerned with the so called 'liberal' tradition of rights but also the civic, republican tradition. Rights are seen as individualistic and also collective. Granting them conveys to the individual they are deeply respected and valued.

The third form of recognition lay in acknowledging that a person possessed unique strengths which could make a contribution to some kind of community of interest. Strengths could take the form of vocational, sporting, cultural, occupational, professional abilities, or character-based attributes. The important issue is that they are acknowledged. The value of recognizing skills in young people in the education system as a way of enhancing their resilience is well known. Having at least one skill 'stress-proofs' the individual and also leads to feelings of self-efficacy and an inner locus of control. Competence in life and showing mastery over the world, even to a limited degree, offsets 'learned helplessness' and builds self-esteem.

It is important at this point to take stock of how Honneth's ideas have been received. Importantly, the conceptual sufficiency of this tripartite model has been questioned. Nancy Fraser (1995), for instance, in a long and protracted polemic against Honneth, opined we need to disentangle, conceptually speaking, 'recognition' from 'redistribution' (see also Chapters 2 and 7). Recognition, she argues, can address cultural needs but not the cleavages in political economy: class-based divisions, inequalities in living standards and material disadvantage. Honneth's model is tipped overly towards questions of cultural identity, Fraser suggests, thus reifying it at the expense of redistributive concerns. The recognition construct allows exploration of who we are as regards the inter-subjective domain of relating to one another, but it cannot enable us to explore a much wider domain of the economy nor of politics, where an egalitarian distribution of goods is to the fore and different kinds of mechanism operate. It addresses, therefore, wounded identities but not social-status injuries.

While there is merit in Fraser's argument, Honneth's (2004) more mature work credibly demonstrated how the recognition concept applied to injustice within political and economic institutions. In doing so, he maintained a leftist-Hegelian critique of contemporary politics, frowning on individualism within liberalism as a political philosophy. While this later work may not provide the reader with a full understanding of the economic basis of modern capitalism, it enables her to gain an understanding of its effects in terms of the manifold injustice it produces – the status injuries it engenders. For example, Honneth draws our attention to the labour market and its institutions. In these domains, some forms of work and not others are recognized. Moreover, some kinds of roles and statuses are recognized while others are ignored. The 'use value' of labour is another area where differences pertain as to what is valued, what is denigrated. Thus, care work, which arguably should command the highest form of societal reverence, is often poorly paid and receives a lowly status (Sevenhuijsen, 1998).

Honneth provides additional examples of how capitalist institutions demand increasingly more of workers in terms of their performance as they compete for advantage in league tables, bench-marking exercises and the market share. Institutions mainly recognize the worker in her capacity to produce, her capacity for entrepreneurial flair. Modern work practices placing emphasis on workers' mobility, flexibility, responsibility and independence have undermined their well-being and collective solidarity and, in doing so, generated psychological distress. Recognition in the workplace is contingent upon productivity as increasingly defined by narrow performance indicators and stretch targets instead of the traditional values of hard work, being a 'team player' and loyalty. Such analysis counters Fraser's claim that Honneth ignores the systemic, operational logic of the market. In all of this, Honneth is arguing if we want to understand the person-in-society nexus, we must do so through the lens of the person's inter-subjective relations, their psychic pain and the communication and action that flows from it. Subjective identity constructed through social interaction is, for

Honneth, made complete in the political moment. At this temporal point, institutions act as mediating domains between social structure and human agency.

Emancipatory Social Work and the Politics of Recognition

Honneth's work has not received the attention it deserves in social work. Houston (2008) explored his recognition model, recognizing its potential in social work. Other commentators, however, have raised concerns about the applicability of Honneth's ideas for social work. Paul Michael Garrett (2010), for instance, eschews recognition theory for its supposed 'psychologization' of human problems and its focus on micro-encounters without a sufficient understanding of structure of the neoliberal state. Houston's response to Fraser's critique, in defence of Honneth, might consequently apply also to Garrett's concerns, even though his points are very well made. Stephen Webb (2010) has also joined the debate. While recognizing the potential impact of recognition theory, he nonetheless wants to tie it explicitly, like Fraser, to the construct of redistribution. Significantly, for Webb (2010), the recognition–redistribution theoretic has the potential to animate ethical social work, as it seeks to respond to the social injustices arising from neoliberal, global capitalism (see Chapter 2).

This is not to say that all responses have been questioning. Froggett (2004) links creative forms of expression and personal development within institutions with interpersonal recognition. The recognition principle is seen as fundamental to struggles for empowerment within other societal domains. In a different vein, Marthinsen and Skjefstad (2011) give credence to the recognition construct in their empirical research of a social work programme in Norway. The social workers were able to develop the service-users' self-confidence by actively recognizing their strengths. Cortis (2007), likewise, showed the explanatory validity of the recognition construct. Service users (women attending a family centre with their children) appeared to value responses to them recognizing their unique worth. Juul (2009) took up a different theme by counterpoising the value of recognition in social work, as an underpinning normative ideal, with the negative judgement found in institutional practices. For Juul, judgement leads to service users experiencing disrespect. The idea that institutions present barriers to recognition is mirrored in Filsinger's (2003) attempt to apply Honneth to psychosocial practice with people with a learning disability. Institutional regimes, it is argued, present sources of misrecognition as witnessed in 'indignities, disregard and restrictions to autonomy' (p. 21). Finally, Fisher and Owen (2008) argued that health and social care workers were able to circumvent audit-based 'economies of performance' with more flexible 'ecologies of practice', wherein a space was created for recognition of the service-users' needs.

Examining this early body of work on Honneth's recognition model, some reservations but also some promising studies recording its empirical utility must be noted. The final part of this chapter contributes to this unfolding debate by outlining a method of social work practice called self-directed groupwork (Mullender & Ward, 1991). Notably, it promotes emancipatory practice for service users who have experienced debilitating forms of misrecognition. In particular, it is argued that self-advocacy and inclusion, two essential aspects of emancipatory practice, flow neatly from the method when buttressed by the three forms of recognition outlined above.

It is salutary to return to Mullender and Ward's (1991) ideas concerning the nature of empowerment. According to them, it is a catch-all phrase, made trendy by the political Right and Left. Despite the rhetoric, they say, insufficient attention has been paid to methodologies involving service users in realizing their own power to make desired changes. Crucially, for Mullender and Ward (1991), methods should tackle the 'personal' and the 'political', for private ills are linked to public issues. Furthermore, they should embrace consciousness-raising approaches and social action. Rather than social workers acting paternalistically on their behalf, service users should be empowered to take action for themselves, to self-advocate when common problems and needs are identified (see Chapter 8).

Table 4.2 presents a summary of how Honneth's recognition model informs the stages and steps within the method. It can be applied in a range of contexts, for example, young care leavers form a group to highlight their relative disadvantage, socially and economically; adults with a sensory impairment seek to realize better practical services from a local authority; or a group of travellers fight to preserve their distinct cultural identity and choice of lifestyle.

The first stage in the process, according to Mullender and Ward (1991), is for the social worker to take stock. This is a pre-planning stage. Here, social workers must reflect critically on their value base prior to engaging with service users in relation to the proposed groupwork. In this context, self-directed groupwork might be captured as an empowering process targeting service-users' struggles for recognition centring on their experiences of disrespect, denigration, shame, outrage and humiliation. Social workers must be receptive to service users, advocating for public recognition of their particular needs, concerns, identities and ways of being. Such demands are morally based but also politically inclined.

Drawing from this value base, self-directed groupwork at this early, pre-planning stage involves assembling a compatible co-worker team, establishing consultancy support and agreeing on empowering principles for the

Table 4.2 Applying self-directed groupwork through the lens of recognition theory

Stages	Aspects of recognition to consider
Stage One: The social workers take stock • Assembling a compatible co-worker team • Establishing appropriate consultancy support • Agreeing on empowering principles for the work	Social workers take stock of their role through recognition theory Teamwork involves reciprocal recognition between co-workers Consultant challenges workers' values using recognition theory as a moral benchmark Empowering principles for the work are defined
Stage Two: The group takes off • Open planning	Social workers seek to maximize service-users' inclusion and engagement to build their self-confidence, self-esteem and self-respect Symbolic interaction and perspective-taking are employed to build social identity, self-efficacy and competence
Stage Three: The group prepares to take action • Asking the 'what' question? • Asking the 'why' question'? • Asking the 'how' question?	Use Table 4.1 as a focal lens to tackle the questions. Examine the enabling and constraining effects of institutions on identity and well-being Examine how they positively recognize identity or engage in negative judgement Use action grid (see below)
Stage Four: The group takes action • Carrying out agreed actions	The group is supported to engage in self-advocacy around the attainment of due rights
Stage Five: The group takes over • Group review Reformulating what? Reformulating why? Reformulating how?	Use recognition model as a counter-factual tool for reflecting on success

work. It is perhaps self-evident that teamwork involves acts of reciprocal recognition between the workers, fuelled by mutual respect, democratic communication and building on one another's strengths. A consultant might highlight gaps or breaches of respect in the worker's preliminary dialogue about the group by using Honneth's tripartite model as a counter-factual tool – a tool highlighting breaches of expected normative standards. In all of this, empowering principles for the work are defined on the basis of the various components of recognition, namely, inclusion, respect, the need for a strengths-based focus, acknowledgement of rights and responses that demonstrate care.

In the second stage, the group takes off. Here, the workers engage with service users as partners to form the group though 'open planning'. In doing so, a particular style of work is inaugurated, enabling service users to set group norms and start the process of defining issues, setting goals and commencing a programme of work. However, advance planning activity by the social workers should be kept to a minimum as the aim is to promote service-user empowerment and maximize their inclusion. In this stage, the workers must seek to actively build the service-users' sense of self-confidence, self-esteem and self-respect. They must be sensitive to the fact that a robust social identity is a product of caring social interaction with solicitous and accurate perspective-taking at its hub. Tuning-in, in the way described, is antithetical to labelling, judgement and a 'looking glass' depiction of the 'other' as deficit-laden. Social workers need to remember that demands for recognition betray some form of personalized psychic injury or cultural ignominy at their very core. The fate of one's identity lies in the inter-subjective realm one inhabits.

In the third stage, the group prepares to take action and asserts its growing autonomy with the social workers receding in their influence. Here, the members are helped to explore the 'what', 'why' and 'how' questions. Specifically, they start with a consideration of 'what' problems need to be tackled. Table 4.1 provides a conceptual tool to focus responses to this question: what rights have been violated; what strengths or contributions have been ignored; what forms of disrespect have been shown; in what manner has identity been misrecognized; what is the impact of a failure to role-take; and what emotional needs have been unmet through neglectful or uncaring responses?

The 'why' question invites an examination of structural factors and their causative powers. Consequently, it has politicized connotations. It is asking why the problems identified in the first stage exist. According to Mullender and Ward (1991), 'introducing the question "why", though the answers may not always extend to global understanding, does consistently widen the areas of concern and potential action that users will identify and hence makes a major difference to the work' (p. 100). Honneth's later theories on institutions, referred to earlier, have much import in this regard. Institutions (workplaces, care homes, day centres, welfare offices, hospitals – to name a few – but also informal institutions, such as the family) are the conduits through which enablements and constraints emerge from wider social structures. Prescribed and proscribed routines, rules, expectations, rituals and imposed hierarchies, the humiliation of the 'self' though depersonalized forms of care, and so on, are the negative aspects of institutions. But on a wider plane, they indicate the low status of care, politically speaking, as Sevenhuijsen (1998) has credibly argued. Honneth's later work is instructive here as it enables service users to reflect on these experiences, gaining understanding of why personal problems are often linked to public issues through the domain of the institution.

The 'how' question is usefully tackled in terms of the action grid shown in Table 4.3, which can be populated by brainstorming ideas for enhancing well-being, status and rights according to different timescales and resources. In addition, attempts can be made to identify situations that can be changed completely, or with help, or cannot be changed at all, or represent situations outside the influence of the service user. An analysis of restraining forces (often institutionally located) that can be weakened and changing forces that can be buttressed provides analytical clarity. The collectivization of hurt, caused by misrecognition, acts as the driver for the 'how' aspect.

The fourth stage is concerned with action. The social workers' role here is to reinforce the group's efforts, promote confidence and create the right climate to enable service users to reflect on their actions. The groups' capacity to advocate for themselves is central and role-playing and modelling may help to develop competence in this area. Through acts of self-advocacy, the group members begin to overcome the social shame concomitant with passive endurance of humiliation and degradation. Such acts can be monitored for their success by again using Honneth's tripartite model of practical self-relation, but also in reformulating the what, why and how questions. At

Table 4.3   Action grid

	Now	Soon	Later
Action taken by us in the struggle for recognition			
Action taken with help in the struggle for recognition			
Action taken by others in the struggle for recognition			

this final stage, the intention is for the group to take over full responsibility for planning their strategy and actions. Typically, they will ask: 'what are the problems we still face?', 'Why do such a range of activities continue to exist?' and 'how can we best act on our renewed understanding to achieve our demands for recognition'?

Conclusion

Honneth (1996) says: 'because engaging in political struggle publicly demonstrates the ability that was hurtfully disrespected, this participation restores a bit of the individual's lost self-respect' (p. 164). By perceiving hurt emotions as the fulcrum tipping action towards normative and political aims, Honneth has harkened back to the original Frankfurt School project concerning the link between political domination and personal moral injuries. Self-directed groupwork is a primary example of how service users can take action through self-advocacy to recover their social and moral worth. For social workers, the method demonstrates inclusive practice with empowerment at its heart.

That said, the method is programmatic and does not reflect the reality that, in many cases, hurt emotions are buried beneath the meniscus of daily functioning. In other words, defence mechanisms are used to protect the self from injury. It is often not a simple case of disrespect automatically leading to demands for recognition in the political sphere. We know from object-relations theories, which Honneth selectively draws on, that defences such as projective identification, denial, reaction-formation, and so on, are galvanized when a threat to the inner working model presents itself. What is more, the wall-to-wall entertainment industry operates to deaden and divert inner attention away from the crippling situation of experienced humiliation. It is in this context that social work has a particular role to play in mediating the translation of hurt feelings to a political demand for recognition. Social workers bring skills of empathy and reflective listening when engaging with service users, as they surmise past hurts as a prelude for tackling aspects of the political order. These skills enable repressed memories to be communicated and ventilated. Thus, relationship-based social work is the medium through which self-directed groupwork ought to be operationalized. This form of social work employs both humanistic and psychoanalytic insights to engender a therapeutic alliance out of which hurt feelings can be accepted unconditionally. From this come trust and the capacity to engage mindfully with the equiprimordial needs for connection and separation, dependence and self-assertion. Social workers must mirror a positive self-image in their dealings with service users so that a propitious emotional relation to the self might flourish. It is only out of relational warmth and compassion that hurt feelings can be safely encountered, analysed and turned into politicized motives for action. In all of this, critical social work draws on recognition theory to give ontological substance to self-directed groupwork.

References

Cortis, N. (2007). Using community services: A case study in the politics of recognition. In J. Connolly, M. Leach, & L. Walsh (eds), *Recognition in politics: Theory, politics and practice*. Cambridge: Cambridge Scholars Publishing.

Filsinger, D. (2003). Reflections on the concept of recognition in psychosocial practice. *Psychiatrische Praxis, 30*, 21–27.

Fisher, P., & Owen, J. (2008). Empowering interventions in health and social care: Recognition through 'ecologies of practice'. *Social Science and Medicine, 67*, 2063–2071.

Fraser, N. (1995). From redistribution to recognition? Dilemmas of justice in a 'postsocialist' age. *New Left Review, 212*, 410–440.

Froggett, L. (2004). Holistic practice, art, creativity and the politics of recognition. *Social Work and Social Sciences Review, 11*, 29–51.

Garrett, P.M. (2010). Recognising the limitations of the political theory of recognition: Axel Honneth, Nancy Fraser and social work. *British Journal of Social Work, 40*, 1517–1533.

Honneth, A. (1996). *The struggle for recognition: The moral grammar of social conflicts*. London: Polity Press.

Honneth, A. (2004). Organised self-realisation: Paradoxes of individuation. *European Journal of Social Theory, 7*, 463–478.

Houston, S. (2008). Conceptualising child and family support: The contribution of Honneth's critical theory of recognition. *Children and Society, 22*, 458–469.

Juul, S. (2009). Recognition and judgement in social work. *European Journal of Social Work, 12*, 403–417.

Marthinsen, E., & Skjefstad, N. (2011). Recognition as a virtue in social work practice. *European Journal of Social Work, 14*, 195–212.

Mead, G.H. (1967). *Mind, self and society*. Chicago: Chicago University Press.

Mullender, A., & Ward, D. (1991). *Self-directed groupwork: Users take action for empowerment*. London: Whiting & Birch.

Sevenhuijsen, S. (1998). *Citizenship and ethics: Feminist considerations on justice, morality and politics*. London: Routledge.

Webb, S.A. (2010). (Re)assembling the left: The politics of redistribution and recognition in social work. *British Journal of Social Work, 40*, 2364–2379.

Wilkinson, R., & Pickett, K. (2009). *The spirit level: Why equality is better for everyone*. London: Penguin.

Winnicott, D. (1971). *Playing and reality*. Harmondsworth: Penguin.

PART II

Politically Informed Social Work Practices

5

Critically Reflective Practice

Carolyn Taylor

The concept of reflective practice is embedded within professional education for health and social work in Anglophone countries (Gould & Taylor, 1996; Johns & Freshwater, 1998; Taylor, 2010) and elsewhere (Nordman, Kasén, & Eriksson, 1998; Yip, 2006). It has been presented as a 'new epistemology of practice', a rejection of attempts within professions such as social work to emulate the natural sciences in their quest for definitive positivist knowledge on which to base practice (Napier & Fook, 2000).

Reflective practice has assumed an important place within the curriculum as a tool for professional learning, often coexisting alongside attempts to make practice more 'evidence-based' or 'research-informed'. Adding the word 'critical' to the term begs several questions: how does this addition alter the concept of reflective practice? What distinguishes critically reflective practice from reflective practice? How can critically reflective practice be used to inform a New Left politics of social work?

To address these questions, the chapter commences by discussing reflective practice and identifies its key elements and the form it takes. It then sets out how critically reflective practice differs in many respects from reflective practice, influenced as it is by critical social science and post-structuralism. An example of reflective practice is given as part of this discussion before examining an alternative approach that attends to 'the politics of representation' within an educational setting (Mehan, 2001). This marks a significant departure from the 'confessional tales' encapsulated in reflective practice. It is argued that critically reflective practice contributes to a new politics of social work, providing it does not slide back into the 'benign introspection' of reflective practice (Taylor, 2003; Taylor & White, 2000). A different set of questions is framed to pose of practice as part of this commitment to a politically-attuned critically reflective form of practice.

Reflective Practice

From the late 1980s, the work of academic and organizational consultant, Donald Schön (1930–97), directly stimulated the rise to prominence of the concept of the 'reflective practitioner' in social work and its subsequent assimilation into the educational curriculum (Schön, 1983, 1987). Schön's starting point for reflective practice was a hard-hitting critique of the professions. He argued that professionals had not lived up to their claims of altruistic service for the benefit of patients and clients using independently verified – and verifiable – knowledge. Professionals have feet of clay: they act for personal gain and self-aggrandizement. They become immersed in, and rendered powerless by, bureaucracies, and they bow to the power and influence of big business and government (Schön, 1983). More tellingly, for Schön, professionals (and Schön had law and medicine primarily in his sights) promote a method of practice – technical rationality – that is not conducive to dealing with the situations of practice:

> In the varied topography of professional practice, there is a high, hard ground overlooking a swamp. On the high ground, manageable problems lend themselves to solution through the application of research-based theory and technique. In the swampy lowland, messy, confusing problems defy technical solution. (Schön, 1987, p. 3)

For Schön (1987), this presents professionals with a clear choice: 'shall he [*sic*] remain on the high ground where he can solve relatively unimportant problems according to the prevailing standards of rigor, or shall he descend to the swamp of important problems and nonrigorous inquiry?' (p. 3). His encapsulation of the messiness and indeterminacy of practice lies at the heart of his ideas. The quest for certainty and the linear problem-solving approach are called into question and the hierarchy of status is inverted: those who grapple with the messiness of practice are engaged in a more difficult and highly prized endeavour than those who adopt a technocratic approach to problems, acting, as it were, as 'handmaidens' to pure science. In place of the generalities common to technical-rationality, Schön (1983) insists upon the 'artful practice of the unique case' (p. 19). In practice, nothing is straightforward and each instance poses its own challenges and dilemmas that have to be worked through. Thus, formal knowledge of an objective, scientific kind tends to remain in the background, while in the foreground the practitioner – note he or she is no longer called a 'professional' – is engaged in negotiating the messy indeterminacies of the 'swampy lowland'.

Schön (1983) deploys three concepts in describing the realities of professional practice:

1. *Knowing-in-action* involves significant elements of tacit knowledge: 'Spontaneous, skilful performance' (p. 191) is in evidence without the person being able to make articulate how it is being done. Here Schön blurs the line between professional practice and everyday activities by drawing on examples such as bicycle riding as examples of knowing-in-action.

2. *Reflection-in-action* arises when our implicit knowing-in-action is disrupted by something that prompts uncertainty and the need to question our actions and thinking, and experiment to find solutions: 'when practitioners reflect in action they describe their own intuitive understandings' (Schön, 1983, p. 276).

3. *Reflection-on-action,* though given less attention in Schön's (1983) work due to his focus on what occurs in the moment of practice, can be summed up as the process of 'making sense of an action *after it has occurred* and possibly learning something from the experience which extends one's knowledge base' (Eraut, 1994, p. 191; emphasis added). Its virtues lie in aiding the development of tacit 'practice wisdom', an ability to practise intuitively.

In social work, Schön's third concept of *reflection-on-action* has been given greatest prominence, aided by Dreyfus and Dreyfus's (1986) idea of a progression in professional development from novice to expert through this reflective process. Thus reflection became a core tool for professional learning and development that occurs not simply through immersion in practice but also by honing one's skills as a reflective practitioner who, by looking back, is enabled to move forward to practise his or her craft skills. To aid such development, a burgeoning literature has emerged, along with a significant number of models for reflection in which the locus of attention is the thoughts and feelings of the individual practitioner as he or she looks back to an incident from his or her practice, and questions and challenges his or her own actions in the professional encounter.

Such is the prominence of reflective practice that some believe it has come to enjoy 'a cult following among curriculum planners and those responsible for professional education' (Ixer, 1999, p. 513). But it has not been immune from criticism. In particular, the concept of reflection-in-action has been subject to intense scrutiny. According to Eraut (1994), Schön fails to analyse everyday practice and, in fact, his examples do not provide evidence of reflection-in-action, but rather concern reflection-on-action oriented to future rather than current action.

Others have raised concerns about the insertion of this 'vague conceptual notion' (Ixer, 1999, p. 514) into the professional education curriculum (Ixer, 1999; Rodgers, 2002). Writing about teacher education, Rodgers (2002) shares Ixer's (1999) concern, noting several problems arising from this lack of clarity, including difficulties in talking about a concept that has no precise definition and distinguishing between systematic reflection and other forms of thought; and problems in assessing 'reflection' and researching its effects on professional practice. Ixer (1999) questions how such a confused concept can be adequately assessed as part of professional learning and expresses concern that student learners who fail to grasp the conventions of reflective practice might be negatively assessed.

However, there is more at stake than greater clarity and refinement of concepts and assessment criteria. Ixer's (1999) critique constitutes a far more profound challenge. He argues that reflection is never purely inductive, nor does it derive simply from experience: 'our preconceived ideas shape the way current action is framed rather than, as Schön saw it, experience being shaped by current action' (Ixer, 1999, p. 519). We do not come to reflection as a *tabula rasa*, rather we bring our understandings and experience to our sense-making in the present. For Ixer (1999), reflection is more than in-the-moment or retrospective action. It is a complex social process in which 'our reflective processes are socially, historically and politically influenced' (p. 519). This is important in exploring how *critically* reflective practice differs from Schön's reflective practice.

In reflective practice the primary focus is individual reflective practitioners and their subjective understanding of experience. In being predicated upon self-understanding and awareness, reflective practice is seen as conforming to a liberal-humanist project of personal growth and self-actualization. It possesses the three dominant features of this rational tradition in asserting that:

> *To be a person is to experience oneself as existing in the world*: subjective experience is always from the perspective of a particular person ...

> *To be a person is to be an active, intentional agent* who engages with, and can influence the world ...

> *To be a person is to possess reflexive awareness*: An extraordinary feature of being human is our capacity for self-awareness, to be aware of our thoughts, feelings, and ourselves hence the notion of the critically reflective self. (Stevens, 1996, p. 153)

This emphasis on the rational individual pervades reflective accounts, where practitioners portray themselves as battling singlehandedly to redress deficiencies in others' practice or heroically display their inadequacies in order to demonstrate how they have developed professionally and learnt to practise sensitively and ethically (Taylor, 2003, 2006). Reflective practice thus starts from a position of 'methodological individualism' in its treatment of people as atomized individuals with particular dispositions and attributes (Burkitt, 2008), albeit ones amenable to change and growth.

Reflective practice adopts a politically neutral stance or represents a depoliticized view of practice in the sense that its overriding goal is practitioners working to the very best of their abilities, attuned to the needs of individual patients, clients, families and carers. Reflective practice implies that, by each practitioner engaging in a process of self-scrutiny, overall professional standards will rise. It displays limited understanding of, and indeed interest in, social structures, instead focusing on individual relationships, be they between practitioners and other professionals or between practitioners and service users.

Reflective practice is broadly accepting of the status quo and the existing parameters of practice, seeing the locus of change as residing in the individual practitioner. For this reason, while reflective and evidence-based practice might have very different ideas about the knowledge–practice relationship, they are both concerned with raising professional standards in a way that sidelines critical political engagement. Neither makes a core political commitment to social justice. Their primary allegiance is to the profession. Reflective practice thus lacks overt analysis of social structures and fails to acknowledge adequately matters of power, hierarchy and domination as they inhere in relations of professional practice.

The following case study in which a critical care nurse challenges a nurse consultant about a decision of 'do not resuscitate' (DNR), recorded in the patient's notes, serves to illustrate this point (Rolfe, Freshwater, & Jasper, 2001). It is reported as a short outburst, *an individual act of resistance* rather than an incident that seriously challenges nurse–nurse consultant relations in the longer term. As far as we can tell as readers, at some remove from the actual incident, it has to be said, it does not act as a catalyst for more collaborative ways of working between nurses and consultants on that ward or in that hospital. It does not alter policy and practice in relation to DNR decisions. Indeed, it seems to have put the nurse in the position of needing to go to some lengths to repair the situation.

In many ways this is a typical example of a reflective account, albeit one that has been published in a textbook. As is common for such accounts, it uses a particular framework – in this instance the rather simple one of 'what, so what, now what?' proposed by Borton (1970) – to present reflection on a recent practice incident. It acts as a heroic confessional tale in which the nurse owns up to conducting herself badly in the heat of the moment and bears some affinity with the kinds of confessional tales that have emerged from ethnographic research (Van Maanen, 1988).

Case example of reflective practice

What happened?

I became very angry at the way in which the nurse consultant took a life-and-death decision about this patient without any consultation with the staff who knew him best. I tried to put across my point of view, but she refused to listen. I eventually lost my temper and shouted at her in the middle of the ward. At this point, she stormed out.

So what am I to make of this?

First, I shouldn't have lost my temper. The consultant probably felt just as uncomfortable as I did about the decision, and dealt with it by asserting her authority ... She might have responded to a rational argument but, by becoming angry, I simply gave her the excuse to storm out. I can see now that any chance of rational communication was blocked by our highly charged emotional states.

Now what can I do to make the situation better?

Now that I am feeling calmer, I think I should make an appointment to see the consultant. We need to talk about the situation sensibly. I may not be able to change her mind but I owe it to myself and to my patient to give it my best shot. I also need to let the consultant see that I am a professional practitioner and that my opinion counts for something. (Rolfe et al., 2001, pp. 27–28)

The situation is rendered authentic by the detail that makes the reader easily able to picture the scene and possibly, without condoning her angry shouting, even to take her side in the argument as the underdog advocating on behalf of 'her' patient (note the nurse's use of the possessive 'my'). There is redemption for the nurse in her subsequent acknowledgement of mishandling the situation and resolving to repair it so that equilibrium in working relationships can be reinstated and trust in her professional competence restored. However, as it is presented, there is no indication that the contentious issue of decisions to categorize certain patients as unsuitable for resuscitation is seriously challenged and that hospital practice will change as a result of this angry exchange and clash of opinions. Instead, it seems confined to an argument about who is best placed to assert this patient's interests on the basis of differing knowledge claims to professional competence: formal medical knowledge of diseases and prognosis on the part of the nurse consultant versus knowing the patient's wishes as a nurse intimately involved in his or her care on a day-to-day basis.

While framing the issues in this way can undoubtedly be important for advancing personal development in one's chosen area of work, a strong argument can also be made for casting the analysis in a different way. Nonetheless, it is essential to point out that conducting a different form of analysis does not mean transforming the heroic author of reflection into a *heroic activist* 'distinguished from orthodox workers by their willingness to rationally recognize systemic injustices and their preparedness to take a stand against the established order' (Healy, 2000, p. 135); the 'disembodied' heroic activist tends 'to stand outside systems of power and speak the truth to them' (Healy, 2000, p. 135). In everyday practice, Healy (2000) argues, agency is 'less a matter of standing out from the crowd in a heroic way than engaging in social change activities through the local networks and systems of which they are a part' (p. 135). Arguably, the heroic activist operates with rather crude binaries of 'them' and 'us' and with a simplified analysis of power that cannot do justice to the complexities of welfare organizations. It is this desire to read the circumstances of practice better, to interrogate them thoroughly and to construct meaningful analyses to which critically reflective practice aspires.

Critically Reflective Practice

Reflective and *critically* reflective practice share a similar starting point in viewing practice as messy and indeterminate rather than orderly and linear. Both reject the idea that externally-generated propositional knowledge – 'knowing that' – is applied to a clearly and easily defined problem in a linear way that privileges theory building or knowledge generation at the expense of the complexities of practising in uncertain terrain. In evidence-based practice, for example, the process of assessment or diagnosis tends to be regarded as unproblematic, with the primary emphasis placed on finding and using empirical evidence to achieve effective outcomes (Gray, Plath, & Webb, 2009; Reynolds, 2000). The messiness of practice situations, such as those in matters of child abuse and neglect or mental health, is not adequately recognized in this schema (Taylor & White, 2001). Hence both claim that 'knowing how' – the knowledge that comes from being in practice and dealing with complex and often intractable situations – is as important as propositional knowledge generated outside practice. Finally, both agree that learning is not solely about doing but also about thinking about actions and experiences. Both are attuned to the idea of *reflection-on-action* prefigured by US educationist John Dewey (1933), who defines reflective thinking as 'active, persistent, and careful consideration of any belief or supposed form of knowledge in the light of the grounds that support it and the further conclusions to which it tends, constitute reflective thought' (p. 9). However, critically reflective practice regards the creation of 'necessary distance' (Rossiter, 2005) from practice as crucial to making sense of it in a critical way. Significantly, it parts company with reflective practice in rejecting its individualism and political neutrality. In contrast, critically reflective practice sees individual selves as produced in interaction with others. We are 'social selves rather than self-contained atoms' (Burkitt, 2008, p. 3). Critical reflection is thus a social rather than individual reflective process.

The form of critically reflective practice proposed has a similar starting point to the form of critical reflection advocated by Jan Fook and Fiona Gardner (2007), with which readers may be familiar. Critical social theory and poststructuralist thought inform our thinking and some of the broader questions are similar in placing social work practice in context. For example, Fook and Gardner (2007) suggest that the process of critical reflection 'is designed to create an environment in which people are enabled to unsettle the major assumptions on which practice is based, making connections between these assumptions and their beliefs about their social world' (p. 25). However, they have stayed closer to the traditions of reflective practice in terms of method: their core focus is on critical incident analysis as a tool for *individual reflection*. While their approach is undoubtedly helpful, my approach moves away from this form of self-questioning to deploy methods drawn from the social sciences to interrogate the spoken and written texts of social workers. My aim is to shift from individual acts of reflection, which themselves are versions produced in particular local contexts (Taylor, 2006), towards a more politically nuanced treatment of social work as collective practice, which examines the everyday routines of practice (see de Montigny, 2013; Floersch, Longhofer, & Nordquist Schwallie, 2013; White, 2013).

The form of critically reflective practice I propose challenges the 'innocent' knowledge of reflective practice, arguing that the very notions of 'helping' and 'caring' cannot be taken for granted as intrinsic to practice by health and welfare workers. In essence, reflective practice regards these notions as unproblematic, ascribing deviance from these ideals to the inevitable human fallibility of individual practitioners, believing self-awareness through reflection can redress these fallibilities. In contrast, critically reflective practice seeks to problematize what it means to 'help' and 'care'. It seeks to interrogate the helping relationship and explore how 'domination may be reinscribed at the moment of helping' (Heron, 2005, p. 342). Where reflective practice glosses over power relations in the 'helping' process, critically reflective practice foregrounds their importance and opens them up to political scrutiny. Its ambitions are not simply for professionals to understand themselves better but for the profession to make a political commitment to 'social work as social justice work' (Rossiter, 2005). In taking this stance, critically reflective practice eschews the crudities of much of the analysis of power within social work, which treats it as a core possession of practitioners, one which can be assuaged by acknowledging one's social location ('race', gender, class, and so forth) *vis à vis* the service user (Thompson, 1993).

Thus, critically reflective practice has turned away from structural analyses of power, often associated with Marxist-influenced radical social work, to embrace poststructuralist thinking about power and subjectivity in order to make sense of, and challenge, the micro-politics of power in everyday practice situations (see Chapters 2 and 3). In doing so, it adopts a particular stance to knowledge/power:

- First, it rejects 'grand narratives', such as totalizing theories of revolutionary change, since these are perceived as giving a 'one-sided, reductive perspective on social reality' (Pease & Fook, 1999, p. 11) rather than offering a multidimensional understanding.

- Secondly, it is asserted that all meaning is unstable and temporary (Weedon, 1987). Social meanings, it is argued, 'are produced within social institutions and practices' (Weedon, 1987, p. 25), and these are always 'historically and contextually situated' (Healy, 2000, p. 39).

This allows for competing interpretations of events and situations although, as will be seen in an example in due course, one interpretation may come to dominate. So, rather than a desire to fix the essence of social work, there is recognition that there are a broad range of locally-situated practices which produce 'social work' (Healy, 2000). To explore these practices, it becomes relevant to examine the way in which social reality is constituted in discourse (see also Chapter 8).

Michel Foucault (1972) described discourse as 'practices which systematically form the objects of which they speak' (p. 49). According to MacLure (2003), discourses can be thought of as 'practices for producing meaning, forming subjects and regulating conduct within particular societies and institutions, at particular historical times' (p. 175). In making 'the discursive turn', critically reflective practice operates with a specific analysis of the conditions in which practice occurs, extending beyond the self-examination of reflective practice to interrogating how social work is constituted in ordinary, everyday settings and encounters by social actors, who are both constrained and enabled by their institutional settings.

An example of work already in the public domain is given to illustrate the possibilities of critically reflective practice. My chosen example is taken from outside social work but is one that I use in my teaching with students on both undergraduate and postgraduate social work programmes. It demonstrates extremely well the way in which examining 'the politics of representation' lies at the heart of critically reflective practice. In order to proceed, critically reflective practice has eschewed the kinds of questions posed within reflective practice frameworks. It has looked instead to academic disciplines in the social sciences and humanities for tools and techniques of analysis. Ethnomethodology, and conversation and discourse analysis, are important influences (for further elaboration, see de Montigny, 2013;

Floersch et al., 2013; Taylor & White, 2000; White, 2013, and for a contrasting form of discourse analysis, see Chapter 8). These enable a different focus on talk and texts in practice. Rather than treating talk and text as resources to be mined for information, they are treated as topics in their own right. This prompts a different set of questions about organizational cultures and the way the business of the occupational group is enacted in everyday settings: 'how do things get done around here?' and 'what are the material effects of the way that things get done?' become key questions. In sum, the focus is analysing and changing the social relations of practice rather than the thoughts and feelings of individual practitioners.

Mehan (2001) explores the process by which a child acquires an educational label of learning disability – or what might today be named a pupil with special educational needs – from a perspective that assumes this involves a conflict between opposing views of the child, and where, ultimately, one view comes to dominate. There are, in effect, conflicting representations of the child and it is possible to study how one version or discourse comes to dominate other modes of representation. In order to do this, Mehan (2001) observed and audiorecorded the following interactions: a 9-year-old child in class with a teacher; his discussion as researcher with the class teacher; and a subsequent professional meeting about the child. We can see at once that this involves a different method from reflective practice, which depends on *post hoc* reports of practice, typically to people (supervisors or assessors) who were not present at the time of the interaction. In effect, reflective accounts act as time travellers that solidify the action in a similar way to case recordings (Taylor, 2008). The mode of analysis adopted by Mehan (2001) takes us much closer to the action. We do not see the teacher–child interactions and the meetings as such, but we are given access to extracts from research transcripts, notably discussion with the class teacher and extracts from the assessment meeting, as well as the psychologist's written report. We are thus enabled to compare our own reading of the text with the author's.

Central to Mehan's (2001) argument is the claim that a lexical formulation does not simply 'reflect unique or exhaustive characteristics [of persons] given in advance' (p. 345). An example given is the difference between the appellations 'guest worker', 'potential citizen', 'illegal immigrant' and 'undocumented worker'. All of these have different connotations, constitute migrants differently and have different material effects in terms of citizenship and belonging within a nation-state. It is this process of competition over modes of presentation of people and 'facts' that Mehan (2001) terms the politics of representation:

> Proponents of various positions in conflicts waged in and through discourse attempt to capture or dominate modes of representation. They do so in a variety

of ways, including inviting or persuading others to join their side, or silencing opponents by attacking their positions. If they are successful, a hierarchy is formed in which one dominant mode of representing the world ... gains primacy over others, transforming modes of representation from an array on a horizontal plane to a ranking on a vertical plane. This competition over the meaning of ambiguous events, people, and objects in the world has been called the 'politics of representation'. (p. 345)

Mehan's (2001) analysis explores how 'labelled social facts are produced from the ambiguity of everyday life' (p. 346). In this instance, he examines the process by which a student becomes constructed as learning disabled. He acknowledges that this operates on at least two planes: one is the broader one in which the category is reconstructed over time. This takes us into the realms of the social history of the category 'learning disabled' and its translation into law and policy as it has changed since the nineteenth century. The other plane is that of the practical application in which 'the historically constructed and legally prescribed categories are articulated with potential instances in actual educational practice at the school site' (p. 347). This involves studying the routine practices of educators as they go through the process of 'referral', 'educational testing' and 'placement' (p. 348).

The child in question is Shane (not his real name), who is referred by his class teacher one month after joining his new school, for his 'low academic performance' and 'his difficulty applying himself to daily class work' (p. 349). Mehan (2001) suggests that, in many respects, Shane seems little different to his peers: they too expressed consternation at the difficulty of certain tasks but, unlike Shane, they were not referred for 'technical assessment'. The testing of his IQ and educational level leads to the transformation of his academic skills into numerical terms, for example 'an IQ of 115, test age 7.5' (p. 351). Shane has now shifted from being an individual pupil to one who is being compared to a normative standard. In this process, his identity is being sharpened from child 'who needs help' to possibly 'a learning disabled child' (p. 351). This sharpening of Shane's identity continues. Despite the mother's concerns about the stigmatizing effects of such a categorization, the process continues apace.

In the next stage, four reports of the child are presented to a meeting of the 'Eligibility and Placement Committee' by the school psychologist, the class teacher, the school nurse and the mother, respectively. Under consideration is Shane's placement in a programme for learning disabled children. The reports varied in three ways: '(1) the manner in which they presented information, (2) the manner in which they founded assertions, [and] (3) the manner in which they presented the child' (Mehan, 2001, p. 351).

With regard to the first of these, the psychologist is given the floor to present her written report without interruption. Other participants – the class teacher, nurse and mother – are treated differently. Their verbal reports are *elicited* by the committee chair rather than delivered. The teacher, the nurse and the parent are questioned and often interrupted. While the psychologist uses her written report as a prop and speaks from her notes, others have to rely solely on memory. The psychologist also uses a different register for talking about Shane. Her discourse is framed in terms of generalized 'troubles' and 'problems', for example 'he cannot switch channels' (p. 355), while the teacher is more positive ('he enjoys math', p. 355), introducing contingencies that affect Shane's performance, such as 'if he's given a sheet where he can fill in answers and work them out he does much better' (p. 356). In contrast to the school psychologist's psychological mode of representation, the teacher speaks 'sociologically, providing contextual information of a locally situated sort' (p. 356). The mother's mode of representation is different again: it is 'historical and biographical' (p. 359), speaking of changes over time (p. 356), for example 'as a small child he ... wasn't interested in sitting on my lap and having a book read to him ... now Shane, at night, lots of times he comes home and he'll write or draw. He's really doing a lot' (p. 354). All three produce different formulations of Shane, but it is the psychologist's that achieves privileged status, effectively trumping the other, more anecdotal versions gained from interacting with the child in the natural setting of home or school.

Mehan's (2001) suggestion as to why this is the case at first seems counter-intuitive, namely that 'the psychologist's discourse obtains privileged status *because* it is ambiguous, *because* it is shot through with technical terms, *because* it is difficult to understand' (p. 357; emphasis added). It is *because of*, and not in spite of, the way the psychologist 'presents information, grounds her assertions and represents the child in discourse' (p. 357) that means her version does not get challenged in the meeting. Speaking from 'an institutionally designated position of authority' (p. 358) and invoking a technical register allows the psychologist's discourse to prevail in this setting. The results of her tests are treated as unchallengeable. Maternal knowledge and teacher discourse cannot match them for objective authority. This has profound consequences for Shane:

> [t]he child becomes an object ... at the outset the child was a participant in discourse with his teachers and his classmates. But, from that point on, the child's contribution to his own career status drops out. The child is only represented in text. The only way we have access to the child is through textual representations of his interactions. The child becomes objectified as the case moves from the classroom to testing to committee meeting. (Mehan, 2001, p. 359)

As the process develops, a 'context-free' view of Shane is developed, one in which he is seen as having a general learning disability. His deficits are not seen as context specific, for example as linked to his move from Montessori to mainstream education. It is institutionally grounded representations formulated from standard tests (WISC-R, the CAT and the Bender Gestalt) (Mehan, 2001, p. 350) that prevail over knowledge derived from experience of and with the child. Noticeably, after the testing process the child is absent, or rather present only as an 'object of concern'.

This worked example provides insight into how critically reflective practice might be realized in social work. It indicates how it might look radically different from conventional forms of reflective practice, with their emphasis on confessional tales by individuals. Instead, by adopting the methods of conversation and discourse analysis (Wooffitt, 2005), critically reflective practice can turn to examine the situated practices that occur in everyday routine practice in social work. There are clear parallels between the process of constructing Shane as a learning disabled child in need of special education and the way in which practitioners and their managers construct social work cases as instances of child abuse and neglect, mental health problems warranting deprivation of liberty, or an older person as at risk of harm. This way of exploring practice moves us away from what is going on in people's heads to an analysis of how, in everyday practice, cases are constituted out of the ambiguities of everyday life. It also enables us to address the micropolitics of power, the way that it operates in social interactions and through texts. It offers an insight into how service users and patients may respond to these institutional processes that deprive them of a voice. Lack of cooperation, resistance and hostility may be ways in which users and patients try, often unsuccessfully, to confront professional domination of the politics of representation. James Scott (2009) sees resistance as a vital precursor to effecting change in social relations. We may further suggest that any complacent rehearsal of 'social work values' as though they inhere in all social work practice, or any easy assumption that textbooks can somehow magically exhort the 'right' values into existence is flawed in its approach. Mehan's (2001) conclusion challenges such complacency:

> More and more often in our increasingly technocratic society, when a voice speaking in formalized, rationalistic, and positivistic terms confronts a voice grounded in personal, common sense or localized particulars, the technical prevails over the vernacular. (p. 361)

Now as an assertion, this may not be warranted. Mehan's (2001) single example does not provide definitive proof. It should be noted that in his example, professionals are neither identical in the representations they produce nor in the extent to which their voice is heard. The class teacher, in effect, is no more successful than the mother at getting her voice and version heard; by refusing to align herself with the psychologist in the technocratic camp, she is effectively silenced. However, Mehan's (2001) work prompts us to consider whether this statement does apply currently in social work and cognate disciplines. To explore this will require close attention to the situated practice of social work and what it is that social work accomplishes in its day-to-day business. Rather than focusing on individual *post hoc* accounts, it suggests that close study of talk or language in use and the production and circulation of texts will be valuable if social work is to learn more about how it operates and to what end. This raises some profound questions about the possibilities for a model of social work based on social justice. (How) can social workers work differently with service users? Does 'making the case' inevitably do violence to users' lives and place practitioners in opposition to users?

Conclusion

This chapter has argued that, to understand critically reflective practice and its potential, it is essential to understand its differences from reflective practice. Where reflective practice seeks to ameliorate practice by individual endeavour, critically reflective practice operates on a broader canvas, with wider goals of social change in its sights interpreted from a poststructuralist perspective. Where reflective practice focuses on the individual practitioner, critically reflective practice seeks to decentre the human subject to focus on practice and how it is constructed and undertaken in specific instances. It does not emphasize practitioners' uniqueness as individuals but rather seeks to understand how social workers shape, and are shaped by, past and present arrangements.

At the heart of the difference between reflective practice and critically reflective practice is the equation of 'critical' with a certain form of emancipatory politics. What does this mean in practice? Much of social work operates as though politics does not exist. Evidence-based practice, for example, is presented as a non-ideological drive to encourage best practice on the basis of the strength of the available objective evidence. Reflective practice also separates practice from its social, economic and political context in favour of a focus on 'in-the-moment' practice examples. Where politics are overtly acknowledged, as for example in radical social work, the tendency is to focus on a critical macro-analysis of how welfare policy and practice are being shaped by globalization and neoliberalism (McDonald, 2006). One of the strengths of that approach is that 'it positions social workers and other human service professionals as players in a much larger game' (McDonald, 2006, p. 59). Critically reflective practice is sympathetic to the tenor of that analysis in the way it sets out the scale of change to economies and welfare regimes in the current era. However, given its poststructuralist stance and its suspicion of 'grand narratives', critically reflective practice is also wary of the panoptic vision of the post-Fordist analytic framework, which can be seen as 'overly deterministic ... and overly silent about the role of human agency' (McDonald, 2006, p. 59). The scope for resistance can appear severely limited. Critically reflective practice positions itself somewhere between the ambitions for social change embraced by radical social work and the modest and ostensibly politically neutral ambitions of reflective practice to effect change at the individual level. Critically reflective practice is politically engaged, not in the sense of being aligned to a specific political manifesto, but in its recognition that 'social work, because of its focus on marginalized people, is a concentrated site of social, political and cultural ambivalence and contradiction' (Rossiter, 2005, p. 7). Once that is assumed, it follows that the core function of critically reflective practice should be to interrogate ambivalence and contradiction not simply for its own sake, but in order to accomplish 'social justice work' (Rossiter, 2005) in the routines of practice.

It is not enough to be self-aware or simply to add to one's expertise and competence through the process of reflection. Critically reflective practice involves, indeed necessitates, taking a longer, harder look at practice and making sense of it differently as a constitutive activity. It is probably better, therefore, to conceive of critically reflective practice as always in process rather than something that can be definitively achieved. It is certainly not a one-off activity, nor is it something that only belongs in formal education and continuing professional development, though these of course make space for such work to occur and are therefore well placed to foster critically reflective practice.

If we are to make it meaningful, whatever our location in social work, a commitment to critically reflective practice is urgently needed. This is not to say that critically reflective practice is easy, particularly for those working in statutory agencies in times of austerity. It most certainly is not. It will, and should, engender feelings of discomfort. Indeed, Dewey (1993) argued strongly that 'one can only think reflectively when one is willing to endure suspense and to undergo the trouble of search' (p. 16). But then, being in (statutory) practice can engender profound feelings of discomfort and inadequacy on the part of practitioners even before engaging in critically reflective practice (see for example Rossiter, 2001). What critically reflective practice offers practitioners is a way to interrogate these feelings of inadequacy and uncertainty by reflecting upon not simply what they were thinking and feeling at the time, but also about how they are positioned in a particular case and how they construct 'the case' and the 'service user'. They can thus seek to reformulate the politics that underpin their practice, having clearly identified how it can do violence to the lives of users. Mehan's (2001) study underlines this point. In order for the psychologist's mode of representation to prevail and the child to be constructed as 'learning disabled', other modes of presentation – the child as in transition from Montessori to mainstream education, the child as a loved, active, and playful son – are silenced. Modes of representation are thus not neutral or simply about 'helping' and 'caring'. As Mehan (2001) states: 'the concrete face–face encounters which generate an instance or a category are also creative moments that reproduce the relations among categories that we see gaining ascendancy historically' (p. 362). It is by making sense of those 'creative moments' (and processes) that practitioners can strive towards critically reflective practice. They will not simply attempt the impossible feat of being a heroic activist (Healy, 2000). Rather, they will interrogate social relations and the possibilities of political change.

In drawing this chapter to a close, it is necessary to flag up a danger for critically reflective practice, namely, that it can easily slide back into a conventional form of reflective practice. In effect, the reflective practice elements of it can easily dominate, or indeed suppress, a critical focus. When this happens, being critical tends to become equated with not taking things for granted, questioning, unsettling one's practice or one's ideas of oneself as a practitioner. While it seems important for any practitioner to ask 'who am I?', 'what prior experience do I bring to my practice?', 'what sort of practitioner am I?' and 'what kind of practitioner do I aspire to be?' such questions alone cannot serve to interrogate the social relations of practice and their material effects for users and for practitioners. The potential of critically reflective practice lies in its capacity to get beyond the 'me' of practice and the obsession with individual narrative that is part of contemporary Western societies. The following questions – and here the work of Rossiter (2005, 2011) is acknowledged – will prove useful for critically reflective practice:

- Making the 'case': How is the service user constituted in different modes of representation?

- How does power operate through the presentation of 'facts' and modes of representation?

- What is obscured or denied expression by the various modes of representation? Whose story or stories are denied expression, and what are the effects of this?

- How has this category of 'concern' been (re)constructed over time in the policy arena?

- What orthodoxies are underpinning or shaping professional discourses?

- What possibilities of change emerge from this analysis?

Clearly, these are very different sorts of questions from the ones posed in the framework for practitioner reflection cited earlier. The ones here are more complex and not amenable to easy answers. They require practitioners to examine how they constitute social work and are constituted in discourse. Critically reflective practice aspires to stay in interrogative mode. There is no magic blueprint for achieving social change and no fixed point on the horizon at which critically reflective practice can envisage rendering itself superfluous. Social work will continue to wrestle with the contradictions engendered by moralizing about and regulating the lives of others. This type of practice provides a means by which to wrestle with those tensions. Of course this is not a recipe for dramatic change to social work. The contribution of critically reflective practice to a new politics of social work lies in its desire to unsettle and reshape the 'politics of representation' so that different voices can be heard and different modes of representation can prevail. By these means, in local, situated contexts of practice, social justice in 'helping' relationships may be accomplished.

References

Borton, T. (1970). *Reach, touch and teach*. London: McGraw-Hill.

Burkitt, I. (2008). *Social selves: Theories of self and society* (2nd edn). London: Sage.

de Montigny, G. (2013). Ethnomethodology. In M. Gray & S.A. Webb (eds), *Social work theories and methods* (2nd edn). London: Sage. 205–217.

Dewey, J. (1933). *How we think: A restatement of the relation of reflective thinking to the educative process*. Boston, MA: D.C. Heath.

Dreyfus, H., & Dreyfus, S. (1986). *Mind over machine: The power of human intuition and expertise in the age of the computer*. New York: Free Press.

Eraut, M. (1994). *Developing professional knowledge and competence*. London: Falmer.

Floersch, G., Longhofer, J.L., & Nordquist Schwallie, M. (2013). Ethnography. In M. Gray & S.A. Webb (eds), *Social work theories and methods* (2nd edn). London: Sage. 195–204.

Fook, J., & Gardner, F. (2007). *Practising critical reflection: A resource handbook*. Maidenhead, Berkshire: Open University Press.

Foucault, M. (1972). *The archaeology of knowledge*. London: Tavistock.

Gould, N., & Taylor, I. (eds) (1996). *Reflective learning for social work*. Aldershot, Hants: Arena.

Gray, M., Plath, D., & Webb, S.A. (2009). *Evidence-based social work: A critical stance*. London: Routledge.

Healy, K. (2000). *Social work practices: Contemporary perspectives on change*. London: Sage.

Heron, B. (2005). Self-reflection in critical social work: Subjectivity and the possibilities of resistance. *Reflective Practice*, *6*(3), 341–351.

Ixer, G. (1999). There is no such thing as reflection. *British Journal of Social Work*, *29*(4), 513–528.

Johns, C., & Freshwater, D. (eds) (1998). *Transforming nursing through reflective practice*. Oxford: Blackwell Science.

MacLure, M. (2003). *Discourse in educational and social research*. Maidenhead, Berks: Open University Press.

McDonald, C. (2006). *Challenging social work: The context of practice*. Basingstoke: Palgrave Macmillan.

Mehan, H. (2001). The construction of an LD student: A case study in the politics of representation. In M. Wetherell, S. Taylor, & S.J. Yates (eds), *Discourse theory and practice: A reader*. London: Sage. 345–363.

Napier, L., & Fook, J. (2000). Reflective practice in social work. In L. Napier & J. Fook (eds), *Breakthroughs in practice: Theorising critical moments in social work*. London: Whiting Birch. 1–15.

Nordman, T., Kasén, A., & Eriksson, K. (1998). Reflective practice: A way to the patient's world and caring, the core of nursing. In C. Johns & D. Freshwater (eds), *Transforming nursing through reflective practice*. Oxford: Blackwell Science. 161–176.

Pease, B., & Fook, J. (1999). Postmodern critical theory and emancipatory social work practice. In B. Pease & J. Fook (eds), *Transforming social work practice: Postmodern critical perspectives*. London: Routledge. 1–22.

Reynolds, S. (2000). The anatomy of evidence-based practice: Principles and methods. In L. Trinder with S. Reynolds (eds), *Evidence-based practice: A critical appraisal*. Oxford: Blackwell. 17–34.

Rodgers, C. (2002) Defining reflection: Another look at John Dewey and reflective thinking, *Teachers College Record*, *104*(4), 842–866.

Rolfe, G., Freshwater, D., & Jasper, M. (2001). *Critical reflection for nursing and the helping professions: A user's guide*. Basingstoke: Palgrave Macmillan.

Rossiter, A. (2001). Innocence lost and suspicion found: Do we educate for or against social work? *Critical Social Work*, *2*(1), 1–8.

Rossiter, A. (2005). Discourse analysis in critical social work: From apology to question. *Critical Social Work*, *6*(1), 1–8.

Rossiter, A. (2011). Unsettled social work: The challenge of Levinas's ethics. *British Journal of Social Work*, *41*(5), 980–995.

Schön, D.A. (1983). *The reflective practitioner: How professionals think in action*. New York: Basic Books.

Schön, D.A. (1987). *Educating the reflexive practitioner: Towards a new design for teaching and learning professions*. San Francisco, CA: Jossey-Bass.

Scott, J.C. (2009). *The art of not being governed*, New Haven, CT: Yale University Press.

Stevens, R. (1996). The reflexive self: An experiential perspective. In R. Stevens (ed.), *Understanding the self*. London: Sage. 147–218.

Taylor, B. (2010). *Reflective practice for healthcare professionals* (3rd edn). Maidenhead, Berks: Open University Press.

Taylor, C. (2003). Narrating practice: Reflective accounts and the textual construction of reality. *Journal of Advanced Nursing*, *42*(3), 244–251.

Taylor, C. (2006). Narrating significant experience: Reflective accounts and the production of (self) knowledge. *British Journal of Social Work*, *36*(2), 189–206.

Taylor, C. (2008). Trafficking in facts: Writing practices in social work. *Qualitative Social Work*, *7*(1), 25–42.

Taylor, C., & White, S. (2000). *Practising reflexivity in health and welfare: Making knowledge*. Buckingham: Open University Press.

Taylor, C., & White, S. (2001). Knowledge, truth and reflexivity: The problem of judgement. *Journal of Social Work, 1*(1), 37–59.

Thompson, N. (1993). *Anti-discriminatory practice*. Basingstoke: Palgrave Macmillan.

Van Maanen, J. (1988). *Tales of the field: On writing ethnography*. Chicago: University of Chicago Press.

Weedon, C. (1987). *Feminist practice and poststructuralist theory*. Oxford: Basil Blackwell.

White, S. (2013). Discourse and reflexivity. In M. Gray & S.A. Webb (eds), *Social work theories and methods* (2nd edn). London: Sage. 218–228.

Wooffitt, R. (2005). *Conversation analysis and discourse analysis: A comparative and critical introduction*. London: Sage.

Yip, K. (2006). Self-reflection in reflective practice: A note of caution. *British Journal of Social Work, 36*(5), 777–788.

6

Critical Management

John Lawler

This chapter discusses recent developments on the management of social work services, particularly focusing on the role and functions of social work managers and the issues that impact upon the firstline management of practice. It summarizes the development of managerialism and markets, and outlines the position of managers and the dilemmas they face. The chapter discusses the potential contribution of critical management studies (CMS) to the understanding of management and managers in social work. It concludes by advocating a more critical understanding of social work managers through the application of Bourdieu's (1990) concept of *habitus*.

Largely, the development of statutory social work in the UK throughout the twentieth and into the twenty-first centuries has been within the context of government – national, but predominantly local, government. Generally such services have been situated in large bureaucratic organizations. Whittington and Bellaby (1979) provide a critical historical account of how hierarchy, rather than horizontalism, became the dominant model for the organization of social services departments in the UK after the Seebohm Report (1968). They show that our taken-for-granted organizational concept of 'professional bureaucracy' in fact only gained impetus in the 1970s through 'public relations' activities of the 'Brunel studies' group of researchers headed by Elliot Jaques. The idea of a social work professional bureaucracy was politically constructed; it did not appear out of nowhere. On this basis, it is perhaps not new to see social work as being 'managed' or 'organized' – it has always been so. However, the ways in which it is managed and organized have changed significantly since the late 1990s (Lawler & Bilson, 2010). Where once there was a relatively comfortable accommodation between the social work 'profession' and the bureaucracies in which it was located and through which it operated – how the service was 'administered' – there is now a different dynamic, where increasingly social work services are 'managed' according to the agenda of the organization in which they are located (Rogowski, 2011). Where previously professional and administrative demands reached a mutual accommodation (Smith, 1979), now the management agenda gains priority and the contradictions between professional practice and professional values, on the one hand, and managerial ideologies on the other, are more obvious and strained. The chapter discusses developments in management in social work, and related developments, with the intention of providing further insights into the implicit assumptions on which they are founded. In order to do this, it first considers a framework within which such developments can be located.

In terms of a New Left politics of social work for analysing managerial developments, a number of possibilities are evident. There has been a growing literature on critical approaches to social work practice providing frameworks following a number of different analyses and philosophies and, not directly related to this development, an increase in critical management studies more generally (e.g., Alvesson, Bridgman, & Willmott, 2009; Linstead, Fulop, & Lilley, 2009; Parker, 2002). Previously, when social work was *administered*, rather than *managed*, there was mutual respect both for the more reflective, professional values and practice and a more objectivist, administrative processes (Harris & White, 2009). The administration model provided a framework of processes – accountability, finance and resource allocation, and human resources processes, among others, which supported social work practice and provided a degree of professional autonomy for social workers to carry out their responsibilities and address the needs of their particular user groups. However, the late 1970s saw a shift away from administration as support to an emphasis on a more active *management* of resources and activities. This saw a change in emphasis, from one where the application of tacit knowledge was supported and its impacts recognized as a matter of subjective evaluation, to one where cause and effect had to be demonstrated more visibly and where subjective professional and user evaluations were given less credence.

Where previously the public sector, the base for most statutory social work, was seen to embody different – pluralist – values from its counterpart organizations in the commercial sector, now the emphasis was on using objectivist 'business' methods in the public sector (Flynn, 2007). Thus increasingly the lines between public administration and business management became blurred.

Managerialism and Marketization of Services

This development did not occur in isolation. With the growth in neoliberal politics and policies in developed economies came the belief that the market was the most appropriate mechanism to allocate resources in meeting the needs of citizens in the public as well as the commercial arena. As market models spread further in the public sector, the language of the market and of business organizations spread increasingly, leading to the development of markets and quasi-markets in social care, as well as the redefinition of different groups in the public sector, the reconstitution of their respective roles, and the development of 'customer choice' in the welfare context (Harris, 2003). Where previously the recipients of social work services had been known and seen as clients, this changed to 'service users' and later, 'customers'. In accordance with this shift, services were expected to respond to customer demands rather than to address client *needs*. This also implied a significant shift in the role of professionals, who traditionally might have identified and addressed the needs of the client, and who now were in the position of responding to the demands identified and expressed by customers. The previous bureaucracies – and the professionals they employed – were seen to offer homogeneous services, defined and organized by the providing agency. Users of services were seen to be relatively passive in this relationship. Increasingly, the role of users has changed to that of active consumer or customer, defining needs and demanding higher quality and more individualized or personalized services. Furthermore, service consumers have come to expect to be able to choose from a range of options as to how their demands might be met, enabling them to select what they considered most appropriate to their situations (Clarke, Gewirtz, & McLaughlin, 2000).

All of the above constitute elements of marketization, an important issue in the growth of managerialism and the role of firstline managers. It is not just the establishment of competitive or quasi-markets but the redefinition of the roles of players in the market – providers, purchasers and consumers. A major role or innovation in this process is that of the manager. In social work, this became a new position – not an erstwhile administrator but a new management role (Lawler, 1992). While initially senior professionals took these positions, there was an expectation that management skills from other sectors would also be incorporated. Where previously administered services would rely on administrators working together with senior professionals to consider the design and delivery of services, developments like the establishment of quality standards, new resource allocation strategies and decision-making processes, the institution of social work managers, together with their privileged position, formed significant developments. Here the description of managerialism provided by Lawler and Bilson (2010) is useful:

> Managerialism refers to the development of the interest of management in how organizations are managed, stressing the role and accountability of individual managers and their positions as that – managers – rather than any other role or

identity, such as senior professional or administrator. The essence of managerial-ism is the belief that many organizations have a great deal in common ... and, given this people equipped as managers should be able to operate efficiently in any domain – in other words there is a belief in the transferability of these skills to other managerial contexts. (p. 4)

While marketization and managerialism might be seen as two sides of the same coin, there is a counter-view (Harris, 2003) that they could, in practice, be contradictory. Marketization privileges the position of the customer as the focus of activity. The institution of management can be seen as an aid to this but, argues Harris (2003), managers' interests on the supply side of the equation have taken precedence over customers' interests on the demand side. He maintains that the former have been more influential in bringing about changes to social work services than any representations of customers or consumer groups.

The position of front-line social workers has been affected considerably by these developments. Whereas previously their caseloads were 'supervised' by senior social workers, now they were managed by 'managers'. This is not a mere semantic difference. The autonomy of the individual social worker diminished with practice driven by procedural guidelines, performance targets and greater regulation (Kirkpatrick, 2006). The role of supervision changed significantly. While traditionally concerned with ensuring that social work practice was in keeping with professional standards, as viewed by the supervisor, now it meant meeting targets and adhering to organiza-tional regulations and procedures. Lost was the reflective aspect of supervi-sion as a learning experience (see Chapter 5). Supervision in the managerial world had a different output or production-oriented focus in keeping with managerial expectations rather than the requirements of professional super-visors and individual practitioner's development. While before individual social workers were accountable to clients and the profession, now they were answerable to line managers and employing organizations. Whereas previ-ously social workers might have been responsible for attending to the 'whole person' through a casework approach, now services had become so frag-mented that different people and agencies could be responsible for different aspects of the service, with social workers chiefly engaged in assessment and service coordination or case management rather than casework. To some extent, this could be attributed to a renaissance in scientific management (Harris, 1998; Taylor, 1911), given that the design of the work was now sepa-rated from its execution. The manager or management designed the elements of the service and established criteria of eligibility while the social worker delivered the service with limited discretion and reduced profes-sional autonomy.

Individualization of services

On a broader level, as part of the so-called modernization process, meaning the move to a business model, public services became increasingly customized for individual service users – citizen-customers – in the neoliberal political agenda (O'Brien & Penna, 1998). The individualized customization of services came to be known as person-centred care. Marketized services provided consumer choice along with individually-tailored personal care packages rather than generalized one-size-fits all programmes (Policy Commission on Public Services, 2004). Social care in the UK provides customers with a range of options, which they can purchase from public, independent or commercial service providers within their personal budget allocation. While social workers have always offered individualized casework services, the development of managed care represented a significant shift in the way resources were allocated and services delivered. The old client categories of children 'at risk', vulnerable adults or people with disabilities gave way to service users or consumers with choice.

A second aspect of individualization relates to the way in which leadership is seen increasingly as an individual rather than a shared or team process. Individualized leadership is fast becoming a necessary requirement for effective twenty-first-century social service organizations (see e.g., Lawler, 2008; Thorpe et al., 2011). A third aspect of individualization relates to the scrutiny of the work of the social worker at an individual level (Dustin, 2007; Kirkpatrick, 2006) now required to meet stringent performance criteria. This has individualized what is required of social workers over sufficient regard for professional standards and requirements. Individualized leadership and performance, regulated by organizational rather than professional standards, makes individual social workers working in high-risk environments extremely vulnerable to scapegoating or blaming when things go wrong – as happened in the case of Baby Peter and the sacking and successful appeal of Sharon Shoesmith in the UK (*Independent*, 2011).

Managerialism and professionalism

Why might tensions between professional and managerial values – or between professional and managerial authority – be an issue? While social workers had always been required to practise in keeping with agency policy, managerialism effectively infused organizations with a set of lawlike principles and privileged managers over professionals. Management principles and practices trumped professional autonomy, knowledge and judgement. Rather than the attainment of professional objectives, management efficiency became the main measure of effectiveness and was seen as a largely objective process in which technical rationality was applied to predict organizational outcomes (Moore, 2008). Largely disregarded were professional knowledge and values, not least relationship-centred intervention, long the cornerstone of social work practice. Managerialism values technical rationality over reflective practice. In other words, the subjective, emotional nature of interpersonal client–worker relationships was eschewed for 'customer satisfaction' – a highly problematic term when working with clients with complex problems. Managers concerned primarily with organizational ends have very different priorities from professionals dealing with clients with complex needs (Moore, 2008). For the most part, social workers favour dialogical over procedural encounters with service users. They favour flexibility and adaptability over predetermined ends.

Clearly, managerialism is not a neutral process, since it is tied to a neoliberal agenda which reduces the role of the state through the marketization of services, and encourages competition and commercialization. In shifting power from social workers to managers, it has effectively reduced professional control over the allocation of resources and services. In essence, it shifts the emphasis from professional social workers to managers as the main instrument of social policy in this area (Rogowski, 2011). Professionalism, too, has political emancipatory aims, which run counter to managerial priorities. With the rise of radical social movements (Dent & Whitehead, 2002), professionals have come under fire for the control they exert over those who are less powerful, less privileged and less educated and who do not have access to resources and opportunities (see Chapter 2).

The issue of managerial–professional contradictions has been the subject of attention for some time but remains and will continue to remain a thorny issue. Any long-term resolution of such tensions is illusory and would reflect objectivist thinking that a 'recipe' for resolution is awaiting discovery. The balancing of these tensions is a 'wicked problem' (Rittel & Webber, 1973) and needs to be recognized as such, that is, there are many ways of addressing it, none of which is perfect, meaning there is no ultimate resolution. Scholars within the public service context more broadly continue to draw attention to this dynamic as being fundamental to public service (and in our context, social work) organizations (see e.g. Friedson, 2001; Henriksson, Wrede, & Burau, 2006). What may be more fruitful to consider from the practitioner's point of view is the triad of manager–professional–consumer noted above and the dynamics of these relationships. The objectivist approach is to focus on defining demand, rationing and allocating resources, on efficiency of output or the service delivered. The front-line worker is growing increasingly accustomed to this focus with the managerial emphasis on target achievement (Dustin, 2007).

There is the associated issue of risk management, which is constant concern in public service generally and in social work specifically. The media attention received by previous cases of spectacular and tragic failure is a constant concern to managers and social workers alike. The challenges within the manager–professional–consumer triad are several. For managers, they include how to support social workers delivering high-quality services while working with (increasingly) restricted resources. This includes all aspects of supervision, but particularly that which develops the confidence and capability of social workers. A further challenge is how to maintain the legitimacy, in the eyes of the various stakeholders, of the organization through which the service is delivered. For the social worker, the challenge includes responding effectively to the perceived needs and expressed wishes of current and prospective users of services. At the same time, social workers have a role in developing the expectations of service users, indeed of managing expectations to some extent. This is not to suggest any manipulation, which might be the case in some directly commercial relationships, but to help the user become more informed themselves. In this way, users might reasonably be clear about what they can expect from services, and can themselves provide some useful input for practitioners and managers in contributing their perspective into the planning for future service development, something akin to the notion of 'expert patient' in healthcare (Lorig, 2002).

The professional–managerial–customer triad has nominally shifted the power balance in favour of the customer, but often overlooked is the involuntary nature of service use, with many service users forced to contact services in times of particular personal emotional distress and mental anguish (Barnes & Prior, 1995). Indeed, service users are often coerced into the service system through their antisocial behaviour arising from mental-health or child-protection issues. Unlike commercial organizations, in social work 'repeat customers' are problematic and social workers are all too familiar with intergenerational family problems. Repeat customers – or recidivists in the criminal justice system – are a strain on overstretched services required under managerial efficiency to do more with less. Developing a dialogue with service users which goes beyond a discussion of their immediate needs to further inclusion of the user voice in policy and service design is a means of addressing both managerial and professional concerns.

However, customer satisfaction is not a term that sits well with a profession working mainly with marginalized, disadvantaged and oppressed groups of people or people with complex problems requiring social work intervention for professionally identified needs. In any event, despite the policy rhetoric, many citizen-customers have little choice given the overstretched and underfunded context of service. Many find that no service can be provided until the situation deteriorates. Essential social work services are restricted to certain categories of need. Encouraging choice in some cases becomes paradoxical or a tokenistic expression of user involvement or empowerment (Harris, 2003). Harris (2003) notes the problematic nature of customer-defined demand rather than professionally identified need. As he argues, the issue of need and how it should be addressed is fundamentally a political issue and cannot easily be supplanted by customer demand and choice. Indeed, Kirkpatrick (2006) notes that increasingly services in some areas are restricted and target only the most severely disadvantaged. This makes the notion of a rational, informed citizen-customer highly problematic within a professional social work context.

Nevertheless, managerialism is unlikely to go away and managerial values and practices undoubtedly have some benefits, not least in relation to the increased transparency and efficiency of services and resource allocation and the privileging of service recipients – citizen-customers. But there is considerable danger that its objectivist ideologies and technical rationality will lead to increasing diminution of the social work role and task (Dustin, 2007). Further, fragmented services – created by increased marketization within a competitive privatized service environment – makes it difficult to achieve service integration, regardless of increasing political rhetoric to this effect. Managerialism tends to overlook people's unique problems and contexts, despite its individualizing tendencies. Its objectivist approach leads to a highly prescriptive service regime which is inimical to reflective, value-based professional social work practice. As Moore (2008) indicates, managers may be unaware of the values underpinning their activities and, therefore, not question them, while social workers are more comfortable deploying their values to promote efficient and transparent services directly suited to the unique needs of service recipients.

Advancing Critical Management Perspectives

Critical management offers a range of further perspectives from which to analyse the concepts discussed in the chapter so far. Critical Management Studies (CMS) present critiques of objectivist perspectives and legitimates the incorporation of subjective elements into the analysis of organizations. CMS itself constitutes an eclectic range of views from the more structural, objectivist approaches, drawing on, for example, Marxist analyses (Adler, Forbes, & Willmott, 2007) to more subjectivist approaches drawing, for example, on the work of Lacan (see, e.g., Arnaud & Vanheulen, 2007). Given the range of sources and perspectives, it is challenging to provide a comprehensive definition of CMS, However, Grey (2005) gives a good summary:

> CMS represents the possibility of drawing together those elements within business schools (and cognate areas) who share some oppositional tendencies. That is:

oppositional to established power and ideology: to managerial privilege; to hierarchy and its abuse: to put it at its most generic, not only the established order but the proposition that the established order is immutable. (p. 187)

It is interesting to note a parallel here: CMS provides a challenge to orthodox thinking and practice in a similar way to the manner in which the radical social work movement provided a challenge to orthodox thinking and practice in social work from the mid-1970s (Bailey & Brake, 1975, see Chapter 2). In both cases, challenges to power – explicit and implicit – are provided and the established order and established practice are problematized. This section highlights specific elements of CMS and points to the potential of using CMS to inform a critical analysis of the role and function of social work managers.

Fleming and Mandarini (2009) highlight a focus of CMS as being to problematize management both in theory and in practice. CMS presents 'an attempt to critique mainstream management scholarship since it de-politicises work and the worker, privileges capitalism as inevitable, unproblematic and beneficial to all' (p. 333). As noted above, managerialism presents a range of particular values, such as the legitimacy or primacy of 'business methods', efficiency and economy, which are being internalized in public service. This, in turn, is likely to affect social work attitudes and practice directly and intentionally and, as importantly, indirectly and in unacknowledged ways. Thus Adler et al. (2007) note how, for example, teamwork within a managerial regime can result in 'the oppressive internalization of business values and goals by team members, who then begin exploiting themselves and disciplining team players in the name of business performance' (p. 179). New public management has provided the means to initiate and perpetuate new structures of subjection and domination. It is argued (e.g., Aronson & Smith, 2011) that managerialism presents management in a male form, promoting and reinforcing stereotypically masculine values and behaviours. This equates with the objectivist approach where management is seen as logical, authoritative, unemotional and procedural, with the balancing values of emotionality and intuition discouraged and viewed as lacking legitimacy (Lawler & Bilson, 2010), thus the 'positivist, value-free model of scientific knowledge [is] enthroned, marginalizing other approaches' (Adler et al., 2007, p. 180).

Critical management approaches view the current status quo as a historical development with the potential for change and more positive development from the contemporary societal context of patriarchy and capitalism. It proposes no 'blueprint' for organization or for society but, by highlighting dominant influences and effects, and problematizing structures and practices, it offers the stimulation to consider how future developments might be made in a more emancipatory direction. Further, it challenges the predominant instrumentalist view that organizations should be managed primarily to ensure that the most profitable and efficient systems can develop. Maximization of output and efficiency are prime goals. Other developments, however (un)humanistic they might be, can be justified only by the extent to which they assist in the achievement of these goals.

Relational issues in social work delivery, once fundamental to effective social work practice, are now valued by the extent to which the managerial agenda is served: using assets effectively, achieving performance targets and demonstrating effectiveness. Thus if it could be demonstrated that 'customer satisfaction' had increased, this might demonstrate managerial or organizational effectiveness despite, in the social work context, individual need not having been (adequately) addressed. If user expectations could be deflated and then met, that too would constitute success. If, for example, visits were withdrawn, existing users might feel the service had deteriorated, but new users not used to home visits would see just one such visit as exceeding expectations, resulting in increased 'satisfaction' even though the service might have declined in terms of other criteria. The use of objective performance targets promotes objective criteria, such as 'consumer satisfaction', which can be relatively easily, if inadequately, 'measured' through user surveys, while eschewing more subjective estimates from social workers and service users.

Social work delivery at the professional interface relies on the establishment of an effective working relationship between social worker and service user and between social worker and manager (Ruch, 2011). This is done through meetings, discussions, negotiations and exchanging perspectives – through a dialogical process – seen as one element of discourse. Within critical management, however, 'discourse' is a term which is not restricted to interpersonal conversation but includes nonlinguistic elements – artefacts, images and constructions (both physical and conceptual) – at micro (social), meso (organizational) and macro (community or policy) levels (Alvesson & Karreman, 2000). In the contemporary context, 'social worker', 'manager' and 'customer' all form part of contemporary discourse influencing identities and affiliations. Laclau (2005) argues that such discourse affects and is affected by beliefs and attitudes – the dominant hegemony. Thus in social work the change in name from client, user and consumer to customer is more than a semantic shift: it constitutes a reshaping of identities, relationships, organizational processes and power relations. Similarly, the shifts from social worker to case manager and from senior social worker or team leader to social work manager promote changing identities and power dynamics. As Aronson and Smith (2011) illustrate, erstwhile social workers who become managers experience a reshaping of identity and understanding of the workplace and positions and roles in the organization. Aronson and Smith's (2011) work is interesting in several respects, not least in demonstrating the dilemmas faced by managers and the extent to which they internalize the roles articulated in contemporary neoliberal discourse and how they resist these influences, taking a stance which legitimates current employment while seeking to undermine some of the implications of the hegemonic discourse in practice.

CMS has continued to develop arguments and analyses made in an earlier era where workers were seen as alienated actors in the production process and under direct control and surveillance throughout their attendance in the workplace. In a post-industrial society, where physical production of goods has decreased and where the direct supervision of the less visible production of services is less obvious, one might expect less surveillance and control. However, CMS, and cultural studies more broadly, note how control has spread beyond the formal work boundaries and throughout society (see e.g. Deleuze, 1992). Fleming and Madarini (2009) point to three aspects of work to consider as sources for theorizing: (1) the activities involved in the direct production of goods and services; (2) activities where workers develop their own particular 'selves' as part of the job – identity work; and (3) social work (not in the welfare sense) or social labour referring to linking activities and linking selves between the workplace and other areas of the social world. There is a certain ambivalence to this, in that such work helps develop relationships and attitudes which act as a means for capitalism to prosper (through maintenance of effective, healthy workers with appropriate commitment to their work) and also helps to form relationships which resist or protect against its worst ravages.

Aronson and Smith (2011) demonstrate, explicitly and implicitly, aspects of identity work and social work or labour. The managers themselves develop 'manager identities', which are not strictly managerial in that they resist or adapt these identities to incorporate resisting elements coherent with their own values and form some protection for social workers to continue their professional activities in accordance with their professional values. At the same time, they focus their activities towards achieving organizational goals. The less obvious or the implicit element of these identities is that of the career professional who, despite their protestations against the negative elements of management, choose to progress their own careers, however reluctantly, by taking management positions. So social work managers can be seen conducting Fleming and Mandarini's (2009) 'social work' in maintaining 'welfare social work' values in the face of pressure from more powerful managerial values. Individual social workers' subjective values and feelings of esteem – the 'worth' of social work – are protected while working towards the objective goals and performance of management.

Towards a New Politics of Social Work

Paradoxes of power are not novel in social work and social work organizations, for example, the contradiction between care and control, or, as already noted, between administration and practice. Social work managers face similar paradoxes in relation to recognizing and dealing with organizational and managerial power in that they can, at the same time, be exercisers and resisters of power (Aronson & Smith, 2010; Dustin, 2007). At a practical level, Aronson and Smith (2010) demonstrate how managers struggle first with the pursuance of objective organizational targets and their own subjective experiences, values and emotions and, secondly, with objectivized – and valorized – masculine managerial stereotypes and their own subjective gendered experience. Critical management, particularly through the use of Bourdieu (1977, 1986, 1990), offers a further means of understanding the relationship between objective and subjective views and of trying to make sense of such contrary perspectives. Indeed, Bourdieu seeks to transcend the objective–subjective distinction. A postmodern view of the manager's situation as described, for example, by Aronson and Smith (2011), might posit the existence of various 'selves' – managerial, professional, work, non-work, feminine and masculine, which presents an interesting dissection of the situation but which ultimately, through constant deconstruction, can produce a somewhat nihilistic result (Capaldi, 1998).

Bourdieu's (1990) concept of *habitus* presents the opportunity to analyse the impact of managerial pressures on those who act against the managerial order while exercising the power endowed by their roles within it. In this way, it is possible to understand that managerial action might not (solely) be a reflection of the structural position of 'manager' but might demonstrate managers' exercise of individual choice within the given organizational and social structures. Bourdieu's approach provides a counter to views of structural – and in this context, managerial – determinism. His concept of *habitus* differs from the other ways in which the concept was used previously (e.g., by Weber and Husserl) in that is constitutes a set of dispositions, which can be seen as individual and or collective. These are distinguishable from 'attitudes' since dispositions are visible and identifiable through preferences in action. Each manager displays a set of dispositions informed by previous experiences, current understandings and potential strategies, and decision-making and problem-solving challenges. Individual autonomy is possible within structural influences and, indeed, those structural influences might then be affected by such themselves. Thus *habitus* can be used to demonstrate the effect of structure on action and the effect of action on structure.

Two other concepts are important in developing understanding of the value of this concept, first that of 'field', which is directly related and, secondly, that of 'capital', which can assist in analyses of managerial action. 'Field' refers to the wider context – social, political and cultural, which develops and maintains general patterns of behaviour and interpersonal relationships and which structures power relations. Thus *habitus* is affected directly by its particular field. Bourdieu also presents different conceptualizations of 'capital', economic, social and cultural, which individuals use in developing their own choices, goals and strategies in and beyond the work context. Özbilgin and Tatli (2005) note how the concept has developed, but argue that its different aspects still await a full integrating theory. For example, drawing on Bourdieu, intellectual and relational capital are related concepts but are not brought together in an overarching theory. Bourdieu refers to 'symbolic capital', which may include any of the above aspects recognized and given value by others. Thus symbolic capital is a collection of resources, actual and ascribed by others, which form a basis for power.

Social work managers have certain powers attributed to them because of their organizational position – rational-legal power, in Weber's parlance. However, the extent of their symbolic capital may vary. It may be restricted to organizational power, should they decide to focus exclusively on the managerial agenda, or they may have more symbolic capital than they currently appreciate, through maintaining their personal legitimacy in the eyes of various, potentially competitive, stakeholder perceptions. So *habitus* represents the strategies which social work managers might adopt, drawing on their objective organizational position, their own subjective experiences and perceptions, and the subjective perceptions of their own staff who attribute value (or not) to the 'dispositions' of their managers.

Social work managers are in a prime position to enhance social capital within their organizations through effective management. CMS is of particular relevance here in that, through its analysis of – unequal – power dynamics, it can aid the development of organizations, still within a capitalist system, which can become more equitable and within which more equitable management can be exercised. It has the potential to be both radical in its promotion of organizations which do not privilege capitalist goals over all else and liberal in promoting equality and fairness.

For the practitioner, the development of critical perspectives is more than an abstract fascination. Social work is fundamentally concerned with issues of power and its inequitable spread and exercise. Including a consideration of critical management perspectives will further inform the necessary analysis professional social workers use to inform both collective and individual standards of practice.

Recent policy initiatives relating to a range of social services focus on developing more customer-focused public services through, among other things, greater delegation of decision-making and extended consumer choice (O'Reilly & Reed, 2010). This focus itself is seen to represent considerable reform. The encouragement to reform applies to managers in identifying possibilities for greater consumer focus and in developing those possibilities into service change. However, it also applies to individual professionals who are also seen as being in key positions to deal with current challenges, being crucial in personalizing services and ensuring 'hard-to-reach' groups are provided for (Prime Minister's Strategy Unit, 2007).

O'Reilly and Reed (2010) argue that much recent policy has also focused on 'leadership' as a major narrative, which has influence both as an underlying ideology and as a technology through which reform can be implemented. Their critical analysis highlights the rhetoric of 'leadership' and its rise accompanying that of 'new consumerism' (p. 917). As their critique indicates, it is useful to recognize the ideological basis of the use of the term and to treat it with some caution. However, there are specific opportunities in the current reform climate to use the implications of greater 'leadership' in improving services and, indeed, that is partly the intention behind its use in policy documents. These come primarily through the exhortation to innovate and inspire more effective and user-focused services as they are increasingly delivered through inter-agency collaboration without reliance on the influence of the traditional management hierarchy in affecting change.

Current managerial developments, including a greater emphasis on leadership, have led to an 'unsettling' of traditional organizational and professional knowledge and influence in public services, with 'new knots' (i.e., combinations of knowledge and power) being formed as different voices are given priority, most notably the voice of the consumer. Such new knots present the opportunity to collaborate and develop services which '(take) account of a more active, participatory, competent public' (Clarke et al., 2007, p. 117). O'Reilly and Reed (2010) see potential here to:

> unravel this new power/knowledge knot by re-positioning service managers and professionals as strategic leaders and operational practitioners, whose job it is to generate the long-term visions and develop the practical technologies through which the needs and choices of the much more demanding and discerning service consumers can be met. (p. 972)

This, then, represents a step beyond the traditional tension of management control against professional discretion to proactive and shared leadership (O'Reilly & Reed, 2010). In the context of healthcare, Ferlie (2012) similarly identifies a rebalancing or 'reverse colonization' of areas now primarily the remit of managers. This increasingly productive dialogue between managers and professionals is leading to the possibility of innovations in governance and policy with implications for change in practice.

Conclusion

Managerialism is now institutionalized in many public services, which employ social workers. New entrants to the profession will not have experience of professional social work outside such a context – managerialism is now a fixed part of Bourdieu's 'field', as noted above. Thus it is relatively easy for managerialism to continue to develop in an unrestricted manner, in serving the aims of the neoliberal agenda with impunity. The values and beliefs which inform it can all too easily go unacknowledged. It is interesting, however, to see the increase in questioning of the dominant capitalist culture in recent months and in the light of the precarious nature of the financial stability of many Western economies. This questioning is reflected in the development of issues in the academic context. Critical management continues to be of increasing interest in academia. As it develops, more specific foci of interest develop also, with CMS more generally. For the practitioner, a critical view of management can be important in the way that a critical view of social structure and relationships is important. With a more detailed understanding of current context, practitioners may develop more effective, innovative ways of operating in the same way as they help service users to develop a clearer understanding of social and power dynamics as they apply to their own situations. As noted above, there is scope to develop innovations in practice, in the delivery of service and in its governance.

One development of particular interest to public service management is the concept of critical governance, still in relative infancy but experiencing a growth of interest (see e.g. University of Warwick, 2011). Work from this and similar sources will help to inform an increasingly robust critique of public service management. So the arguments on using specific critical concepts to analyse social work management and these contemporary developments, ways of developing analyses which go beyond the managerial evaluation of effectiveness and efficiency alone, become clear. Such critical perspectives are crucial in three main respects: as contributions to the debate regarding managerialism itself; in the development of alternative models and practice in organizations employing social workers; and in the engagement with users of social work services. The extent to which the potential of such perspectives is realized is yet to be seen.

References

Adler, P.S., Forbes, L.C., & Willmott, H. (2007). Critical management studies. *Academy of Management Annals*, *1*(1), 119–179.

Alvesson, M., Bridgman, T., & Willmott, H. (eds) (2009). *The Oxford handbook of critical management studies*. Oxford: Oxford University Press.

Alvesson, M., & Karreman, D. (2000). Varieties of discourse: On the study of organizations through discourse analysis. *Human Relations, 53*(9), 1125–1149.

Arnaud, G., & Vanheulen, S. (2007). The division of the subject and the organization: A Lacanian approach to subjectivity at work. *Journal of Organizational Change Management, 20*(3), 359–369.

Aronson, J., & Smith, K. (2010). Managing restructured social services: Expanding the social? *British Journal of Social Work, 40*(2), 530–547.

Aronson, J., & Smith, K. (2011). Identity work and critical social service management: Balancing on a tightrope? *British Journal of Social Work, 41*(3), 432–448.

Bailey, R., & Brake, M. (1975). *Radical social work*. London: Edward Arnold.

Barnes, M., & Prior, D. (1995). Spoilt for choice? How consumerism can disempower public service users. *Public Money and Management, 15*(3), 53–58.

Bourdieu, P. (1977). *Outline of theory of practice*. Cambridge: Cambridge University Press.

Bourdieu, P. (1986). The forms of capital. In J. G. Richardson (ed.), *Handbook of theory and research for the sociology of education*. New York: Greenwood Press. 241–258.

Bourdieu, P. (1990). *The logic of practice*. Stanford, CA: Stanford University Press.

Capaldi, N. (1998). Scientism, deconstruction, and nihilism. *Argumentation, 9*(4), 563–575.

Clarke, J., Gewirtz, S., & McLaughlin, E. (eds) (2000). *New managerialism, new welfare?* London: Sage.

Clarke, J., Newman, J., Smith, N., Vidler, E., & Westmarland, L. (2007). *Creating citizen-consumers: Changing publics and changing public services*. London: Sage.

Deleuze, G. (1992). Postscript on the societies of control. *October, 59,* 3–7.

Dent, M., & Whitehead, S. (2002). *Managing professional identities: Knowledge, performativities and the 'new' professional*. London: Routledge.

Dustin, D. (2007). *The McDonaldization of social work*. Aldershot, Hants: Ashgate.

Ferlie, E. (2012). Concluding discussion: Paradigms and instruments of public management reform – the question of agency. In C. Teelken, E. Ferlie, & M. Dent (eds), *Leadership in the public sector: Promises and pitfalls*. Abingdon, Oxon: Routledge. 237–251.

Fleming, P., & Mandarini, M. (2009). New perspectives on work and emancipation. In M. Alvesson, T. Bridgman, & H. Willmott (eds), *The Oxford handbook of critical management studies*. Oxford: Oxford University Press. 328–344.

Flynn, N. (2007). *Public sector management* (4th edn). London: Sage.

Freidson E. (2001). *Professionalism: The third logic*. Cambridge: Polity Press.

Grey, C. (2005). Critical management studies: Towards a more mature politics. In D. Howcroft & E.M. Trauth (eds), *Handbook of critical information systems research: Theory and application*. Aldershot, Hants: Edward Elgar. 174–194.

Harris, J. (1998). Scientific management, bureau-professionalism, new managerialism: The labour process of state social work. *British Journal of Social Work, 28,* 839–862.

Harris, J. (2003). *The social work business*. London: Routledge.

Harris, J., & White, V. (eds) (2009). *Modernising social work: Critical considerations*. Bristol: Policy Press.

Henriksson, L., Wrede, S., & Burau V. (2006). Understanding professional projects in welfare service work: Revival of old professionalism? *Gender, Work and Organization, 14*(2), 174–192.

Independent. (2011). Sharon Shoesmith in line for compensation, 2 August. Retrieved 2 September 2011 from http://www.independent.co.uk/news/uk/home-news/sharon-shoesmith-in-line-for-compensation-2330560.html.

Kirkpatrick, I. (2006). Taking stock of the new managerialism. *Social Work & Society*, 4(1), 14–24.

Laclau, E. (2005). *On populist reason*. London: Verso.

Lawler, J. (1992). The social services manager. Ph.D. thesis, University of Bradford.

Lawler, J. (2008). Individualization and public sector leadership. *Public Administration*, 86(1), 21–34.

Lawler, J., & Bilson, A. (2010). *Social work management and leadership: Managing complexity with creativity*. Abingdon, Oxon: Routledge.

Linstead, S., Fulop, L., & Lilley, S. (2009). *Management and organization: A critical text*. Basingstoke: Palgrave Macmillan.

Lorig, K. (2002). Partnerships between expert patients and physicians. *The Lancet*, 359(9309), 814–815.

Moore, G. (2008). Re-imagining the morality of management: A modern virtue ethics approach. *Business Ethics Quarterly*, 18(4), 483–511.

O'Brien, M., & Penna, S. (1998). *Theorising welfare: Enlightenment and modern society*. London: Sage.

O'Reilly, D., & Reed, M. (2010). 'Leaderism': An evolution of managerialism in UK public service reform. *Public Administration*, 88(4), 960–978.

Özbilgin, M., & Tatli, A. (2005). Book Review Essay: Understanding Bourdieu's contribution to organization and management studies. *Academy of Management Review*, 30(4) 855–877.

Parker, M. (2002). *Against management: Organization in the age of managerialism*. Cambridge: Polity Press.

Policy Commission on Public Services. (2004). *Making public services personal: A new compact for public services*. London: Policy Commission on Public Services Report to the National Consumer Council.

Prime Minister's Strategy Unit. (2007). *Building on progress: Public services*. HM Government: Cabinet Office.

Rogowski, S. (2011). Managers, managerialism and social work with children and families: The deformation of a profession? *Practice*, 23(3), 157–167.

Rittel, H.W.J., & Webber, M.M. (1973). Dilemmas in a general theory of planning. *Policy Sciences*, 4(2), 155–169.

Ruch, G. (2011). Where have all the feelings gone? Developing reflective and relationship-based management in child-care social work. *British Journal of Social Work*. First published online 5 October 2011, doi:10.1093/bjsw/bcr134.

Seebohm Report. (1968). *Report of the Committee on local authority and allied personal social Services*. Cmnd 3703. London: HMSO.

Smith, G. (1979). *Social work and the sociology of organisations*. London: Routledge & Kegan Paul.

Taylor, F.W. (1911). *The principles of scientific management*. New York: Harper.

Thorpe, R., Gold, J., & Lawler, J. (2011). Locating distributed leadership. *International Journal of Management Reviews Special Issue*, 13(3), 239–250.

University of Warwick. (2011). *WBS Research Projects*. Retrieved 11 November 2011 from http://www2.warwick.ac.uk/fac/soc/wbs/projects/orthodoxies/inaugural_conference.

Whittington, C., & Bellaby, P. (1979). The reasons for hierarchy in social services departments: A critique of Elliott Jaques and his associates. *Sociological Review, 27*(3), 513–539.

7

Critical Best Practice

Harry Ferguson

In this chapter, two claims are made. First, whatever a new politics of social work is founded upon, it can only have credibility if it focuses on practice, *on what social workers actually do*. Despite the huge literature that exists on social work, virtually none of it is based on evaluations of what social workers do, especially how they practise when face-to-face with service users. An aim of this chapter is to contribute to correcting this by drawing on data from a participant observation study of social work practice in child protection. The second claim the chapter makes is that, while it is appropriate to focus on the things that go wrong and how systems fail in social work, one important emphasis for critical analysis needs to be on what constitutes *best* practice. The mass of data that a research study generates needs to be allowed to speak for itself in the sense of revealing whatever the findings are, whether that be in showing good, bad or average practice. How such things are defined and assessments made are, of course, contested issues, and need to be part of the critical discussion and justified through the use of theory. I attempt to show how it is possible to identify practice that is 'best', and the basis upon which such claims might be made.

The broader agenda the chapter seeks to address is the need for a more positive orientation towards critical social work practice. In some respects, the radical/critical tradition has contributed to social work becoming dominated by a 'deficit approach', where the focus is always on what does not get done (well) and on how social work supposedly 'fails' (Ferguson, 2003a; Saleebey, 2009). The chapter argues instead that what is needed is a meeting of critical practice and best practice, what I have elsewhere called a critical best practice perspective (Ferguson, 2003a; see also Gordon & Cooper, 2010; Howe, 2009; Jones, Cooper, & Ferguson, 2008). The central aim of a critical best practice perspective is to promote positive learning about social work by setting out examples of best practice informed by critical perspectives. The focus is on outlining and analysing actual practice where it can be shown that what social workers did was done well, with all the benefits that could accrue from this for service users. A key reason why such practice might be regarded as 'best' is because it contains a 'critical' component, where social workers have used their powers and capacities to reflect critically in a theoretically informed way that is both skilful and deeply respectful to service users, being mindful of their often marginalized social position and vulnerability, while at the same time using key skills, judgement, and what I call 'good authority'. Social work needs to showcase what it routinely does well by developing knowledge of best practice on which to base learning and positive growth, and making this visible both within the profession and to the public. The kind of critical theory needed is that which can operate at the level of the 'intimate' and illuminate as well as critique the lived experiences of practice and everyday life (Ferguson, 2011).

What's 'Critical' in Social Work?

What does, or should, it mean to be 'critical' in social work, or about social work? The 'critical' in critical best practice is meant in the sociological sense of critique, as opposed to being negative or censorious. This does not mean always trying to be 'nice' and constructive. Asking awkward questions and being contrary in questioning the nature of power and the ways society is structured is a vital part of what being an academic or intellectual should include (Fuller, 2005). 'Critics', as Ian Shaw (2005) observes of social work, 'are not universally liked' (p. 1244). Shaw argues, however, and correctly in my view, that the approach to critique in social work has resulted all too often in 'critical' meaning 'censoriousness'. The academic social work critic takes the moral high ground as he analyses all that is wrong and unequal in capitalist society (Garrett, 2013). A legitimate agenda to pursue social justice and social transformation is adopted, but without careful attention to the messy realities and complexities of the actual social work practices under consideration. At best, consciousness of inequalities and injustice has been raised, but we are no further forward in understanding what social workers do or might actually do differently. Meanwhile, approaches that do not conform to this radical orthodoxy are caricatured as having sold out to the seductions of 'bourgeois', individualized consumer capitalism (Garrett, 2003, 2004). Shaw (2005) is surely right in arguing that the introduction of practitioners' voices in the research process is a key way to achieve a wiser, grounded knowledge of what social work and critical practice involve.

What seems common to all 'critical theorizing' in social work is a commitment to using such critique not merely to understand the world but to try to change it to enhance service-users' lives. But key questions concern what precisely social work should be seeking to change, what it has the capacity to change, and *how* social work might go about actually improving the lives of those it seeks to help. My argument is that too often the vision of change and level of transformation demanded by radical/critical social work has been and remains hopelessly idealistic and unrealistic. The 'emancipatory politics' (Garrett, 2003, 2004, 2013) being called for address social problems and human suffering from the perspective of large-scale social and political processes (see Chapter 3). The alternative approach argued for here addresses concerns at the level of the personal and people's lived experience and practices, what, over a decade ago, I called 'life politics' (Ferguson, 2001, 2003b, 2003c, 2004). This involves accounting for power and structural factors that contribute to people's problems by addressing them through analysis of how they materialize in service-users' lives and relationships in actual social work practice. It means engaging in deep analyses of what I call 'intimate practice' (Ferguson, 2011), focusing on encounters between service users and social workers, paying attention to the impact of where the work goes on (such as when children are interviewed in intimate spaces like their bedrooms), and the dynamics of relationships in how physically and emotionally close to service users practitioners need to get in order to protect and be of therapeutic value to them.

The radical or 'critical' imagination in social work began to engage in such analysis with the birth of the 'radical social work' movement in the early 1970s (see Chapter 2). It was a response to the dominance of social casework, with its alleged tendency, under the influence of theories such as psychoanalysis, to reduce all problems to the individual failings of clients. Social work courses were dominated by psychological theories, with minimal use of ideas drawn from sociology or politics. Bailey and Brake's (1975) pioneering *Radical Social Work* defined it as being about 'understanding the position of the oppressed in the context of the social and economic structure they live in' (p. 9). At first, radical social work was concerned solely with social class and drew heavily on the theories of Karl Marx (Corrigan & Leonard, 1978). In the 1980s, with the influence of feminism and the women's movement, gender, sexism and sexuality reached social work's radical agenda, while racism (Dominelli, 1988), disability rights (Oliver, 1996) and gay and lesbian rights (Brown, 1997; Hicks, 2000) soon followed. Thus by the 1990s, notions of anti-discriminatory practice, anti-oppressive practice, and empowerment of a diverse range of service-user groups had become part of the mainstream of theory and practice in social work (Dalrymple & Burke, 2006; Thompson, 1993). Indeed, the very language of 'service user' entered social work at this time, replacing 'client', as another way of embedding the principle that those receiving services deserved to be treated equally and to be routinely worked with in dignified and empowering ways. The radical tradition is also being renewed through a return to Marxist approaches (Ferguson & Lavalette, 2004a; Ferguson & Woodward, 2009; also see Chapter 12).

The explicit notion of 'critical social work' or 'critical practice' has been taking shape since the late 1990s and is a step forward in that it represents a more grounded and practically useful radicalism (Adams, Dominelli, & Payne, 2009; Brechin, Brown, & Eby, 2000; Fook, 2012; Gray & Webb, 2013; Healy, 2000, 2005; Pease & Fook, 1999). In other words, there is more of a concern with giving at least clues as to how 'critical' practitioners might actually *practise*. I sense a growing awareness of the need to transcend the often idealistic theoretical prescriptions of critical theorizing to include greater clarity with regard to what needs to be skilfully done in practice, as well as thought and aspired to. However, problems persist in how critical social work theory remains at the level of negative critique, idealistically prescribing what should *not* be done (don't be sexist, racist, classist, and so on), while the actual practicalities of what *can* and often *should* be done, and *how*, are ignored or left at the level of aspiration. Largely, critical social work literature has avoided any encounter with actual practice, especially leaving out how critical practice can be done well. So, for instance, when students and practitioners look for examples of how to avoid being oppressive, while using statutory powers and authority and their skills in ethical, creative ways, there is nowhere for them to go.

A further implication of what I am arguing is that once the effort is made to come down to earth and engage at the level of intimate practice – to step into the shoes of the social worker, to walk with them up the garden path into the service-user's home to face the dilemmas and challenges involved in the complex interactions between service users and social workers – it becomes clear that much more needs to be done to recognize the complexity of social work practice and service-user's lives. A whole landscape opens up and demands our critical attention, ranging from the use of the body, gestures, touch, types of questions, the management of emotion, the constructive use of statutory powers, to changing professional attitudes and dominant beliefs about situations, providing advocacy, practical and material support, and changing service-users' beliefs and behaviours (Jones et al., 2008; Saleebey, 2009). Nowhere is the challenge of such analysis more urgent than with respect to the use of power and authority. The radical/critical tradition in social work has tended to set up crude oppositions between the 'bad social worker', who is always oppressive, and the 'good service user', who is always oppressed and invariably innocent. Sometimes service-user's problems are significantly influenced by their oppression. But, in many areas of practice – child and adult protection, mental health, probation, and young offenders – it is never so simple. Most social work literature is written as if the service user were voluntary, stressing the importance of respect for them and their rights and 'empowerment'. In the childcare literature, this is frequently expressed in terms of the goal of 'working in partnership' with parents and families. Radical/Marxist social work goes so far as to advocate collectivist approaches where social workers seek to work in partnership with service-user groups to challenge oppressive institutions and forces (see Chapter 12). But how are social workers to work 'in partnership' with people who are 'involuntary clients' and do not want a service? The neglect of such questions in the critical social work literature has resulted in limited analytical attention to the complexity of the work when risk is involved and service users are a million miles away from being the idealized fictional characters created by radical social workers. We have to face up to the fact that not only do such service users not want a service, but many try to avoid and even deceive or intimidate social workers. Given the risks some people represent to others and themselves, very often the best practice issue is not *if* constraint is valid, but *how* it is applied in a respectful, critically reflective way, which provides as much scope as possible for the service user to plan his or her own life.

Once this is accepted, theoretical perspectives other than those that provide 'structural' analyses of capitalist social relations become deeply relevant to critical social work. For instance, the work of Freud, and the psychoanalytic literature in general, has much to offer because it helps to reveal the complexity at the heart of humanity, the impact of the unconscious and the capacity we all have for sabotaging and destroying ourselves and others, as much as good intentions, resilience and creativity (Bower, 2005; Cooper & Lousada, 2005; Froggett, 2002). Such theories provide a means to incorporate an understanding of relationships and people's emotions and inner lives and how they interact with external influences and processes (Keeping, 2008; Trevithick, 2003). Being open to such human complexity is necessary to enable us to go beyond the purity and simplicity that has dogged so much theorizing in social work. We need to be far more honest about the struggle involved in being 'critical', the human challenge of practising empathy, and values such as tolerance, while so often dealing with the pain, cruelty and suffering that comes from its opposite, with all the feelings and inner conflict this can provoke.

The kind of new politics of social work I am arguing for demands that we seek to understand the complexities involved by recognizing how contradictory and multi-layered social work practice is. When statutory powers are used to detain adults under mental health legislation or to remove children from home, rarely can there be a straightforward 'good' outcome for all involved, or sometimes even for anyone involved. Such work very often involves serious infringements of rights and adding to the suffering of some (relatives, parents and siblings) in pursuit of promoting the safety and well-being of the vulnerable child or adult (who may not even want or appreciate it). And despite (or even because of) such infringements of rights and causing of distress, the practice involved may be entirely ethical and proper. Power in and of itself is not oppressive. It can be and sometimes is in how it is unethically exercised. But, equally, it is a positive and necessary resource, depending entirely on whether how it is used constitutes 'good authority' (Ferguson, 2011). It is precisely the setting out of how such ethical work is done that is at the heart of a critical best practice approach.

The (Best) Practice of Social Work

There is a remarkable absence of research into how social workers actually practise, and what they say and do when face to face with service users (Forrester et al., 2008; Hall & Slembrouch, 2009). My recent research has sought to correct this neglect by shadowing social workers from child and family teams, in particular as they go about their day-to-day child protection work. Adopting ethnographic methods, I shadowed workers wherever they saw children and parents, which, in the majority of cases, was in the service-user's home (Ferguson, 2011). I sought to capture the very 'work' that *is* social work, the movements, stillness, actions taken, talk and its consequences. The research made no assumptions and had no agenda to study only particular kinds of practice that could, for instance, be viewed as 'best', good or bad. The participant-observation method was open-ended, with the aim of finding out *what social workers actually do* by studying them going about their routine work. A large amount of qualitative data was gathered from observations and audio recordings of practice encounters and interviews with workers, which produced a wide variety of insights into different issues and kinds of social work practice. Given that the standpoint of this chapter is to focus on the dynamics of practice that can be identified as 'best', I am being very selective in focusing on a piece of work from the study, which, I will argue, constitutes 'critical best practice'.

The social worker I shadowed in this case had been involved with the family for 18 months. There were two children, a 15-year-old girl and a 12-year-old boy. Their mother had been living with a violent, controlling and emotionally abusive partner, whose behaviour impacted on the children and their mother alike. In turn, the mother's ability to care for her children was being adversely affected by her heavy drinking. The children had been on a child protection plan since the early days of involvement and the social worker had done a lot of direct work with them around their level of safety in the home and their self-esteem. The social worker felt the time had come for the children to come off the child protection plan and this was to be recommended at a case conference which was due in a week's time. The findings from the day's visit had confirmed the social worker's view.

It was clear from my observations of the children and how they and the social worker related to one another, and from the social worker's own account afterwards, that she had been instrumental in creating significant change and improvement in the children's level of safety. The turning point was when, after a great deal of patient input from the social worker, the mother decided that the abusive partner would have to leave. The social worker described the children as being jubilant when he left, after which they revealed even more about the full extent of the controlling regime to which this man had subjected them, and the liberation they felt when he had gone. The mother had had a relapse recently where she met up with this man again and stayed away overnight. Having done more work with her on the issues, the social worker's view was that matters had improved for the children and the mother to the extent that social work involvement had run its course and the time was approaching for her to withdraw.

On the visit, the two children were present, along with a family friend who was caring for them after school while their mother was at work. On arrival, the music system was playing at full volume. The social worker began to take control by excitedly engaging with the 12-year-old about his birthday cards and asking about the presents he had received. Prior to the home visit, the social worker had described the children as being quite weary of social work involvement, insofar as she suspected they had tired of having to come home directly from school at times when she had arranged to see them, which meant they could not spend time with their friends. Consequently, she felt that time spent with them seemed rather forced and contrived in terms of looking for things to focus on. But, to my eyes, the children's engagement was much more active and fulsome than I had been led to expect. As was often the case, the social worker was being overly modest and humble about the depths of her skills at communicating with young people in a respectful, authoritative and nurturing way. The children had given her nothing less than their full attention. The distractions we had walked into – the loud music and TV, the computer and mobile phone screens – had been quickly turned off. Faced with these distractions 18 months ago, when she had first started to visit the family, the social worker had negotiated a ground rule that everything would be turned off and stay off. This had happened for the entire duration of the one-hour visit.

The social worker's practice was distinguished by deep displays of enthusiasm, curiosity and readiness to express a viewpoint in response to what the children had presented to her. When she crossed the threshold and entered physically into a child's world – their sitting room, kitchen, bedroom – she skilfully took the next crucial steps of entering their emotional world. She had achieved this immersion on this occasion by using the relationship she had built with the children in the previous 18 months and referring back to prior concerns about their welfare and safety, past events and decisions, going back to the issues that had placed them at risk, especially their mother's ex-boyfriend, and talking about their mother herself and how they felt she was coping. This reflective work had also included mentioning joyful things, such as when she had accompanied them to the park in the summer. Her questioning style was open-ended, successfully drawing their feelings about their own level of safety from them. She had asked them whether there was anything she needed to be worried about and, if social care were withdrawn, what they would do should they have concerns in the future. Many months ago the social worker had given them the phone numbers for emergency social care services and they had confirmed that they had kept those numbers hidden in secret places in the home (away from adults) in case they should need them. Here we see the social worker skilfully negotiating what I earlier called the multi-layered complexity of practice: she had become an ally and protector for the children, while simultaneously working at challenging the mother to recognize her partner's abusive behaviour and supporting her to make the right choices.

By seeing them at home like this, the social worker was respecting the children's request not to see them at school due to their fear of the stigma of having a social worker visit there and the embarrassment of being seen to be a teenager in need of professional help. The family friend who was caring for the children in the mother's absence had respectfully stayed out of the sitting room and 90 per cent of the visit involved the social worker talking to the 12- and 15-year-olds on their own. In the latter part of the visit, the social worker asked the children whether she could have a look upstairs. They agreed and accompanied her there. When upstairs, the social worker skilfully used the children's possessions – their CDs, make-up and photographs – to connect more deeply with them, commenting jokingly on a photograph of one of them on the wall, generating some fun and laughter. She asked them about TV and popular culture references and expressed her own opinions about who would win the reality TV talent competition. Afterwards she explained how she had done this deliberately in the belief that showing even a little of her private self was a useful engagement strategy.

Requesting to see upstairs felt risky, given how cooperative the family had been up to this point and the potential for resistance it might create. The social worker explained afterwards that she nearly always checked upstairs, particularly children's bedrooms, where a child protection plan was in place. She did this in part to check on their sleeping and home conditions, but also in case there were risks to the children that they could not talk about but which she would be able to see by looking for herself. The social worker's spatial awareness provided further evidence of best 'intimate practice' in that she was deeply aware of the need to speak to the children in places where they felt comfortable and could not be overheard by adults. The worker was able to be with young people in different parts of the house, which was crucial to entering the depths of the children's physical and emotional worlds. This showed a worker who understood how notions of

'empowerment' and 'partnership working' were too simplistic in this kind of
work and who enacted a complex understanding of power that went beyond
comfortable discussions where the service users alone set the agenda. This
constituted the use of good authority because it ensured that an important
element of the protection task was carried out and due to the timing of it in
the session and the skilful, tactful and playful manner in which it was
performed. 'Critical best practice' has been characterized as practice that is
skilfully supportive, therapeutic and challenging of power structures, yet
authoritative (Jones et al., 2008). This worker's practice deserved to be called
'best' because of how it enacted a soulful combination of all these elements.

Shortly before ending the home visit, the social worker had received a
mobile phone call from the office advising her that a male service user (not
connected to the current case being visited) had phoned to say that he was
on his way to the office and was 'going to make her pay' for the trouble she
was bringing to bear on his family. It was now after 5 o'clock, and the office
was warning her not to go back that evening, and she did not. This was one
of many vivid examples I experienced in the research of the routine risks
and threats that social workers had to put up with. The social worker's
response suggested there was nothing particularly unusual about the threat
and she emphasized how she coped with it, motivated by a desire to connect
with children to make their lives better.

Conclusion

This chapter argued that, to have credibility, a new politics of social work
must be founded upon analyses of practice, upon evidence *of what social
workers actually do*. Out of this form of empirical inquiry, which inevitably
touches on numerous elements and issues, critical analysis needs to pay
attention to what constitutes *best* practice. This approach represents a strategic attempt to develop a more positive perspective on researching, learning
about and, most importantly, doing social work from critical perspectives.
The pervasive negativity of so much critical social work theory and the
crisis-driven obsessions of media-scapegoating of social work have left us
without a knowledge base of best practice and devoid of a tradition of celebration, pride or sense of achievement on which to build or fall back upon.

Producing a different kind of knowledge and politics means adopting
theories and methods that give primacy to understanding people's actions
and experience, and the meanings it has for them. Theory and understandings of practice are developed out of the everyday experience of professionals and service users and how they interact with one another. This
ethnographic approach proceeds by observing and gathering 'narratives'
from the key actors involved that provide for making sense of practice, and

out of which some key evidence and claims about *best* practice can be made. As I have argued, this contrasts with those approaches that focus on 'structures' and 'systems' at a distance, remote from what social workers actually have to do.

We need a politics of, and knowledge base for, social work that understands it as a creative endeavour shaped in crucial ways by how practitioners, teams and organizations are able to act and go about doing their work. However, best practice is categorically not something that floats free of the organizational and social context in which it goes on. It derives its legitimacy from the State and its laws and is, at all times, embedded in organizational processes. In recent years, social work has become a much more bureaucratised, regulated, managed and procedural enterprise (Broadhurst et al., 2010; Munro, 2011). Some interpret this as having led to the almost total erosion of autonomy and discretion for practitioners. Whereas once the lament of radicals was a fear of social workers being 'agents of social control' or 'social police', now it is equally a fear of being policed and held captive by an all-encompassing regulative managerial system (Webb, 2006; see Chapter 7). Such apparently highly managerial conditions makes it even more important that research seeks to find out what it is that practitioners actually do. Forms of theorizing are needed which must be able to work effectively at a number of interrelated levels, incorporating the personal, the organizational and the social/political. As I have tried to bring to life through the case study, this means addressing head-on the intimacies of people's lives and how social work practices, at best, 'wrap' themselves around people's vulnerabilities, strengths, dangerousness, suffering and resilience. Such research can develop knowledge that equips social workers with the skills to practise in the kinds of authoritative, nurturing ways I have profiled in this chapter. The urgent task of critical best practice analysis is to help social workers recognize their capacity for action and how they can and do make a difference.

References

Adams, R., Dominelli, L., & Payne, M. (eds) (2009). *Critical practice in social work.* Basingstoke: Palgrave Macmillan.

Bailey, R., & Brake, M. (1975). *Radical social work.* London: Edward Arnold.

Bower, M. (2005). *Psychoanalytic theory for social work practice.* London: Routledge.

Brechin, A., Brown, H., & Eby, M. (eds) (2000). *Critical practice in health and social care.* London: Sage.

Broadhurst, K., Wastell, D., White, S., Hall, C., Peckover, S., Thompson, K., Pithouse, A., & Davey, D. (2010). Performing initial assessment: Identifying the latent conditions for error at the front-door of local authority children's services. *British Journal of Social Work*, 40(2), 352–370.

Brown, H.C. (1997). *Social work and sexuality: Working with lesbians and gay men.* Basingstoke: Palgrave Macmillan.

Cooper, A., & Lousada, J. (2005). *Borderline welfare: Feeling and fear of feeling in modern welfare.* London: Karnac.

Corrigan, P., & Leonard, P. (1978). *Social work practice under capitalism: A Marxist approach.* London: Macmillan.

Dalrymple, J., & Burke, B. (2006). *Anti-oppressive practice, social care and the law.* Buckingham: Open University Press.

Dominelli, L. (1988). *Anti-racist social work: A challenge for white practitioners and educators.* Basingstoke: Palgrave Macmillan.

Ferguson, H. (2001). Social work, individualisation and life politics. *British Journal of Social Work, 31*(1), 41–55.

Ferguson, H. (2003a). Outline of a critical best practice perspective in social work and social care. *British Journal of Social Work, 33*(8), 1005–1024

Ferguson, H. (2003b). In defence (and celebration) of life politics in social work, *British Journal of Social Work, 33*(5), 699–707.

Ferguson, H. (2003c). Welfare, social exclusion and reflexivity: The case of child and woman protection, *Journal of Social Policy, 32*(2),199–216.

Ferguson, H. (2004). *Protecting children in time: Child abuse, child protection and the consequences of modernity.* Basingstoke: Palgrave Macmillan.

Ferguson, H. (2011). *Child protection practice.* Basingstoke: Palgrave Macmillan.

Ferguson, I., & Lavalette, M. (2004). Beyond power discourse: Alienation and social work. *British Journal of Social Work, 34,* 297–312.

Ferguson, I., & Woodward, R. (2009). *Radical social work in practice.* Bristol: Policy Press.

Fook, J. (2012). *Social work: A critical approach.* London: Sage.

Forrester, D., Kershaw, S., Moss, H., & Hughes, L. (2008) Communication skills in child protection: how do social workers talk to parents? *Child & Family Social Work, 13*(1), 41–51.

Froggett, L. (2002). *Love, hate and welfare.* Bristol: Policy Press.

Fuller, S. (2005). *The intellectual.* London: Icon Books.

Garrett, P.M. (2003). 'The trouble with Harry': Why the 'new agenda of life politics' fails to convince. *British Journal of Social Work, 33,* 381–397.

Garrett, P.M. (2004). More trouble with Harry: A rejoinder in the 'life politics' debate. *British Journal of Social Work, 34,* 577–589.

Garrett, P. M. (2013). *Social work and social theory.* Cambridge: Polity Press.

Gordon, J., & Cooper, B. (2010). Talking knowledge – practising knowledge: A critical best practice approach to how social workers understand and use knowledge in practice. *Practice, 22*(4), 245–257.

Gray, M., & Webb, S.A. (2013). Critical social work. In M. Gray & Webb, S.A. (eds), *Social work theories and methods* (2nd edn). London: Sage. 99–109.

Hall, C., & Slembrouch, S. (2009). Communication with parents in child welfare: Skills, language and interaction. *Child and Family Social Work, 14*(4), 461–470.

Healy, K. (2000). *Social work practices: Contemporary perspectives on change.* London: Sage.

Healy, K. (2005). *Social work theories in context: Creating frameworks for practice.* Basingstoke: Palgrave Macmillan.

Hicks, S. (2000). Sexuality. In M. Davies (ed.), *The Blackwell Encyclopaedia of Social Work*. Oxford: Blackwell. 141–153.

Howe, D. (2009). *A brief introduction to social work theory*. Basingstoke: Palgrave Macmillan.

Jones, K., Cooper, B., & Ferguson, H. (2008). *Best practice in social work: Critical perspectives*. Basingstoke: Palgrave Macmillan.

Keeping, C. (2008). Emotional engagement in social work: Best practice and relationships in mental health work. In K. Jones, B. Cooper, & H. Ferguson (eds), *Best practice in social work: Critical perspectives*. Basingstoke: Palgrave Macmillan. 71–87.

Munro, E. (2011). *Munro Review of Child Protection, Final Report: A child-centred system*. London: Department for Education.

Oliver, M. (1996). *Understanding disability: From theory to practice*. Basingstoke: Macmillan.

Pease, B., & Fook, J. (eds) (1999). *Transforming social work practice: Postmodern critical perspectives*. London: Routledge.

Saleebey, D. (ed.) (2009). *The strengths perspective in social work practice* (5th edn). New York: Longman.

Shaw, I. (2005). Practitioner research: Evidence or critique? *British Journal of Social Work*, *35*(8), 1231–1248.

Thompson, N. (1993). *Anti-discriminatory practice*. London: Macmillan.

Trevithick, P. (2003). Effective relationship-based practice: A theoretical exploration. *Journal of Social Work Practice*, *17*(2), 163–176.

Webb, S.A. (2006). *Social work in a risk society*. Basingstoke: Palgrave Macmillan.

8

Critical Discourse Analysis

Greg Marston

This chapter outlines the reasons why discourse analysis is an important dimension of critical social work practice. It brings to the forefront the very significant new contributions that sociologists focusing on the politics of recognition and redistribution, such as Nancy Fraser and Axel Honneth, can make in casting a New Left politics of social work (see also Chapters 2 and 4). In making this case, it begins by discussing some key developments in discourse theory and analysis within the social sciences and how they relate to the normative concerns of social work, specifically social justice and its multiple interpretations. Developing an appropriate analytical framework for critical social work practice can be difficult because there are conflicting and overlapping definitions of discourse formulated from various theoretical and disciplinary standpoints (Fairclough, 1992; Macdonell, 1991). Many different accounts of discourse have developed in the social sciences, partly due to recent interest in discourse theory among a wide range of academic disciplines. Whether language has assumed a more central focus as a result of this, or whether there has been an increase in the social importance of language in the operations of power, is open to question. In *Discourse and Social Change*, Norman Fairclough (1992) argues that it is more the latter:

> I believe there has been a significant shift in the social functioning of language, a shift reflected in the salience of language in the major social changes that have been taking place over the last few decades. Many of these social changes do not just involve language, but are constituted to a significant extent by changes in language practices. In many countries there has been an upsurge in the extension of the market to new areas of social life, such as education and health care. A major part of this impact comprises changes in discourse practices, that is, changes in language. (p. 6)

As an analytical category, discourse is concerned with language use in social contexts. Discourse contributes to the construction of social identities; secondly, discourse helps construct social relations between people and institutions; and thirdly, discourse contributes to the construction of systems of knowledge and belief (Fairclough, 1992). Nancy Fraser (1991) contends that a theory of discourse can help us: (1) understand how people's social identities are fashioned and altered over time; (2) understand how, under conditions of inequality, social groups are formed and unformed; (3) illuminate how the cultural hegemony of dominant groups is secured and contested; and (4) shed light on the prospects for social change and political practice.

This chapter argues that critical discourse analysis is complementary to the way in which the editors of this volume conceptualize critical social work. In the introduction to this book, Mel Gray and Stephen Webb define different dimensions of critical social work, one of which involves analysing the coercive workings and organization of power, especially as they are manifest in relations of domination and hierarchy. Like other forms of power that congeal in certain configurations of time and space, discourses that represent the social world are also structured hierarchically within fields of practice, with some discourses being dominant and institutionalized, while others are actively suppressed or marginalized. This process of establishing what Foucault (1972) called 'orders of discourse' involves struggle and contestation over whether certain topics are permissible and who gets to speak in the name of 'truth'. From the outset, it is important to recognize that the coupling of discourses is not fixed and static and it is important to resist the temptation to divide the discursive world too neatly into dominant and counter-discourses. For example, while the professional knowledge of social workers or lawyers can be a disciplining force on ordinary citizens, legal knowledge can also become a device of resistance, allowing subordinated groups to claim legal rights. To put it simply, no discourse is a permanent weapon of either dominant or marginalized groups. The uses of discourses are dynamic and ultimately unpredictable. What matters is that social workers have a clear and conscious appreciation of how discourse supplement forms of power in late modern societies. This will help guide action towards redressing social injustice.

An argument advanced in this chapter is that social workers have a responsibility to be critically aware of their own discourse when they represent and intervene as agents of change in public spaces, therapeutic relationships and organizational contexts where they work. As agents of change, it is also important to see that part of a responsibility in challenging social injustice is to interrogate the discourses that become institutionalized in certain spaces and times. Interrogating discourse has the explicit social justice objective of opening up a space for other subject positions and discourses to be acknowledged and for a wider range of actors to participate in naming and framing social problems.

While critical social theory has furnished the applied social sciences with the conceptual resources to think through the connections between language and social change, particularly the connection between economic and cultural injustice (see Chapter 2), there has been less guidance about how discourse analysis as a method of critical inquiry can be used by social work practitioners. This chapter seeks to contribute to addressing this gap. After covering some of the main conceptual issues concerning social justice discourse in the first part of the chapter, it outlines how the contributions from cognitive social science and sociolinguistics can offer social workers some practical ways to use discourse theory in their everyday practice, at both the micro and macro levels. To this end, it shows how a concentration on discourse at the micro and macro levels can contribute to thinking about a new politics of social work.

Developments in the Social Sciences and Implications for Practice

This section opens with an account of how I became acutely aware of the effects of discourse during my time working for a national peak organization in the field of housing and homelessness. This experience is used as a starting point to develop an example of poverty and structural injustice that can be used to highlight the importance of discourse to social work practice, particularly with respect to policy activism. The final part of this section discusses some of the main social theorists that support an explicit focus on discourse in pursuing social justice ends, particularly the insights of two key theorists: Nancy Fraser (1997), with her interest in the connections between economic and cultural justice, and the critical discourse analysis framework developed by Norman Fairclough (1992), which combines an analysis of how discourse operates as a form of power in society with a more textually oriented form of discourse analysis that uncovers the way the language shapes and structures social relations.

My own interest as a practitioner and later as a researcher in the social effects of language was sparked in the context of a rapidly changing discursive landscape in the field of homelessness and public housing policy in Australia during the mid-1990s. Within a relatively short period of time, I found myself in a policy community that was rapidly adopting a heavily market-oriented language to describe service users. Public housing tenants were being recategorized as generic 'customers' in official policy documents and proposals. I started to think about what this discourse signalled in terms of ongoing state obligations for the social protection of citizens and, more substantively, what this language meant for facilitating the political legitimacy of a mixed economy of welfare that was creating a larger space for managerial and marketized solutions to public problems.

At the state-government level, this marketization discourse was being coupled successfully with a political and media discourse that was socially conservative in its representation of public housing tenants. State governments were reactivating an historical discourse of 'bad tenants' to justify policies that effectively weakened security of tenure in public housing. The 'bad tenant' discourse constructed individuals as solely responsible for their position in a segmented housing system, and allowed the state government to say it had no obligation for tenants who did not respect the social institution of the law. Another important effect of this discourse in framing the nature of the issue was to divert public interest away from the structural problems in Australia's housing system, such as increasing income inequality, rising land prices in metropolitan areas, long waiting lists for public housing and discrimination in the private rental market.

There is no single 'culprit' when identifying the causes of structural social injustice. Identifying one agent or one factor as solely responsible for housing injustice, such as a neoliberal government or an exploitative lessor, has the effect of absolving other social actors and reifying social structures. This is not to suggest that individuals should not be held accountable for their actions. In the case of real-estate agents who ignore anti-discrimination legislation in allocating housing properties, there is a moral need for these individuals to be brought before a tenancy tribunal to account for their actions. However, a justice discourse that operates by seeking to identify degrees of liability of past actions does not take us very far in working towards solutions for a more just future. Vulnerability to housing deprivation for large numbers of people, for example, is an entirely predictable outcome of contemporary housing markets, particularly in the absence of aggressive regulatory intervention to prevent it (Young, 2011). The dominance of a moralizing and individualizing discourse of 'bad tenants', however, works against the possibility of recognising structural problems and long-term solutions.

Carol Bacchi's (2009) work in theorizing policy analysis helps in considering the relevance of discourse analysis in making certain policy options appear rational and reasonable and others implausible and unrealistic. One of her arguments is that there is a need to deconstruct critically how the social problem is framed, as the discursive framing of the problem inevitably informs the solution proposed by decision makers. If the problem is framed predominantly as one of 'bad tenants', then it should come as no surprise that state governments propose tougher tenancy laws to exclude certain classes of tenants from accessing public housing. In other words, policy discourses make some interventions possible, while closing off the possibility of others materializing. To engage in these discursive struggles requires a recognition that policy discourses can distort as much as they reveal. For example, it is disingenuous to suggest that persons living in neighbourhoods with poor schools, few shops and dilapidated housing, kilometres away from the closest job opportunities, have an equal opportunity with other persons in the same metropolitan area. Yet this is precisely what a moralizing self-sufficiency discourse does. It assumes that the background conditions that these people face are not unjust and that structural difficulties have been overcome through the march of modernity and the achievements of a range of social movements (Young, 2011).

Another questionable assumption in a self-sufficiency discourse is that it is only the responsibility of the poor that we need to worry about. The self-sufficiency discourse seeks to isolate the deviant poor and render them blameworthy for their condition, which then justifies the application of paternalistic and punitive policies towards them. What would happen, however, if poverty were found to be relatively common, at least for a certain period of time in many peoples' lives? (Rank, in Young, 2011) Or what would happen if citizens acted with determination and collective purpose on the evidence that privileged irresponsibility harms millions of people, such as was the case with the recent example of the 2008 global financial crisis where speculation in mortgage-backed securities led to widespread financial collapse? What might be concluded is that any worry about irresponsibility ought to be directed to all citizens, not just those made more visible by the mass media and state surveillance. It might also be concluded that those citizens who are not poor, at least at the moment, participate in the same structure of advantage and disadvantage, constraint and enablement as those who fall below the poverty line at some point. After arriving at this conclusion, it becomes that much harder to absolve ourselves from having no responsibility for social injustice (Young, 2011).

Having a hope of transforming these material realities requires that social workers pay critical attention to the way in which policy actors construct responsibility and irresponsibility, justice and injustice, and privilege and opportunity. What the above example suggests is that it is not enough for social workers to rally against the unequal distribution of goods and resources within society. They must also intervene in cultural politics to make economic justice possible. Socially conservative discourses that circulate in the public sphere about disadvantage are referred to by Fraser (1997) as 'adding cultural insult to economic injury' (p. 15). The case of refugees and the conservative politics of border protection are good illustrations of this connection. When refugees are demonized by politicians and the mass media as 'illegals' or 'queue jumpers' – as they regularly do in Australia and other countries – it becomes possible to deny this group of people material resources granted to others, such as settlement services and jobs. The discourse of illegality is powerful precisely because it resonates within a society that supposedly respects and upholds 'the rule of law'. Constructing people as unlawful puts them on the side of a moral binary that works against their claims to be recognized as persons with rights. To address this injustice requires that social workers intervene on the cultural and the material, and they may need to become involved in social movements that actively seek to reframe social identities in the public sphere (see Chapter 12).

To be effective political agents, social workers must also be prepared to contest the scope of the social justice frame itself, which, in an international sense, means questioning the state-territorial frame of justice claims making. It is no longer sufficient to discuss the structural conditions for the 'good life' in what Fraser (2010) refers to as the 'Westphalian frame', which means that the subjects of sociopolitical justice are constituted with reference to national territorial states, but what is required are other principles that can supplement this national frame to deal with the new realities of global governance. In the following extract, Fraser (2010) explains this point in relation to the need to rethink the Western welfare state so that other political spaces can be brought into the picture:

> The idea that state-territoriality can serve as a proxy for social effectivity is no longer plausible. Under current conditions, one's chances to live a good life do not depend wholly on the internal political constitution of the territorial state in which one resides. Although the latter remains undeniably relevant, its effects are mediated by other structures, both extra and non-territorial, whose impact is at least as significant. (p. 25)

The effect of these developments, Fraser (2010) argues, is a lack of consensus, even among professed social democrats and egalitarians, as to how to understand the injustice, let alone redress it. This acknowledgement of confusion and uncertainty is not an argument for taking no action or standing still until a reform path becomes clear – by definition, political agency requires action in the public sphere. However, what is required is rethinking the scope of political action. One of the insights from discourse theory is that it is not possible to stand outside discourse. Social workers intervene as political agents full of potential and possibility, but also know that it is not possible to be certain about the outcome. As stated in the introduction to this chapter, political discourses are dynamic. Conflicting transnational forces mean that the terrain is shifting more quickly than it has in the past. Capitalism is constantly changing and its reach, through new technologies, is extending into what were once spaces outside the influence of market forces.

In his book *Speeding Up Fast Capitalism*, Ben Agger (2004) argues that fast production made possible by advances in technology also requires fast consumption and the creation of new markets. The result of these developments in accumulation regimes is that the forces of capital 'have colonized what used to be off limits to the social and political ... subjecting all of life to scheduling, producing, connecting, messaging, immersing oneself in the quotidian and therefore losing sight of the bigger picture' (p. 132).

Under these circumstances, the self-sufficiency discourse becomes a kind of comfort zone. Nancy Rosenblum (in Young, 2011) argues that part of the reason a self-sufficiency discourse thrives in present conditions is because we have a declining faith in our own political agency and 'the less confidence we have in our own democratic political agency the more we demand of others' (p. 40). This argument helps explain the dominance of the self-sufficiency discourse. Consequently, citizens come to passively regard the complex workings of society whose effects are fortunate for some individuals and unfortunate for others, as solely the result of individual effort and, therefore, not a matter of justice for which all citizens should take collective responsibility (Young, 2011). The following section theorizes a more active version of political agency, but one which is also balanced by the need to recognize that the scope and scale of social justice concerns are being rapidly transformed. The first part of the discussion sets out a way in which discourse analysis helps the task of reflexivity, while the second sketches some ways in which discourse analysis can be part of everyday political action.

Connecting Critical Discourse Analysis to Social Work Practice

As a professional project, social work educators must constantly confront the question about how they should teach students to respond to the conditions of the present. In the push towards a 'new politics', what should social work programmes instil in students about the prospect for social justice in a globalizing world? It remains the case that social work education continues to include curricula on political economy and sociology, which are social science disciplines that seek to identify structural explanations for social problems. Moreover, social work professional associations and textbooks continue to espouse professional norms of emancipation, liberation, social justice and empowerment. However, in both cases, the reference point for claims making and needs interpretation often comes back to the national state. In 2000, the International Federation of Social Workers (IFSW) produced a much-cited statement about the purpose of social work: 'The social work profession promotes *social change*, problem solving in human relations and the *empowerment* and *liberation* of people to enhance wellbeing' (emphasis added). Later in the same statement, it claims:

> Social work addresses the barriers, inequities and injustices that exist in society … Interventions also include agency administration, community organisation and engaging in social and political action to impact social policy and economic development. The holistic focus of social work is universal, but the priorities of social work practice will vary from country to country and from time to time depending on cultural, historical, and socio-economic conditions. (IFSW, 2000, n.p.)

Despite these pronouncements about structural issues, it is also the case that beginning social workers are likely to be influenced by the dominant societal discourse of self-sufficiency and the muted political agency that this discourse gives rise to. Presented with a sociocultural discourse of passive agency and a professional discourse about the possibilities that arise when 'heroic agents' confront social structures presents contradictions that may be difficult for beginning practitioners to reconcile. As Amy Rossiter (2005), in her insightful analysis of these contradictory discourses of agency and responsibility, argues: 'Social workers as people suffer when the results of practice seem so meagre in comparison to the ideals inherent in social work education, in agency expectations, and in implicit norms which define professional activity' (p. 4). The result of this asymmetry can be ambivalence, uncertainty and doubt.

Rossiter (2005) goes on to argue that discourse analysis can help practitioners work through the gap between theory and action in practice contexts. She offers a way to think about this contradiction in reflecting on social casework, which is useful in displacing the notion of the 'heroic' social work activist towards a more nuanced, sophisticated understanding of practice. She does this by getting her students to analyse case studies from their practice experiences. Students are asked to identify: (1) 'ruling' discourses in the case studies; (2) the oppositions and contradictions between discourses; (3) positions for 'actors' created by discourses which, in turn, shape perspectives and actions; and (4) the constructed nature of experience itself.

These elements are intended to help students shift from 'what I did' to how the case was constructed, and how their feelings arose from the complicated constructions of their practice within particular locations and time. Rossiter (2005) argues that once discourses were identified, students could discover how those discourses created subject positions for themselves, their clients, and others involved in the case. This is one example of how discourse analysis can displace the individualism of the 'heroic activist' in favour of a more nuanced, complex and sophisticated analysis. Discourse analysis enables a critical distance to be drawn from ambivalent and contradictory values, and permits social workers to acknowledge how their identities as professionals are constructed, and how the people they work with are constructed in often messy and ambivalent practice contexts.

Using discourse analysis as a tool for reflexivity can also assist in recognizing that what is expressed by a social worker as an ethical dilemma can also be understood as an attempt to reconcile conflicting and contradictory discourses, as in the case of front-line social workers being asked to apply a financial sanction to a young unemployed person for non-compliance with a welfare-to-work policy measure (McDonald & Chenoweth, 2006). In this example, discourse analysis would not only normalise client resistance as an expression of agency in the face of a paternalistic policy discourse, it would also assist in identifying the clash for the worker between professional ethics and potentially punitive policy. Having identified the competing discourses, the worker can identify the political actors that form various 'discourse coalitions' and how they might work with these to challenge and change government policy. And as a minor act of rebellion, the worker might refuse to use the term 'customer' or 'job-seeker' when talking about people experiencing unemployment in their regular team meetings. They might argue that these marketized identities do not fit the sort of state obligations more fully captured by a social citizenship discourse.

The social worker would recognize that how people were called to participate mattered; that this naming and framing of those who become the targets of social policies must be respectful of difference. They would recognize that stigmatizing some people limits their options, while, at the same time, elevating others to a higher status, with a wider array of more rewarding options (Young, 2011). They would insist on a more fully-fleshed subjectivity when talking about ordinary people experiencing disadvantage, arguing that people in social contexts do not exist one-dimensionally as 'poor people', 'black people' or 'people with disabilities'. The unequal distribution of wealth, income and cultural resources flows through a variety of social categories. In theoretical and political terms, the social worker would recognize that it is a form of 'symbolic violence' (Bourdieu, 1991) to fix upon a partial social categorization and impute it to a limited set of social characteristics.

In using discourse analysis as a tool for critical reflexivity, it is possible to see how social workers can reflect on their role in promoting social justice. It allows both beginning and experienced practitioners to decentre expert knowledge and reconsider the value of a professional identity constructed as the 'all-knowing subject' – the one who possesses unique insight to transform various forms of oppressive practice. Blom (2009) argues that maintaining a tension between the unknowing and knowing professional expert can create a critical potential in social work practice, as it opens up a possibility for challenging rigid routines and assumptions. Another problem with the professional subject position of the 'all-knowing subject' is the idea that agency is only attributable to the liberator, that is, the actor who possesses the expertise and actions to determine the 'who' of justice claims-making. The effect of this expert authority is to neglect the importance of public autonomy, the freedom of all social actors to participate in framing the justice issues that bind them (Fraser, 2010). As such, some versions of professionalism can work against the democratization of discourse practices, and this is something that critical social workers need to guard against in their own practice. Associated with this decentring of expert knowledge, it is also important to recognize that a faith in science and evidence are unlikely to be sufficient props in the face of political and social uncertainty. McDonald (2003), for example, argues in her critique of evidence-based social work, which came to prominence in the late 1990s and early 2000s in countries like Australia, the USA and the UK, that evidence-based practice fails to acknowledge the diversity of knowledge and ways of knowing, particularly those that arise from social and political movements. Similarly, Webb (2001) argues that evidence-based practice traps social work within a technocratic and positivist scientific framework.

Decentring the version of professionalism that comes from a faith in evidence-based practice allows other possibilities to emerge, other ways of critical thinking and acting that are more consistent with the complex networks of late modernity and more inclusive of notions of citizenship and policy deliberation. In many ways, this more humble starting point for political action is a liberating proposition, as it implies a connected and collective responsibility for social injustice, but it also suggests that one cannot be certain about the most effective pathway. This conceptualization is similar to what Iris Marion Young (2011) refers to as the idea of the *perhaps* in conceptualizing political agency and possibility:

> This active stance opens up a future that can be made, but is risky and uncertain. Let us try together to alter the social processes that we understand produce injustices, and *perhaps* we will have some success. People in solidarity for the sake of justice are determined to improve social relations, but they are also tentative and humble. (p. 120)

So while some ambitions may seem unrealistic in present political circumstances, the active political agent realizes that political circumstances will change over time as a result of a constellation of social, political and economic forces. Social workers can also think about changing discourse about disadvantage, poverty and injustice in the same way. Reframing dominant discourses is something social workers can engage in during their everyday practice with colleagues, managers, government officials, clients, friends and family. However, they can also appreciate that a large-scale shift in discourse practice requires mobilizing a coalition of forces and resources, and change may be gradual. With the benefit of historicizing discourse, they can see that discourses do indeed change. The conceptualization of disability, for example, or the construction of gender and sexual norms or family form, have changed considerably over time, sometimes reawakening much earlier discourses, other times inventing new hybrid discourses.

The relationship between discourse and material change is dynamic and dialectic. In this respect, as Fraser (1997) notes, both cultural and social politics must be recoupled, both practically and intellectually, if we are to conceive of provisional alternatives to the present political and social order:

> A critical approach must be 'bivalent', in contrast, integrating the social and the cultural, the economic and the discursive. This means exposing the limitations of fashionable neo-structuralist models of discourse analysis that dissociate 'the symbolic order' from the political economy. (p. 7)

One approach that fits with the different levels of social work practice and seeks to have a social analysis and detailed textual analysis of language is 'Critical Discourse Analysis' (CDA). CDA is based on recognition that changes in language use are linked to wider social and cultural processes and vice versa, and language analysis is an important method for studying social change (Fairclough, 1992). Fairclough's (1992) CDA approach involves a three-dimensional framework whereby:

> Any discursive event (i.e. any instance of discourse) is seen as simultaneously being a piece of text, an instance of discursive practice, and an instance of social practice. The text dimension attends to language analysis of texts. The discursive practice dimension ... specifies the nature of the processes of text production and interpretation. The social practice dimension attends to issues of concern in social analysis such as institutional and organisational circumstances of the discursive event and how that shapes the nature of the discursive practice, and the constitutive/ constructive effects of the discourse referred to above. (p. 4)

Further, in coupling CDA with a dialectic perspective, Fairclough (1992) underscores the dynamic relationship between social practice and text, mediated through discourse practices. Put simply, language change has implications for social practice, and changes in social practice may generate changes in language use. In Hajer and Versteeg's (2005) view, discourse analysis has three particular strengths in social work and social policy analysis: the capacity to reveal (1) the role of language in politics; (2) the embeddedness of language in practice; and (3) mechanisms to answer 'how' questions about the function of language.

Cognitive science also offers social work something to consider in working with discourse as a category of political change. George Lakoff's influential book *Don't Think of an Elephant!* (2004) provides practical advice on how to change political discourse. First, be clear about your beliefs and values, and then be confident and unapologetic about declaring them in political debates and discussion. In contrast to a 'faith in facts' approach to changing the world – identified earlier as part of the evidence-based practice approach in social work – Lakoff (2004) argues that frames – or mental structures – are more powerful than facts – hard evidence – in changing behaviour and political attitudes. His approach seeks to make these frames more transparent, since they shape the goals we seek, the plans we make, the way we act, and what counts as a good or bad outcome of our actions. In other words, thinking or seeing differently requires speaking differently. In terms of policy change, Lakoff's (2004) argument helps us to realize that, when a politician or policy maker is confronted with a fact or a piece of information that contradicts his or her mental frame, the inconvenient fact will often be rejected.

Returning to the example of social justice, it is possible to see how these insights from cognitive science and critical discourse analysis might be applied. If poverty were understood as a personal or moral failing then social workers would most likely seek out information to confirm this bias. They would understand any form of state dependency as moral failing, while, at the same time, encouraging market-based dependency as a sign of independence. Politicians and mass-media reports of 'welfare fraud', unemployed 'scroungers' or 'dole bludgers' are social identities that symbolize this dominant social policy discourse. Reframing self-sufficiency and moral deficiency requires that social workers take apart the value assumptions and policy logic that lie behind these sentiments and the silences in the text about connected responsibility. Taking the concept of social inclusion as an example, which governments in the UK and later in Australia appropriated as a way of talking about poverty, one sees how reframing works in the interest of promoting a structural measure of injustice. In her insightful analysis of New Labour's social exclusion discourse in the UK, Ruth Levitas (1998) identified three ways in which this term was given meaning, ranging from a moral underclass discourse (MUD) to a social integrationist discourse (SID) to a redistribution discourse (RED). This framework provides social workers with a way to step back and consider whether the programmes being promoted under the banner of 'social inclusion' are simply pushing and prodding people into various markets that, by definition, discriminate.

A CDA framework allows social workers to consider whether the 'inclusion/exclusion' binary is the most appropriate way to consider the relations of economic advantage and disadvantage. Does it lead to a distorted gaze on the 'excluded', at the cost of allowing little or no critique about the risks associated with a market society? Who gets to name the excluded? What sort of society is imagined in this conception, and is it more productive than an older discourse of poverty? Similar to what was discussed earlier about the risks of anchoring social work in a technocratic world-view of evidence-based practice, social work must also be careful that, under the banner of social inclusion, it does not settle for market compliance as a signifier of its legitimacy as a profession. Critically reflective practitioners must ask themselves whether the language of inclusion and exclusion is sufficient for promoting a social justice framework oriented towards a relational approach that includes an analysis of the relationship between the housed and the unhoused, the wealthy and the poor, the overemployed and the underemployed. As Hilary Silver (1995) argues, in her critique of social inclusion/exclusion binary, 'exclusion involves two parties, the excluders and the excluded' (p. 58). The challenge is to frame social inclusion as a relational concept, otherwise it ends up being a 'weak discourse' (Levitas, 2005). This example from social policy highlights the importance of being thoughtful about the language used in seeking to redress injustice, particularly in regard to social problems. As Majone (in Fischer & Forrester, 1993) states: 'As politicians know only too well, but social scientists often forget, public policy is made of language. Whether in written or oral form, argument is central in all stages of the policy process' (p. 2).

Conclusion

Discourses about how society works function at their most effective when they are naturalized, accepted as taken-for-granted social facts. The role of the social worker as discourse analyst is to uncover the contingent and historical basis of sociocultural, organizational and professional discourses, to show that they are constructs with multiple interpretations. On one level, discourse analysis – like all forms of criticism – can be a real source of change, depriving some practices of their self-evidence while extending the bounds of the thinkable to permit the invention of others (Burchell & Miller, 1991). In its significance, the discursive dimension of social change and its role in reproducing material injustices is unlikely to diminish in the future. As Poynton (2000) argues:

> Possibilities for an oppositional stance – for any kind of resistance to the operations of new forms of power – are giving way to very different kinds of engagement with issues of power, government and their legitimation. Discourse remains at the heart of these issues, however, rendering critical forms of discourse analysis – current and future – of ongoing importance. (p. 38)

The challenge for social work is to recognize that intervening in the socio-cultural realm is a legitimate and necessary aspect of social work practice. Identifying the discourses operating in organizational environments, or broader policy communities, allows practitioners to get some critical distance from their everyday contexts and helps them to appreciate the role of language in facilitating organizational or policy change. Ultimately, social workers using discourse analysis in their practice would acknowledge that working in the interests of a more socially just world requires interventions in the material and the symbolic order.

Acknowledging the significance of discourse in political action requires a wider definition of resistance – that goes beyond the idea of open rebellion – to enable social workers to recognize that changing the way they frame social problems or refusing to use devalued social identities are significant political actions at the local level. A simple binary between 'open rebellion' and 'consent' misses low-level refusals and disobedience. Within organizational environments where much social work practice takes place, politically adept social workers are often required to be 'bilingual' in their use of discourse, strategically adopting a managerial frame when communicating with funding bodies or senior managers to secure funding and other resources, while using a more explicit social justice discourse when connecting with ordinary citizens and their struggles. Some might see this 'double speak' as a form of conservative resistance, which ultimately legitimates the colonization of managerialism in human service organizations. A better starting point is to acknowledge and validate the multiple forms of resistance that can exist at the local level of social work practice, formal and informal, discursive and material. Symbolic refusals and covert resistance within seemingly disconnected local spaces can sometimes amount to a seismic shift in framing questions of justice, a point acknowledged by Scott (1990) in his work on the potential power of practical resistance in confronting domination:

> These are the forms that political struggle takes when frontal assaults are precluded by the realities of power. At another level it is well to recall that the aggregation of thousands upon thousands of such 'petty' acts of resistance have dramatic economic and political effects. (pp. 191–2)

References

Agger, B. (2004). *Speeding up fast capitalism: Cultures, jobs, families, schools, bodies.* Boulder, CO: Paradigm.

Bacchi, C. (2009). *Analysing policy: What's the problem represented to be?* Frenchs Forest, NSW: Pearson Education.

Blom, B. (2009). Knowing or un-knowing? That is the question in the era of evidence-based social work practice. *Journal of Social Work, 9*(2), 158–177.

Bourdieu, P. (1991). *Language and symbolic power.* Ed. and intro. J.B. Thompson. Cambridge: Polity Press.

Burchell, G.G.C., & Miller, P. (eds) (1991). *The Foucault effect: Studies in governmentality with two lectures by and an interview with Michel Foucault.* Chicago: University of Chicago Press.

Fairclough, N. (1992). *Discourse and social change.* Cambridge: Polity Press.

Fischer, F., & Forrester. J. (eds) (1993). *The argumentative turn in policy analysis and planning.* Durham, NC: Duke University Press.

Foucault, M. (1972). The discourse on language. In M. Foucault, *The archaeology of knowledge.* New York: Pantheon Books.

Fraser, N. (1991). The uses and abuses of French discourse theories for feminist politics. In P. Wexler (ed.), *Critical theory now.* London: Falmer. 98–117.

Fraser, N. (1997). *Justice interruptus: Critical reflections on the 'postsocialist' condition.* New York: Routledge.

Fraser, N. (2010). *Scales of justice: Reimagining political space in a globalising world.* New York: Columbia University Press.

Hajer, M., & Versteeg, W. (2005). A decade of discourse analysis of environmental politics: Achievements, challenges, perspectives. *Journal of Environmental Policy & Planning, 7*(3), 175–184.

International Federation of Social Workers (IFSW). (2000). *Definition of social work.* Retrieved 2 June 2011 from http://www.ifsw.org/f38000138.html.

Lakoff, G. (2004). *Don't think of an elephant! Know your values and frame the debate.* White River Junction, VT: Chelsea Green Press.

Levitas, R. (1998). *The inclusive society? Social exclusion and New Labour.* Basingstoke: Palgrave Macmillan.

Levitas, R. (2005). *The inclusive society? Social exclusion and New Labour* (2nd edn). Basingstoke: Palgrave Macmillan.

MacDonell, D. (1991). *Theories of discourse: An introduction.* Oxford: Basil Blackwell.

McDonald, C. (2003). Forward via the past: Evidence based practice as strategy in social work. *The Drawing Board, 3*(3), 123–142.

McDonald, C., & Chenoweth, L. (2006). Workfare Oz-style: Welfare reform and social work. *Australia Journal of Policy Practice, 5*(2/3), 109–128.

Poynton, C. (2000). Linguistics and discourse analysis. In A. Lee & C. Poynton (eds), *Culture and text: Discourse and methodology in social research and cultural studies.* Sydney, NSW: Allen & Unwin.

Rossiter, A. (2005). Discourse analysis in critical social work: From apology to question. *Critical Social Work, 6*(1), 1–8.

Scott, J. (1990). *Domination and the arts of resistance: Hidden transcripts.* New Haven, CT: Yale University Press.

Silver, H. (1995). Reconceptualizing social disadvantage: Three paradigms of social exclusion. In G. Rodgers, C. Gore, & J.B. Figueiredo (eds), *Social exclusion: Rhetoric, reality, responses.* Geneva/New York: IILS/UNDP. 57–80.

Webb, S.A. (2001). Some considerations on the validity of evidence based practice in social work. *British Journal of Social Work, 31,* 57–79.

Young, I.M. (2011). *Responsibility for justice.* Oxford: Oxford University Press.

PART III
Transformative Social Work Practices

PART III

Transformative Social Work
Practices

9

New Practices of Empowerment

Viviene E. Cree

We are living in dangerous times. The world is becoming an ever-more risky place for those on the margins, in the developing and developed world (Bauman, 2007; Beck, 1999). Just as drought, famine and war are forcing millions of people in the developing world to leave their homes in search of safety, so the economic recession and austerity cuts in public services are hitting hardest those most need in the developed world (Ferguson & Woodward, 2009; Hugman, 2010). It is tempting, in such difficult times, to latch onto a concept which seems to offer something positive: empowerment is one such idea. Who could fail to agree that it is a 'good idea'? And yet, like so many commonly used terms in social work – advocacy, participation, human rights, anti-oppressive practice – it has not been sufficiently scrutinized or analysed. To seek to empower others seems a noble aspiration, and one which is self-evidently appropriate for social workers. But it is not at all clear what it is and how social workers might do it. Saleebey (2006) goes so far as to suggest that empowerment is 'rapidly becoming hackneyed' (p. 9). Nevertheless, this chapter argues that empowerment remains a valuable concept for social work today and must be understood as part of a radical response to the problems faced by individuals, groups and communities. In this respect, it cannot offer a 'cheap and cheerful' solution to tough economic times. Moreover, social workers cannot give power to anyone. Instead, those who hold power over others – social work practitioners, managers, policy makers, educators and researchers, as the case may be – must strive to establish conditions through which those with less power – service users, junior colleagues, citizens, students and research informants, for example – are able to feel empowered and valued, or empower themselves. This conceptualization of empowerment builds on a particular way of thinking about power as not only 'top-down', but also as something which

145

everyone has, to varying degrees, in different ways and at different times. The chapter begins by exploring what empowerment is, before examining contrasting approaches and considering how the term has been used in social work. It then takes a step back to consider what is meant by power, before exploring what empowerment might mean in contemporary service environments. The chapter concludes by relocating empowerment within a critical social work paradigm.

Understanding Empowerment

In a textbook on empowerment now in its fourth edition, Adams (2008) suggests that the roots of empowerment can be found in a number of antecedents, each of which has contributed something to the ways in which it has developed as an idea. He identifies eight strands, which may be summarized as two competing responses to the human condition. The first, often described as 'self-help' – or self-sufficiency (see Chapter 8), builds from the idea that individuals are responsible for themselves, their families and their problems and any help given by external agents – the State, the Church, voluntary bodies – should seek to encourage individual independence and self-reliance. In contrast, the second stresses the 'social' nature of problems and the need for social approaches and solutions. The tensions between these two responses are still visible in contemporary debates within and about social work, most noticeably in critiques of its heavily individualistic focus.

Empowerment as an individual response

There is nothing new about the idea of empowerment as self-help. On the contrary, a number of popular catchphrases and proverbs demonstrate the history of this resilient concept. For example, the adage 'God helps those who help themselves' is said to have originated in ancient Greece (Panati, 1999). It is closely related to the Chinese proverb, 'Give a man a fish and he will eat for a day. Teach a man to fish and he will eat for the rest of his life.' This catchphrase came to public attention in 2008 with a high-profile Oxfam campaign.

The establishment of the Charity Organization Society (COS) in London in 1869 demonstrated the self-help approach. The COS acted as a clearing house, dealing with claims for charitable help. Caseworkers investigated the amount and nature of help to be given on the basis of this assessment (see Cree & Myers, 2008). A typical COS grant to a widow might be the gift, or perhaps loan, of a mangle – a machine for squeezing dry and pressing wet laundry – so that she could do other people's washing for payment. The COS Organizing Secretary, Charles Loch (in Fraser, 2009), explained, 'We must use charity to create the power of self-help' (p. 143). This was the rationale behind campaigns against the provision of free school meals, public housing and the welfare state in general. Similar arguments were rehearsed again in 2010 in the USA as Republican politicians and media pundits railed against Barack Obama's reform which brought near-universal healthcare coverage to US citizens for the first time.

Commentators, such as Adams (2008), have noted that the idea of self-help has been criticized because it 'reflected the values of middle-class society' (p. 9; see also Cruikshank, 1999). While this undoubtedly is the case, in reality, the concept of self-help has had widespread appeal, and might be considered as much an integral feature of working-class ideology as a middle-class imposition on the working classes. A key example of this can be found in the trade-union movement, which also emerged in the nineteenth century in Europe and the USA. Trade unions were built on the principle of self-help, as predominantly male workers banded together to achieve common goals, such as better pay and working conditions. They also provided benefits and services for their members and their families. Although they were concerned for the greater good of society, demonstrated, for example, in their support of the Labour Party in the UK, their primary focus was on their members' interests, not those of the working class in general.

By the 1980s, a new spirit entered the self-help discourse, one which was unapologetically anti-professional in tone. Here it was argued that the welfare state 'produces' the poor and had to be dismantled if people were to have any chance of managing themselves and their lives (Cruikshank, 1993, 1999). Self-help also re-emerged as a major political theme in the UK with the election in May 2010 of the Conservative–Liberal Democratic coalition government intent on 'rolling back the frontiers of the state', just as Margaret Thatcher had promised 30 years earlier. The Prime Minister, David Cameron's (2010) vision was of a 'big society' in which people would be given greater power and control over their communities. His manifesto begins:

> We want to give citizens, communities and local government the power and information they need to come together, solve the problems they face and build the Britain they want. We want society – the families, networks, neighbourhoods and communities that form the fabric of so much of our everyday lives – to be bigger and stronger than ever before. Only when people and communities are given more power and take more responsibility can we achieve fairness and opportunity for all. (p. 1)

The idea of the 'big society' has been challenged on a number of fronts – political, economic and social. Some have suggested that without the power to raise taxes, there is little additional power available to give to communities. More crucially, it is unclear how communities will be able to do more for themselves, faced with cuts in government spending to education, health, police and, of course, social work services. In reviewing this policy, Jordan (2011) argues that the rationale for the 'big society' is twofold:

> On the one hand, it offers to deliver citizens from the technocratic formalism of the new public services, with their obsessions about rules, systems and checklists; it invites participation, enthusiasm and commitment. On the other, it promises to restore to professionals the power to exercise judgement, critique and expertise – to take back decision-making from the government, managers and inspectors. But behind these appeals lies a deeper one to the question of what social services (and the politics which informs them) are really about. (p. 3)

The 'big society' is also tied to another 'self-help as empowerment' buzzword, namely, 'personalization'. In neoliberal policy terms, personalization is the 'way in which services are tailored to the needs and preferences of citizens' and the means by which the state empowers citizens 'to shape their own lives and the services they receive' (UK Department of Health, 2008, p. 4). The stated aim of personalization is, therefore, for services to meet the needs of the person, rather than the person having to 'fit in' to suit the service provided. Those using services, for their part, are described as having more choice, control and responsibility over the support they receive. This has been operationalized through 'individual budgets' or 'direct payments', where cash is paid directly to service users so they might acquire their own support, rather than having it delivered by a statutory agency, such as a Social Services Department or Health Board (see Chapter 6).

While the disabled peoples' and mental health consumer movements – and the social model of disability – have long advocated for service-user rights, personalization in the organization and delivery of social services under welfare reform stems from neoliberal rather than empowerment ideology. Hence it was introduced at a time of significant restructuring of welfare services towards welfare-to-work programmes focused on the unemployed, through the rhetoric of consumer choice. Given that some service users might end up with less support or lower-quality care, it remains to be seen whether empowerment of this kind will produce positive results for those who use services and their carers. Clearly, personalization is unpopular with professionals since it leads to new challenges in terms of employer–employee relationships, working conditions, and security for service users and care workers alike. Service users might choose to use unqualified care workers over professional help and support. Thus, from a professional perspective, while it might be empowering for service users to be able to purchase the personal assistance of their choice, how are the personal assistants whom they employ to be protected or empowered? And what if a service user does not wish to become an 'employer', preferring the safeguards which the prior, arguably more paternalistic, system offered? Who decides what empowerment means in this context, and who is to be empowered?

Lloyd (2010) explored this in her research on older people's experiences of personalization (see also Ferguson, 2007). She points out that personalization is a very individual response to human need, prefaced on the assumption that being 'in control' is 'an unquestionable benefit for service users' (p. 193). But, she argues, an ethic of care perspective 'raises a more complex picture by highlighting differences in needs and priorities between care providers and receivers' (p. 194). Moreover, if care giving and receiving are understood as reciprocal in nature, then ideas about the location of power become rather more diffuse (Tronto, 1993). This highlights the reality that 'no one is an island'. It is through relationships with one another that individual identities are forged. This suggests that, in order to retain the positive qualities and outcomes of empowerment, it must be understood as a social rather than an individual – or personalized – response. While social workers have always claimed to offer personalized services, tailored to the unique needs of their clients, they assumed a ready supply of care, equally available to all. As Lloyd (2010) and others have noted, the contemporary neoliberal environment has altered the playing field, giving rise to 'an ethic of care' and rights discourse to safeguard people's entitlements to adequate and compassionate care (Gray, 2010a; Tronto, 1993; Sevenhuijsen, 1998).

Empowerment as a social response

As with care, a social approach to empowerment builds on the idea that social problems, like poverty, unemployment, illness, crime and delinquency, are not individually but structurally caused and, because of this, cannot be solved by individual effort or personalized care alone. Social – structural or institutional – problems are seen as rooted in social inequalities and social conditions. Sociologist C. Wright Mills first wrote about this in 1959, when he made the connection between 'personal troubles and the public issues of social structure' (p. 8). The Women's Liberation Movement in the late 1960s and 1970s took this idea further, arguing that the 'personal is political'. From this perspective, empowering others became a political and, indeed, politicizing act in which empowerment concerned social transformation, and social workers claimed to engage in transformative or emancipatory practice (see Chapter 2). Nevertheless, self-help remained an ongoing feature of consensus-oriented community development (Craig & Mayo, 1995).

The origins of this political approach to empowerment can be traced to the settlement movement and, more specifically, to the work of Jane Addams in the USA. Addams visited Toynbee Hall – the first university settlement – in the east end of London in 1884 and, on her return to the USA, established Hull House in Chicago. She gave three reasons for doing so:

1. The desire to make the entire social organism democratic, to extend democracy beyond its political expression.

2. The impulse to share the race of life, and to bring as much as possible of social energy and the accumulation of civilisation to these portions of the race which have little.

3. A certain renaissance of Christianity. (in Soydan, 1999, p. 109)

The language here may seem old-fashioned and at odds with empowerment as a radical phenomenon. Yet Addams went on to create Hull House as a living demonstration of her beliefs that the causes of problems lay in society and not with individuals. Three very different kinds of activities took place in Hull House: direct social service; cultural, educational and leisure activities; and social reforms – for example, Addams campaigned against child labour in the clothing industry.

Highly influential in social work was radical Marxist educationalist Paulo Freire (1972), who argued that the people who knew most about oppression and could do something about it were those who were oppressed, not those who were trying to 'help', because help might increase the disempowerment of individuals who took on mainstream ways of seeing the world and came to accept the establishment's lack of confidence in them:

> To surmount the situation of oppression, men [*sic*] must first critically recognize its causes, so that through transforming action they can create a new situation – one that makes possible the pursuit of a fuller humanity ... Although the situation of oppression is a dehumanized and dehumanizing totality affecting both the oppressors and those whom they oppress, it is the latter who must, from their stifled humanity, wage for both the struggle for a fuller humanity; the oppressor, who is himself dehumanized because he dehumanizes others, is unable to lead this struggle. (p. 24)

As a Marxist, the answer for Freire (1972) was 'conscientization' – or the development of a critical consciousness – through a process in which the oppressed were first enlightened to examine their experience – and the contradictions within this – and then, with this new awareness, to change it.

Barbara Bryant Solomon's (1976) *Black Empowerment* has been described as the starting point of empowerment practice in social work (Lee, 1994). Solomon, a black faculty member at the – then – white University of Southern California, explored what she had learnt from teaching on an experimental course, 'Social Work in Black Communities', delivered from a black, inner-city disadvantaged neighbourhood in Los Angeles. She argued that mainstream, universal services and standardized approaches to problem solving in social work reinforced feelings of powerlessness among black and other minority clients because they failed to confront the concept of personal, social, economic and political power, working at the direct – individual – and indirect – community – levels. Most especially, she pointed to the ways in which individuals and groups had unequal access to resources in society, while society itself created power 'blocks' that inhibited people through a process of 'institutionalized discrimination'. Solomon (1976) concluded that empowerment, as process and a goal, offered a way forward for working with those who bore the brunt of discrimination:

> a process whereby the social worker or other helping professional engages in a set of activities with the client aimed at reducing the powerlessness stemming from the experience of discrimination because the client belongs to a stigmatized collective. These activities are specifically aimed at counteracting such negative valuations. (p. 29)

Solomon's (1976) next sentence presented a challenge to social work: 'The success or failure of empowerment is directly related to the degree to which the service delivery system is an obstacle course or an opportunity system' (p. 29). In other words, social work actions – and support systems – could make things worse or better for people. More recently, several writers have argued that it is more challenging today to employ empowerment approaches in neoliberal services (Gray, 2010b, 2011; McDonald, 2006).

In another classic text, Lee (1994) claimed empowerment 'resides in the person, not the helper' and has 'three interlocking dimensions':

> the development of a more positive and potent sense of self; the contribution of knowledge and capacity for more critical comprehension of one's environment; and the cultivation of resources and strategies for achieving personal and collective goals. (p. 13)

'Transformation', Lee (1994) wrote, 'occurs as people are empowered through consciousness raising to see alternatives' (p. 14). This is a very different way of thinking about empowerment practice from that offered by ideas of self-help. More recently, feminist sociologist Hill Collins (2000) took this further by suggesting that becoming empowered 'requires more than changing the consciousness of individual Black women via Black community development strategies. Empowerment also requires transforming unjust social institutions that African-Americans encounter from one generation to the next' (p. 273). This leads, inevitably, to a discussion of power.

What is Power?

The concept of power, like empowerment itself, is highly contested and open to different interpretations. In a classical Marxist sense, power inhered in the wealthy owners of production – the capitalists – who had power over the lives of the proletariat – the workers – through their control over the means of production. Marx believed that the internal contradictions within capitalism would lead inevitably to its self-destruction and replacement by a new system, socialism, and later, communism.

Feminists in the 1970s and 1980s challenged this characterization, pointing out that women had been oppressed by men whatever economic system had been the order of the day. Women's experience was determined primarily, they argued, by discrimination based on gender, not class (see Gray & Boddy, 2010). Analyses since then have become much less polarized, far more complex, and arguably, ambiguous. Challenges to feminism from working-class women, as well as lesbian and black women, have led to the acceptance of the paradigm of 'intersecting oppressions of race, class, gender, sexuality and nation, as well as individual and collective agency' (Hill Collins, 2000, p. 273).

At the same time, postmodern ideas, particularly emanating from the work of French philosopher Michel Foucault, have introduced a new understanding of the creative capacities of power. In *Discipline and Punish*, Foucault (1977) explored a shift in industrialized societies from a regulation of the population through physical punishment of the body – torture, beating, whipping, and the ultimate sanction, capital punishment – to a society in which regulation was achieved through surveillance and supervision. Foucault (1977) argued that power was not a negative construct existing only to forbid or repress. It was omnipresent, diffused throughout society, and both regulatory and productive. In an interview towards the end of his life, Foucault (in Kritzman, 1990) suggested there was little point in studying power in its own right. Instead, it was better to study 'strategies of power': 'the strategies, the networks, the mechanisms, all those techniques by which a decision is accepted and by which that decision could not but be taken in the way it was' (p. 104).

From this perspective, empowerment might be seen as another 'strategy of power' whereby people control and are controlled through empowerment, as well as the very many other discourses which compete for primacy in social work theory and practice. If this were so, then the onus would be on social workers to practise empowerment in a self-conscious way, building from the realization that, like other forms of knowledge, it has the capacity to be used for good or ill, to justify practices which sustain people's oppression or encourage their emancipation. Here lies the challenge for those who have entered a career in the 'helping' professions – how to encourage others to empower themselves – as individuals, groups and communities – in such a way that they or we do not become part of the problem.

Practices of Empowerment

A host of social work textbooks offer advice on 'how to practise' in an empowering way. In one such example, Dalrymple and Burke (1995) assert that the first stage of empowerment involves 'making the links between our personal position and structural inequalities' (p. 51). For them, this was the core of the empowerment process, just as consciousness-raising was the starting point for Freire and the Women's Liberation Movement in the 1970s. Following on from this, they suggested that empowerment sought to replace powerlessness with 'some sense of power'. If empowerment practice were to be effective, they argued, it would be 'essential to understand the process which leads from feeling powerless to powerful' (p. 52). They described empowerment as a three-stage process, involving a linear progression from 'the [personal] level of feelings' – personal biography – to 'the [cognitive] level of ideas' – developing a sense of control, initiative and ability to act, through new insights and a new language to explain experience – and, finally, reaching 'the level of [political] action'. In this way, the personal became political, and individuals or groups would be motivated to take action to change their situations. Later Thompson (2006) followed this approach, suggesting that empowerment had to take place at the personal, cultural and institutional levels. But the question is, how? Disability campaigners, such as Mike Oliver (1995), have argued that empowerment is not a gift of the powerful, whoever they might be. It is something people can only do for themselves collectively. As Solomon (1976) noted, the inevitable question remains: what can social workers really do to contribute to others' empowerment?

Writing as service users, and hence as people who might be portrayed as members of a less powerful group, Wilson and Beresford (2000) have pointed out that anti-oppressive theory and practice, despite having emancipatory aspirations, have 'regressive potential' because service users and their organizations were not involved sufficiently in their development, which involved 'expert' appropriation of service-users' knowledges and experiences, and had 'failed to address the use of social work and social care services as an area of difference and category of social division' (p. 553). The same might be said about the theory and practice of empowerment. While championed by members of oppressed groups, empowerment has been appropriated by others and become part of the definition of professional social work (IFSW, 2000) and is no longer a threat to the status quo.

Empowerment coheres with long-held individualistic social values like 'self-determination'. It has become strongly implicated in individualistic rights and strengths-based approaches which stress individual, not collective, solutions to personal and social problems (see Bell, 2011; Foster, 2011; Gray, 2011), and with consumerist approaches which see poverty as the fault of the 'flawed customer' (Bauman, 2004). Empowerment ideas have even been absorbed into management practices which stress the importance of 'self-efficacy' and 'personal competence' (see Chapter 6). For example, Conger and Kanungo (1988) argued against empowerment being allowed to go too far, since it might lead to 'overconfidence and misjudgments on the part of subordinates' (p. 480). It has been co-opted in policy discourse as well, though the practices built around this rhetoric are anything but empowering. They are a reminder that empowerment is not necessarily a positive experience for the 'empowered' or for others. In a wide-ranging review of empowerment, Weissberg (1999) claimed that securing power for an oppressed, poverty-stricken or excluded population might achieve little that was positive, but much that was negative.

New Practices of Empowerment

So where does this leave us? How can we think, talk and carry out new practices of empowerment for a new politics of social work? To answer these questions, we must first challenge the binary opposition at the heart of the idea of empowerment: that there is a powerful 'us' (who hold power) and 'them' (who are powerless victims). At the same time, we must challenge the notion that we inevitably have the means and authority to give power to others. In reality, many social workers, particularly in the developed world, are employed by the State in gatekeeping or surveillance roles and, to a lesser degree, by voluntary organizations in the non-governmental sector, where they are often contracted to offer remedial and individualized – case-management – services. They have little power to manage their own working lives, let alone to give power to others. And yet, daily acts of resistance are apparent in their willingness to step outside the normal rules of engagement with service users to challenge discriminatory policies or punitive practice (see Chapter 12). They also demonstrate a capacity to care for others, and this may mean being prepared to do things for service users, such as making a phone call or accompanying someone on a visit, rather than showing them how to do this themselves (a typical example of a so-called empowering approach).

Those who use services also exert power, sometimes over their social workers as well as the bureaucratic and, at times, authoritarian State. They may refuse to open the door when the social worker visits; not tell the truth when asked about their offending behaviour; deliberately mislead, prevaricate or even use their own power to frighten or silence a social worker. They may also, however, demonstrate care for their social worker, by asking about their lives, or simply making them a cup of tea. As Foucault (1977) has noted, power is not something we *possess* but something we *exercise* in relationships. We cannot, therefore, give it to someone. We can only make it possible for it to be explored by encouraging others to examine their own capacity for power in the lives – their individual, cultural and social power. This introduces a new possibility for social workers to play a part in supporting resistance and encouraging alternative – subjugated – discourses (see Pease, 2002 and Chapter 8). By 'taking a stance', by foregrounding social rather than individual explanations and solutions, and being willing to entertain alternative views, social workers might begin to identify new empowering practices. Critical social work has this potential, since it emphasizes the structural nature of oppression, and the need for strategies that bring people together as active agents of their own lives.

Conclusion

This chapter has argued that empowerment, as understood and practised in social work, owes little to the emancipatory aspirations of the collective imagination. Much that passes as 'empowering practice' is little more than individualistic, consumerist and conservative in scope. A truly empowering practice would be much more unsettling and radical. It would also more likely come from forces outside social work – from service-user and advocacy groups, community activists and social movements – rather than from local-government bureaucrats or social work academics. There are, nevertheless, glimpses of what might be possible, for example, through the Social Work Action Network (SWAN) in the UK, where practitioners, service users, academics and students collectively campaign for 'a profession worth fighting for' (see Chapter 12). At the same time, the idea of empowerment encourages social workers to rethink the larger questions they confront in light of theories of power and powerlessness, dependence and independence, and care and welfare. Bauman (2000, 2001) has argued that society has a duty to take care and responsibility for its citizens. To gain independence, individuals must first experience dependence. Similarly, if social workers are to embrace truly the emancipatory potential of empowerment theory and practice, they must first be willing to accept their own power – and powerlessness – as well as that of the people they are seeking to empower. Only then will they begin to understand the nature of the human – and social – condition and its political ramifications.

References

Adams, R. (2008). *Empowerment, participation and social work* (4th edn). Basingstoke: Palgrave Macmillan.

Bauman, Z. (2000). *Liquid modernity*. Cambridge: Polity Press.

Bauman, Z. (2001). *The individualized society*. Cambridge: Polity Press.

Bauman, Z. (2004). *Work, consumerism and the new poor* (2nd edn). Buckingham: Open University Press.

Bauman, Z. (2007). *Liquid times: Living in an age of uncertainty*. Cambridge: Polity Press.

Beck, U. (1999). *World risk society*. Cambridge: Polity Press.

Bell, M. (2011). *Promoting children's rights in social work and social care: A guide to participatory practice*. London: Jessica Kingsley.

Cameron, D. (2010). *Building the Big Society*. Retrieved 4 May 2013 from http://www.cabinetoffice.gov.uk/media/407789/building-big-society.pdf.

Conger, J.A., & Kanungo, R.N. (1988). The empowerment process: Integrating theory and practice. *Academy of Management Review, 13*(3), 471–482.

Craig, G., & Mayo, M. (1995). *Community empowerment: A reader in participation and development*. London: Zed Books.

Cree, V.E., & Myers, S. (2008). *Social work: Making a difference*. Bristol: Policy Press/BASW.

Cruikshank, B. (1993). Revolutions within: self-government and self esteem. *Economy and Society, 22*(3), 327–344.

Cruikshank, B. (1999). *The will to empower: Democratic citizens and other subjects*. Ithaca, NY: Cornell University Press.

Dalrymple, J., & Burke, B. (1995). *Anti-oppressive practice: Social care and the law*. Buckingham: Open University Press.

Ferguson, I. (2007). Increasing user choice or privatizing risk? The antinomies of personalization. *British Journal of Social Work, 37*(3), 387–403.

Ferguson, I., & Woodward, R. (2009). *Radical social work in practice: Making a difference*. Bristol: Policy Press.

Foster, S. (2011). *Human rights and civil liberties* (3rd edn). London: Longman.

Fraser, D. (2009). *The evolution of the British welfare state: A history of social policy since the industrial revolution*. Basingstoke: Palgrave Macmillan.

Foucault, M. (1977). *Discipline and punish: The birth of the prison*. New York: Pantheon Books.

Freire, P. (1972). *Pedagogy of the oppressed*. London: Penguin.

Gray, M. (2010a). Moral sources: Emerging ethical theories in social work. *British Journal of Social Work*, *40*(6), 1794–1811.

Gray, M. (2010b). Social development and the status quo: Professionalisation and Third Way cooptation. *International Journal of Social Welfare*, *19*(4), 463–470.

Gray, M. (2011). Back to basics: A critique of the strengths perspective in social work. *Families in Society: Journal of Contemporary Social Services*, *92*(1), 5–11.

Gray, M., & Boddy, J. (2010). Making sense of the waves: Wipeout or still riding high? *Affilia: Journal of Women and Social Work*, *25*(4), 368–389.

Hill Collins, P. (2000). *Black feminist thought: Knowledge, consciousness and the politics of empowerment* (2nd edn). London: Routledge.

Hugman, R. (2010). *Understanding international social work: A critical analysis*. Basingstoke: Palgrave Macmillan.

International Federation of Social Workers (IFSW). (2000). *Definition of social work*. Retrieved 24 October 2011 from http://www.ifsw.org/f38000138.html.

Jordan, B. (2011) Making sense of the 'Big Society': Social work and the moral order. *Journal of Social Work*, published online 6 May 2011. doi: 10.1177/1468017310394241.

Kritzman, L.D. (1990). *Michel Foucault: Politics, philosophy, culture. Interviews and other writings 1977–1984*. London: Routledge.

Lee, J.A.B. (1994). *The empowerment approach to social work practice*. New York: Columbia University Press.

Lloyd, L. (2010). The individual in social care: The ethics of care and the 'personalisation agenda' in services for older people in England. *Ethics and Social Welfare*, *4*(2), 188– 200.

McDonald, C. (2006). *Challenging social work: The context of practice*. Basingstoke: Palgrave Macmillan.

Oliver, M. (1995). *Understanding disability: From theory to practice*. Basingstoke: Palgrave Macmillan.

Panati, C. (1999). *Words to live by: The origins of conventional wisdom and commonsense advice*. Penguin: New York.

Pease, B. (2002). Rethinking empowerment: A postmodern reappraisal for emancipatory practice. *British Journal of Social Work*, *32*, 135–147.

Saleebey, D. (2006). *The strengths perspective in social work practice* (4th edn). Boston, MA: Pearson Education.

Sevenhuijsen, S. (1998). *Citizenship and the ethics of care*. London: Routledge.

Solomon, B.B. (1976). *Black empowerment: Social work in oppressed communities*. New York: Columbia University Press.

Soydan, H. (1999). *The history of ideas in social work*. Birmingham: Venture Press.

Thompson, N. (2006). *Anti-discriminatory practice* (4th edn). Basingstoke: Palgrave Macmillan.

Tronto, J. (1993). *Moral boundaries: A political argument for an ethic of care*. London: Routledge.

UK Department of Health. (2008). *Transforming Social Care*. Local Authority Circular DH (2008)1. London: Department of Health.

Weissberg, R. (1999). *The politics of empowerment*. Westport, CT: Praeger.

Wilson, A., & Beresford, P. (2000). 'Anti-oppressive practice': Emancipation or appropriation? *British Journal of Social Work*, *30*(5), 553–573.

Wright Mills, C. (1959). *The sociological imagination*. Oxford: Oxford University Press.

10

Rights-based International Social Work Practice

Richard Hugman

Human rights and social justice are claimed as major principles providing the foundation for social work, as stated by the International Federation of Social Workers (IFSW) and the International Association of Schools of Social Work (IASSW) (IFSW/IASSW, 2004). These principles bind together the twin objectives of 'problem solving in human relationships and the empowerment and liberation of people to promote human well-being' (IFSW/IASSW, 2004). That is, the principle of human rights, along with that of social justice, underpins both micro- and macro-level practices.

This chapter focuses specifically on rights-based international social work practice. In doing so, it draws on this definition as the basis for two important points. First, social work must be conceived broadly. Not only is it either micro-level, individually oriented and confined to small-scale personal change, nor is it only about macro-level, social structural change. It is about both of these things, sometimes separately and sometimes together. In short, social work is about the personal *and* the political. As this chapter proceeds to argue, it is very often about the relationship between the two – the personal as the political and the political as the personal. It is in this context that human rights can be seen clearly as vital to all forms of social work practice.

International social work here means any form of social work that involves two or more countries (Healy, 2008). It can take the form of practitioners working in 'other' countries, such as in humanitarian work; helping people who have come from 'another' country – working with refugees or migrants; working with international organizations, whether or not the practitioner travels; exchange or partnership between social workers in two or more countries; and working with issues that originate in another country or are impacted by inter-country relations (Dominelli, 2007; Healy, 2008;

Hugman, 2010; Lyons, Manion, & Carlsen, 2006). Human rights are a central issue in all such practice, whether or not it is immediately obvious on the surface.

To examine human rights as the basis of international social work, this chapter first examines the concept itself. This idea has a long history and has been understood in particular ways within social work. Then, secondly, some recent examples of rights-based practice are considered to show ways in which the principle of human rights might inform practice in many contexts. Yet at the same time they pose several questions for thinking about the politics of social work at both the micro- and macro-levels. So, thirdly, the chapter proceeds to draw out some implications for ways of approaching the politics of social work through a human rights base.

Human Rights as a Principle

As an idea, human rights have their origins in the European Enlightenment period, growing out of struggles against the authoritarian rule of absolute monarchs. Modern approaches to human rights owe their foundations to the theories of philosophers like Thomas Hobbes (1588–1679) and John Locke (1632–1704), who shared the view that human beings are naturally free and equal in a moral and political sense, and must find ways to agree on how to live together in ordered societies. From this is derived the concept of government as the expression of the collective will of the people comprising a society. Subsequently, out of these ideas, come the modern debates of political theory, as to whether society is best understood as a form of contract, or as shared values, or some other model for understanding the processes by which people achieve stable societies.

As Hinman (2008) notes, human rights has had a greater impact on the world in the twentieth century than any other principle or ideal. He suggests that not only relationships between people but also between humanity and the natural environment are often infused with the language of rights. Most significantly, it is embodied in the *Universal Declaration of Human Rights*, approved by the United Nations in 1948, which has come to define a standard of international relations and guide judgements about the actions of nations and individuals (UN, 1948). The application of human rights thinking to a wide range of different groups of people have been developed out of the *Universal Declaration*, including the rights of women, children, people with disabilities and indigenous peoples. However, at the same time the idea of rights and some of the details in the specific UN documents are fiercely contested, with many countries attaching 'reservations' to particular aspects (Gasper, 2006) – indeed, despite itself having the earliest national Bill of Rights, the USA has never ratified the *Universal Declaration*.

Wronka (1998) applies the concept of 'generations' to thinking about human rights in social work and links these to the goals of the French Revolution: liberty, equality and solidarity. First came civil and political rights, which in Europe and North America emerged slowly over centuries as increasingly larger sections of populations gained the standing of citizens with a legally recognized status to make decisions about government, own property, make contracts, and so on. However, such rights were not enjoyed universally in these countries until the twentieth century, when women gained the same rights as men, or, in some countries, when people of all ethnicities also finally gained these rights.

The second generation of rights are economic, social and cultural rights. These are often associated with the claims that citizens make on their societies to goods such as health, education, employment, housing, and so on, or, in broad terms, 'social services'. The major difference between the first and second 'generations' of rights is that whereas the first are based largely on freedom from constraint and certain well-defined legal freedoms (to vote and enter into contracts), the second depend on states making positive provisions for their citizens. Thus they are more deeply contested, as they rest on ideas not only about what it is to be human (such as 'to be free'), but also about what a decent human life might look like. In so far as they seek 'equality', this too remains widely disputed as a goal.

The third generation, which Wronka (1998) calls 'solidarity rights', are less well defined and still emerging. A clear example would be claims to the environment, such as a right to clean water and air. The relationship between nations might also be recognizable as such a right, in that the international order affects the capacity of people to enjoy other rights. These rights are even more contested, as they are based on ideas about common humanity that transcend nations, ethnicities and other ways of dividing humanity ethically and politically.

A particularly influential development of this model of human rights is that proposed by Ife (2008). In particular, he notes the extent to which all three generations of rights depend on the capacity of people to make claims on a 'duty bearer'. That is, all statements of rights are, in effect, claims on how each person should be treated by others. These may be 'negative' in that the duty of others is not to get in the way of the exercise of a right, but in many situations they will be 'positive' in that a rights claim is actually a claim on others to do something. Ife (2008) argues, correctly, that social work practice is usually more directly concerned with the second- and third-generation rights. However, where first-generation rights are denied, this may cause social work quite reasonably to join with law, politics and other professions, as well as with communities themselves, to work towards the achievement of these rights.

Ife (2008) goes further, and regards the third-generation rights as including rights to the expression of culture. He has in mind here the right of cultural 'minorities', such as Aboriginal people in Australia and other settler societies, to live according to their own traditions – both lore and law (Ife, 2008). This leads him to question the notion of 'common humanity' and to argue for a view of rights that stems primarily from the varying nature of humanity in each different culture (Ife, 2009, 2010).

While the valuing of cultures is important, this last aspect of Ife's argument seems to go too far. Social workers like Lundy (2006), Reichert (2003) and Staub-Bernasconi (2007) all base their understanding of human rights on a universal view of humanity – what all people have in common and share *as human beings* establishes claims to these facets of life as rights. The underlying logic is that without these things no person can live a basically decent human life and so to deprive people of these things – whether deliberately or by default – is to deny them their humanity. The common aspects of what it is to be human are identified by Doyal and Gough (1991) as health and freedom. Similarly, Sen (1983) and Nussbaum (2000) have argued for the concept of 'human capabilities', which for Nussbaum include bodily health and integrity, relationships, emotion, senses and thought and practical reason. However, if human needs are regarded solely in terms of cultural difference, then claims to them as rights have insecure foundations, disconnected from their basis in a core of 'what it is to be human' and partial to any given perspective. While this may appear to deal with the difficult question of the important differences between cultures (for example, in terms of what a family might look like or how community obligations are understood), at the same time it opens the door for the subordination of cultures because it removes the capacity to make cross-cultural moral and political judgements.

Lundy (2006) and Staub-Bernasconi (2007) clearly make the point that, insofar as social work focuses on human needs, and the detail of these needs may differ between people, including on cultural grounds, unless these needs are understood as *rights*, they remain captive to hostile political perspectives. Social programmes and services require legitimation, whether from the State or from communities. Hence unless they are grounded in an agreement that these things represent what is necessary for all people to live a decent human life, then they can easily be cancelled. As Lundy (2006) puts it, the view of addressing poverty that people have a right to the basic requirements of life, such as food, clothing and shelter, is very different to suggesting that these things are needs which may or may not have to be provided. Indeed, since the 1980s, many governments have increasingly defined such things as needs, a perspective that has been promoted by the International Monetary Fund and the World Bank. This position forms the basis for denying the unjust structural conditions that underpin poverty, and makes individual moral responsibility the basis for social policies. Against this, for Staub-Bernasconi (2007), Lundy (2006), Sen (1983) and Nussbaum (2000), it is only by grounding rights claims in a view of the human condition as common to all human beings that such claims have any greater force than statements of sectional interests.

For Webb (2009), this is the crux of the argument. He critiques the notion of 'difference' as the basis for human rights precisely because it obscures the single starting point on which assertions of equality might firmly rest, namely, that rights attach to all people equally because all are human. Following from this, Webb (2009) is concerned that the postmodern focus on 'difference' lets neoliberalism in by the back door. The expression of rights within this framework, he argues, is not an expression of solidarity but an 'aggregated free expression' of personal preference that follows a market model.

In saying this, Webb (2009) is in agreement with the arguments already described. But, curiously, he then goes on to lump together Ife's (2008) and Reichert's (2003) arguments, and criticize international social work organizations for promoting a vision of human rights that is 'as hollow as it is absolutist' (p. 312). This seems mistaken. First, Ife (2008) and Reichert (2003) are not proposing the same view of human rights. Indeed, Ife's (2008) critique of a 'common humanity' could be read as a rebuttal of Reichert's (2003) position. Conversely, the assertion that human rights must be based on more than statements of preference, in other words to be grounded in a sense of the commonalities of humanity, stands against Ife's (2008) arguments.

However, just as Ife's (2008) conclusion seems to go too far, so does Webb's (2009). We can agree that any understanding of exactly what should be regarded as a right will always be incomplete (Nussbaum, 2000, also makes this very point), but this does not prevent us from seeking to use such claims effectively in assisting people to achieve a better life (compare Hugman, 2008). Ultimately, Webb (2009) appears to be linking the principle of rights too tightly with relativist arguments for difference, so wanting to reject all arguments for rights on the basis of a position against the predominant view of rights in social work. As a result, Webb (2009) appears not to notice that there are various positions on human rights in social work, so, in throwing out the relativist 'bathwater' of 'difference', he also disposes of the 'baby' of common humanity.

Although they are approaching human rights from very different standpoints, Ife (2008) and Webb (2009) both appear to conflate 'universalism' and 'absolutism' (compare Renteln, 1990). It is more helpful to see these as distinct positions. In this sense, it is possible to understand a universal view of rights as that which seeks sufficient commonality in what it is to be human, while allowing that values are modified and changed over time and subjected to debate such that the same core values might be interpreted differently in different contexts. Approaching the principle of rights in this way allows for the firm foundation of common humanity while at the same time recognizing that this is always subject to historical, cultural and other contingent interpretations and applications.

Human Rights in International Social Work Practice

Having reviewed the principle of human rights, it is helpful to look at how it is used in social work practice internationally by considering three examples of the work of social workers in several parts of the world. All in different ways embody a concern with human rights as already discussed. The final section then considers the implications of these illustrations for thinking more generally about human rights in international social work practice.

Community versus economic development

Kuruvilla (2005) presents an analysis of an economic development initiative in the Indian state of Kerala that ultimately had a serious negative impact on local communities. The original government-sponsored project was based on a three-way agreement – between India, Norway and the UN in the 1950s – to develop the fishing industry and local fishing communities. In the 1970s, India assumed responsibility for the programme, which became known as the 'Integrated Fisheries Project' and resulted in two decades of intervention by numerous professionals and volunteers (Kuruvilla, 2005, p. 47). As Kuruvilla (2005) notes, its focus was the provision of technical aid whereby communities were 'shocked into immobility' (p. 47). Overall, the outcomes were highly detrimental to the fishing communities, resulting in environmental degradation; the introduction of technologies unsuited to the region; licensing of foreign fishing companies (that excluded local fishers); and economic gains accruing to external interests, thus damaging local fishing markets to the extent that people who had previously met their own nutritional needs could no longer afford to buy fish (Kuruvilla, 2005).

In response, social workers in local and national non-governmental organizations (NGOs) began to assist local fishing communities, often with international support and assistance. In contrast to the government-sponsored programme, these interventions focused on helping communities to develop internal strategies to counter external forces. But the 'integration of marginalized people' (Kuruvilla, 2005, p. 50) was pursued at the expense of attention to wider issues like the valuing of traditional knowledge and local cultures. For Kuruvilla (2005), the particularistic concerns of international donors thwarted community-focused social development approaches and undermined their human rights focus. Hence she argued for an approach in which human rights were central to the development of local agency and social workers 'partnered' local communities.

Post-war social reconstruction

Dada Maglajlić (2010), a social worker from Croatia, reflected on post-war reconstruction work undertaken by local and international organizations in Croatia and (what was then) Bosnia-Herzegovina. She described a partly successful programme – 'Suncokret' – run by UNICEF to provide a brief intervention with children affected by the war through which social workers and others assisted displaced people living in camps, organizing access to services, including health and social welfare, and establishing programmes such as one for unaccompanied children. Later, local workers were joined by volunteers from other countries. Although led by local professionals, the programme was run in partnership with those living in the camps.

Subsequently, Maglajlić (2010) worked for a number of years in community mental health in Bosnia-Herzegovina (as it was at that time), where projects again involved a combination of local professionals and international organizations from Italy, Sweden, the USA and the UK, and were influenced by radical approaches to psychiatry that emphasized deinstitutionalization and supported the active participation of mental health system survivors in designing and running services. However, the stability of these developments was fragile as they depended on international donor funding and, after several years, the donors' attention shifted to other countries (Afghanistan and Iraq) and the promotion of institutional childcare provision (orphanages).

Maglajlić (2010) noted the dominance – and variable impact – of international agencies and donors in these projects: where they employed rights-based practice and focused on enabling and supporting local people to formulate and direct programmes, outcomes were positive in terms of strengthening communities to find solutions to their own needs. However, when they imposed external agendas, obstructed possibilities for the development of grassroots leadership, and used 'cut-and-paste' (Maglajlić, 2010, p. 112) approaches – bringing in strategies and practices developed in other contexts, without tailoring them to the new situation – they were less successful. From this we can conclude that outcomes are clearly better when local community participation – understood as a right – is integral to practice.

Human rights overboard

In 2001, a Norwegian container-freight ship the *MV Tampa*, on its way to Australia, picked up 438 people, including 46 children, from a sinking boat in the Timor Sea (Gentry, 2007). It was then denied entry to Australian territorial waters and, when the captain decided to proceed because of the developing humanitarian crisis in the conditions for the people on board, while it was still in international waters the ship was intercepted by Australian troops and the asylum seekers were taken to the island state of Nauru.

This event changed the political tone in Australia concerning refugees and asylum seekers. While it is widely regarded as having given the then governing party a boost in the national elections held shortly afterwards, it also focused opposition to policies of mandatory detention of asylum seekers arriving in Australia 'without authorization'. The diverse range of organizations that has since come to oppose and campaign against these policies includes community groups, religious groups, trade unions and the professions. Social workers in Australia have often been actively involved in the promotion of asylum seekers' rights to asylum under the Refugee Convention (UN, 1951/1967) through representations to government and politicians and demonstrations in cities and at detention centres.

One particular action by social workers was a 'people's inquiry' into mandatory detention after the Australian government ignored calls from all sections of society for an official inquiry. So, in 2005, following the wrongful lengthy detention of an Australian citizen with mental health needs, the Australian Council of Heads of Schools of Social Work agreed to sponsor an independent inquiry. Sessions were held in each Australian state, at which interested people could present evidence about the reality of life for refugees and asylum seekers, especially their experiences of mandatory detention, and of the alternative steps that community members were taking to counter the damaging impact of the policy on those who were incarcerated.

Briskman, Latham and Goddard's (2008) comprehensive report provided graphic detail of the unjust treatment of asylum seekers within the detention system created. The report has played an important role in informing action and debate by many opposed to Australian policy. In 2008, in the early days of a new centre-left Rudd government, some of the recommendations of the report were considered as the basis for possible policy changes, such as avoiding the detention of children. However, this change stalled as the government struggled to hold office.

Human Rights in Practice

Each of these examples concerns international social work. Social workers, their agencies and policies cross borders, as do the problems and issues with which they are concerned. In all of this, the profession carries with it a claim to the principle of human rights but often encounters difficulties in making it a reality in practice.

First, social workers need to consider the charge that human rights claims are culturally loaded and represent yet another incursion of Western values into other parts of the world. Against this charge, it is important to consider that the idea of human rights does not describe 'things', nor should it involve detailed descriptions of particular ways of living. Rather, human rights language enables us to examine areas of agreement on what 'promoting a decent human life' entails, which, in turn, would provide a basis for challenging oppression, rights violations and disadvantage. In this regard, Nussbaum's (2000) conceptions of 'human capabilities' can help social workers consider what this might look like: having bodily integrity and being able to form valued relationships, pursue life goals (including being able to secure a sustainable livelihood) and exercise one's own judgement (practical reason) are widely recognized as important in deciding what might constitute a 'decent human life'. That Nussbaum (2000) developed this list from her work with local women's groups in India points to the cross-cultural plausibility of her claim to their 'universal' recognition. This is where Renteln's (1990) distinction between 'universal' and 'absolute' becomes important. It can be agreed between cultures that these things are valuable (the universal view), without them having to look exactly the same across different contexts (the absolute view). This view of universal but not absolute values can be seen in the three examples above.

Secondly, these examples show that, if the principle of human rights were approached in this way, international social work practice would give explicit attention to facilitating and promoting the agency of communities and individuals. This cannot be done without making participative, community-based practices the central focus. Both Kuruvilla (2005) and Maglajliĉ (2010) described weaknesses not only in the types of practice and policy that informed international interventions but also in the definition of the underlying problems based on external understanding and knowledge. While better than the exclusively economic focus used previously in Kerala and certainly better than the surrounding conflict in the Balkans, both programmes in question still failed to achieve ongoing social development in several key respects.

Hence a major question, especially in less economically developed parts of the world, is the international donors' dominance in funding such work. Whether UN agencies and entities or independent international non-governmental organizations (INGOs), all have particular interests and mandates dictated by the political or public interests in the countries from which they obtain their resources. This can compromise rights-based practice by distorting goals: focusing on 'integration' rather than other aspects of the situation in Kuruvilla's (2005) account and shifting attention to other 'hot spots' and leaving behind highly institutionalized social services in Maglajlić's (2010) account. These policy imperatives also restrict social work agendas in international social development programmes. In these circumstances, it is not human rights but human needs that are being addressed – needs as perceived by people external to the particular situation rather than as defined from within.

Thirdly, all three examples demonstrate that rights-based social work can, at times, conflict with governments and others holding authority within communities, even in representative democracies, such as Australia and India. Further, in most Western countries, including Australia, neoliberalism has come to dominate economic policy and this has been accompanied by a more restrictive view of the roles of professions, especially those funded by the State. Hence the authority of professions to speak about policies has been challenged to the extent that taking a stand on human rights issues is seen as 'beyond the competence' of professions. In Australia, opposition to the policy of mandatory detention of unauthorized asylum seekers from psychiatrists, nurses, teachers and others, who are in direct contact with detainees, has been attacked by various governments on these grounds as much as has the stance of social workers.

The response to this, in many instances, is for collective voices to be developed, in which members of various professions, and community members join together to find ways to continue to assert human rights claims. Maglajlić (2010) described how local and international professionals in Croatia worked together in an NGO under the direction of local leadership. In Australia, Briskman et al. (2008) noted the actions of particular social workers to organize the 'people's inquiry' were supported by the wider profession and drew in members of other professions and wider society.

Social workers can engage with change from inside their organizations, contributing to policy and planning processes. Kuruvilla (2005) showed that practices could be presented in a way that fit donors' agendas while still allowing scope to address what was actually needed in the local context. She also suggested that international social work dialogue could assist by acknowledging this problem more explicitly as a basis for acting to seek changes in the way in which such policies were established in the first place. Maglajlić (2010) claimed social workers played key roles in many INGOs and were ideally placed to do this. Where this was not possible, they could seek opportunities in other places.

The Contribution of Human Rights to a New Politics of Social Work

So far this discussion has focused primarily on practice in social development, policy and advocacy. However, the challenges for social work presented by the principle of human rights impacts on all practices. Rights-based social work, as with other forms of critical social work, is partisan: it means taking a stance. Even in institutional service provision characteristic of social work practice in Western countries, there remains the need to recognize and respond to human rights implications. Childcare, child protection, human trafficking, mental health services (acute and long-term), people with disabilities, family and domestic violence, services for older people, HIV and AIDS, drug and alcohol abuse, community and social development – in other words, in all areas of social work, the way in which social workers practise should be explored for human rights implications. Even where social workers exercise statutory authority, perhaps especially in such circumstances, both as individuals and professionals, we need to continue to seek to develop reflexive practice that enables us to consider and support human rights. For example, in these circumstances, do we make sure that least restrictive alternatives are used; do we argue for them when they are not available; do we take the time to check that people know what is happening, why, and what their rights are; do we take responsibility to persist with difficult situations; and do service users have a substantive say in the way that decisions are made about their lives? While not always recognized as human rights issues, these aspects of practice are core to the micro-politics of social work.

Service users feature strongly in rights-based social work: morally and politically it asserts that 'what it is to be human' is based on an understanding of agency – so 'being human' requires that, to the greatest extent possible, a person should have an active role in making choices and setting plans about her or his life. Practices that turn people into passive recipients of the actions of others, including social workers as well as governments and multinational companies, breach human rights because they deny aspects of humanity. In ethics such practices are called treating a person as a 'moral patient', whether this is a fishing community, children who have been internally displaced by civil war, or a refugee family. It is now widely questioned in social work ethics discussions (compare with Webb, 2010, pp. 113–14). (The same argument is also applied in social work practice in Western contexts, such as with disabled people – see Postle & Beresford, 2007.)

It is important to understand that this view of agency and the rights of service users does not remove the responsibility of social workers to inform, advise and guide service users in forming plans and making choices. Rather, it emphasizes the way in which this becomes focused on helping service users to achieve their rights through effective access to services and policies. Nor does it conflate the notion of rights with consumerism. To take Maglajlić's (2010) example, she is not proposing a simplistic form of attention to children's 'preferences', but rather that the whole community should be part of developing appropriate responses, in the structures and practices of services provided to children displaced by civil war. This way of working not only assumes attention to needs, drawing on the idea that people benefit more when they are involved in this way – although it does incorporate that notion to good effect – but also, more importantly, that people ought to be involved in this way because otherwise they continue to be oppressed. In this sense, the outcomes sought by social work are moral and political, as well as social and psychological.

The question these examples pose for social workers and members of other 'caring professions' is whether practices and policies should, therefore, be based on a universal understanding of universal rights, or whether claims to 'difference' should lead to distinct services. The Kerala fishing communities had particular cultural issues, as did children in the Balkans or asylum seekers arriving in Australia. Should there be distinct responses according to the service users' cultural background and the issues they face? Or should the same responses be offered, even if this is in a way that ensures that the cultural backgrounds of all people are recognized equally? Within such questions, there is then the issue of how to ensure that those who wish to access these interventions are able to do so, while those who do not are not denied human dignity as a consequence.

Considering these issues as the 'micro-politics of practice' points to the problem of 'recognition' debated by Honneth (Fraser & Honneth, 2003) (see Chapter 2). According to Honneth, disadvantage and discrimination stem from a failure to accord 'recognition' to the subjective humanity of each person (see Chapter 4). Applied to social work and welfare systems, this notion suggests that not providing appropriate responses for a diverse range of service users comes from inadequacies in the way in which the moral and political identity of each person is grasped. From this perspective, without recognition people are not accorded their full humanity because their subjectivity is ignored. Such a view can sit comfortably with social work, insofar as its underlying ethos has long been to personalize social issues and problems (Timms, 1983). We respond to this person, in these circumstances. Yet, in contrast, Fraser (Fraser & Honneth, 2003) argues that claims of recognition can only be understood as a form of injustice that constitutes a denial of the right to live a fully human life. Thus, from this view, the problem with the way in which members of fishing communities, children displaced by civil war, or asylum seekers are offered assistance is not whether their subjective identity is damaged by discrimination, but whether they are unjustly denied the common status of humanity. This is a universal argument about shared values of justice not a particularistic argument about diverse identity.

It is not that different identities do not matter. Fraser provides the example of an African American Wall Street banker who cannot get a taxi because of racial discrimination (Fraser & Honneth, 2003, p. 34). Compared to white American bankers successfully getting taxis, this is an issue of 'recognition'; yet, compared to many African Americans, to be a banker provides the means to overcome many structural inequalities. However, the claims concerning discrimination, oppression and exclusion voiced by service users, whether in the form of communities, families and social groups or individuals, tend overwhelmingly to be arguments against structural injustices and inequalities. They are issues of the social systemic distribution of resources, both material and relational, that institutionalize disadvantage. Issues of recognition are overlaid and intertwined. This relationship is complex and often fluid. Issues of (re)distribution and recognition are both important, with the balance shifting between instances and over time. Yet the shared reality for service users is more often that of (re)distribution. Problems of recognition can divide as well as unite the disadvantaged or oppressed.

As Young (1990) puts it, the central problem is oppression. Injustice prevents people from living human lives; understood in this sense, the problem of partiality – of 'taking sides' – is reframed. While the underlying rights claim is based on shared humanity, the experience of oppression is contextualized, so that it is not only possible but actually necessary for social workers to attend to the particular situations of service users. So these can be seen both in terms of the common challenges faced by people with disabilities, older people, children, people with mental health problems, and so on, and at the same time in terms of structural disadvantage arising from ethnicity and culture, sex, social class, age, (dis)ability or sexuality. While focusing on the rights of local Kerala fishing communities in a developing country exploited by international business, we must also understand broader relations between Asian, European and North American cultures. Likewise the rights of asylum seekers arriving in Australia might be seen in light of objective rights established by international law, the ethnic identities of those involved, and their particular needs and interests. Responding to the particularities of an individual's context can appropriately be grounded in the notion of universal human rights. In this way, a micro-politics of social work attends to this service user, in this community, and draws on the commonality of claims to what is necessary for a decent human life. In other words, social work practice enjoins human rights and social justice as the two ethical pillars of social work (see above). Too often, however, this connection is not spelled out and this lack of integration leads to attempts to prioritise one value over the other (compare with Solas, 2008).

Conclusion

Developing human rights as the basis of social work is as much an orientation as it is a single model of practice. This chapter considered some key debates about the principle and examines examples of international social work practice informed in different ways by this orientation. It then proceeded to make the case that such ideas are necessary also in other areas of practice, arguing for an understanding of human rights as foundational to the micro-politics of social work generally. In doing so, it has argued that human rights, though not absolute, are universal and cannot be ignored if a new politics of social work is to accomplish its goals of helping people to resolve problems in social relationships, challenge oppression and achieve freedom to live decent human lives.

References

Briskman, L., Latham, S., & Goddard, C. (2008). *Human rights overboard: Seeking asylum in Australia*. Melbourne, NSW: Scribe Publishing.

Dominelli, L. (ed.), (2007). *Revitalizing communities in a globalizing world*. Aldershot, Hants: Ashgate.

Doyal, L., & Gough, I. (1991). *A theory of human need*. London, Routledge.

Fraser, N., & Honneth, A. (2003). *Redistribution or recognition? A political-philosophical exchange*. London: Verso.

Gasper, D. (2006). Cosmopolitan presumptions? On Martha Nussbaum and her commentators. *Development and Change*, *37*(6), 1227–1246.

Gentry, K. (2007). *How Tampa became a turning point*. Retrieved 25 August 2011 from http://www.amnesty.org.au/refugees/comments/how_tampa_became_a_turning_point.

Healy, L.M. (2008). *International social work: Professional action in an interdependent world* (2nd edn). New York: Oxford University Press.

Hinman, L. M. (2008). *Ethics: A pluralistic approach*. Belmont, CA: Thomson-Wadsworth.

Hugman, R. (2008). Ethics in a world of difference. *Ethics & Social Welfare*, *2*(2), 118–132.

Hugman, R. (2010). *Understanding international social work: A critical analysis*. Basingstoke: Palgrave Macmillan.

Ife, J. (2008). *Human rights and social work: Towards rights based practice* (2nd edn). Melbourne: Cambridge University Press.

Ife, J. (2009). *Human rights from below: Achieving rights through community development*. Melbourne: Cambridge University Press.

Ife, J. (2010). Human rights and social justice. In M. Gray & S.A. Webb (eds), *Ethics and value perspectives in social work*. Basingstoke: Palgrave Macmillan. 148–159.

International Federation of Social Workers (IFSW) and International Association of

Schools of Social Work (IASSW) (2004). *Definition of social work.* Retrieved 22 August 2011 from http://www.ifsw.org./f38000138.html.

Kuruvilla, S. (2005). Social work and social development in India. In I. Ferguson, M. Lavalette, & E. Whitmore (eds), *Social work, globalisation and social justice.* London: Routledge.

Lundy, C. (2006). Social work's commitment to social and economic justice: A challenge to the profession. In N. Hall (ed.), *Social work: Making a difference. Social work around the world IV.* Berne and Oslo: IFSW and FAFO. 115–128.

Lyons, K., Manion, K., & Carlsen, M. (2006). *International perspectives on social work: global conditions and local practice.* Basingstoke: Palgrave Macmillan.

Maglajlić, R.A. (2010). International organisations, social work and war: A 'frog's perspective' reflection on the bird's eye view. In M. Lavalette & I. Ioakimidis (eds), *Social work in extremis: Lessons for social work internationally.* Bristol: Policy Press. 105–114.

Nussbaum, M. (2000). *Women and human development.* New York: Cambridge University Press.

Postle, K., & Beresford, P. (2007). Capacity building and the reconception of political participation: A role for social care workers? *British Journal of Social Work, 37*(1), 143–158.

Reichert, E. (2003). *Social work and human rights.* New York: Columbia University Press.

Renteln, A.D. (1990). *International human rights: Universalism and relativism.* Thousand Oaks, CA: Sage.

Sen, A. (1983). *Commodities and capabilities.* Amsterdam: Elsevier.

Solas, J. (2008). Social work and social justice: What are we fighting for? *Australian Social Work, 61*(2), 124–136.

Staub-Bernasconi, S. (2007). Economic and social rights: The neglected human rights. In E. Reichert (ed.), *Challenges in human rights: a social work perspective.* New York: Columbia University Press. 138–161.

Timms, N. (1983). *Social work values: An enquiry.* London: Routledge & Kegan Paul.

United Nations (UN). (1948). *Universal Declaration of Human Rights.* New York: United Nations.

United Nations (UN). (1951/1967). *Convention and protocol relating to the status of refugees.* Geneva: United Nations High Commission for Refugees.

Webb, S.A. (2009). Against difference and diversity in social work: The case of human rights. *International Journal of Social Welfare, 18,* 307–316.

Webb, S.A. (2010). Virtue ethics. In M. Gray & S.A. Webb (eds), *Ethics and value perspectives in social work.* Basingstoke: Palgrave Macmillan. 108–119.

Wronka, J. (1998). *Human rights and social policy in the twenty-first century* (2nd edn). Lanham, MA: University Press of America.

Young, I.M. (1990). *Justice and the politics of difference.* Princeton, NJ: Princeton University Press.

11

Femocratic Childcare Governance

Tammy Findlay

This chapter sees childcare as a 'zone of political engagement' in which childcare policy is analysed within a framework of democratic governance. Like critical social work generally, femocratic childcare values the perspectives of service users and envisions a childcare system designed around the needs and interest of children and families. Through the lens of feminist Nancy Fraser's critical social theory, the chapter examines what a democratic-feminist, or femocratic childcare system might look like by exploring two of Fraser's central conceptual pairings: (1) redistribution and recognition; and (2) étatism and contra étatism. Sharing Fraser's interest in reconciling principles existing in tension with one another, the chapter analyses the gendered contradictions inherent in two models of childcare governance in Canada: school-based and community-based models.

The school-based model – reflected in recent proposals in Ontario, Canada, as well as in Norway, Scotland and the Netherlands – embodies welfarist and feminist principles of universal citizenship, social entitlement and redistribution (Sainsbury, 1999). But, at the same time, it raises the spectre of feminist critiques of welfare-state hierarchy and paternalism and provides weak recognition (Fraser, 1997a). The school-based model favoured by some childcare advocates is built on a feminist-inspired ethos of participatory democracy, popular control and service-user empowerment, and advances strong recognition. However, its effects are less redistributive, running the risk of reprivatizing responsibility for social reproduction, and reinforcing neoliberal paternalism (Arneil, 2006; Bezanson & Carter, 2006; Schram, 2012).

The chapter proceeds in five sections. It begins by outlining the key concepts and theory on governance and its relationship to Fraser's framework. Thereafter, it describes the school- and community-based models, respectively, identifying their strengths and weaknesses. It then considers whether Fraser's proposals regarding 'post-neoliberal anti-étatism' and her 'critical theory of recognition' provide a way forward in childcare 'governance', arguing that Fraser's framework can be used to build practical policy alternatives in Canada and elsewhere. In fact, the concepts of governance, étatism and contra étatism, and redistribution and recognition can be important guides for the women's movement as it struggles to imagine a femocratic childcare system (see, for instance, Coalition of Child Care Advocates of British Columbia (CCCABC), 2011; Child Care Advocacy Association (CCAAC), 2004).These concepts can also provide a foundation for building a new politics for critical social work as it pertains to childcare and women's equality. For this political project of critical social work – as a social movement seeking radical social transformation – Fraser maps out a *praxis* for confronting ideology and power. She shows that challenging gendered relations of domination, regulation, control, coercion and management relies on empowering service users without simply offloading responsibility, and repositioning practitioners as active agents in this process of democratization and governance for social justice.

Femocratic Childcare Governance and its Links to Social Work

This chapter relies on several concepts and theories that require some clarification: femocratic, childcare, governance, and their connection to social work. 'Femocratic' means centred on women's interests and 'femocratic institutions' might be staffed largely by women or represent women's interests and advance feminist causes. They are gender-based – advancing women's equality, autonomy and emancipation – and democratic, favouring participatory processes in which women as service users are involved and empowered. Femocratic institutions seek positive outcomes for women (Findlay, 2008). Femocratic social services aim to find a balance between Fraser's étatism – top-down bureaucratic welfare-state provision based on professional expertise – and contra étatism – bottom-up, citizen- or service-user induced community-based provision – and redistribution – of wealth and power – and recognition of the rights and interests of minority or subordinated groups, such as women in a paternalistic society. Thus 'femocratic childcare' would seek institutional recognition that responsibility for social reproduction, such as the care of children, whether in the family or public domain, is done largely by women and if women are to be able to participate in the labour market – as is the primary goal of contemporary neoliberal social provision – quality, regulated, affordable, community-based childcare services must be publicly provided. At the same time, women constitute the bulk of the childcare workforce, working in a context historically staffed by under-resourced, underpaid or unpaid and untrained workers. Feminists have long pushed for recognition of their unpaid work in society and for standards of care that can only be provided by well-trained, properly compensated and adequately resourced childcare workers. They have also been at the forefront of campaigns not only to recognize women's rights but also children's rights and the rights of minorities. 'Femocratic childcare', therefore, means services that recognize and respect that communities, especially women in communities – parents, childcare workers, child and family advocates and researchers – must have a say in how childcare services are organized and delivered. To this extent it is rights-based (see Chapter 10).

Femocratic childcare also challenges the artificial institutional and ideological division that has been created between early care and learning, recognizing that 'good care educates and good education cares' (Canadian Union of Public Employees (CUPE), 2009). The separation of care and learning has served to undervalue the caring *and* education work women do in the childcare sector and undermines the role early learning should play in supporting families. An *integrated* childcare system views learning and care as mutually reinforcing elements of holistic services for families (CCCABC, 2011).

Here, childcare should not be confused with services provided by the child welfare or protection systems more usually associated with social work. In this context, 'childcare' refers to the non-parental care of children, while their parents are working, studying or participating in the community, which provides early learning opportunities. Childcare policies include 'preschool care' as well as 'early childhood education' (ECE), 'early education and care' or 'early learning and childcare'. Internationally, childcare services range from services located almost entirely within the informal or private for-profit sector, to near-fully public services. Within marketized neoliberal provision, such as in Canada, there is an increasing emphasis on government-contracted or private services run on a business rather than a non-profit or public model. In Canada, only 25 per cent of families with young children have access to formal regulated childcare services (Friendly & Prentice, 2009). The remainder rely largely on informal caregiving by relatives, friends and neighbours, and increasingly on commercial services.

Given this situation, feminists and childcare advocates in Canada have long sought a comprehensive, public system of childcare, raising issues of 'governance', which concern the organization of institutional and interpersonal relations of power: Whose responsibility is it to provide childcare services while parents are at work? Who should pay for childcare services? Where should they be located? Who should have access to them? What should the services look like? Who should be involved in making these decisions? The CCCABC (2007) uses the Institute on Governance's definition of governance as the 'process whereby societies or organizations make important decisions, determine whom they involve and how they render account' (p. 3). Governance structures determine who does what in a system: 'who has "the power to make decisions" about child care' (p. 3). Governance issues have become even more significant in neoliberal public policy, where roles and responsibilities are rebalanced between complex institutional structures, diverse partnership arrangements between the public, voluntary and community sectors, and the free market (Phillips, 2003). The women's and childcare movements in Canada largely agree that neoliberal governance solutions that emphasize either informal or market-based childcare arrangements are incompatible with advancing women's equality. There is less consensus, however, about two other modes of governance, one centred on schools and the other on community-based organizations. While both seek to combine care and learning, in each, questions of control, management, participation and responsibility are addressed quite differently.

Foucault's theory of governmentality has been crucial to understanding how the regulation, control and management of 'welfare clients' has been managed through neoliberal paternalism, which shifts the locus of social responsibility – responsibility for collective welfare or well-being – onto the individual, family and community (Gray, 2010, 2011; Larner, 2000; Pacini-Ketchabaw, 2007; Schram, 2012). It also aids understanding of how social service professionals, such as childcare workers and social workers, become complicit in disciplining and managing service users. Pacini-Ketchabaw (2007) demonstrates how immigrant children are managed differently through a discourse of multiculturalism: the language of 'acceptance', 'cultural sensitivity', 'tolerance' and 'flexibility' so central to Canada's multiculturalism policy effectively regulates the behaviour of immigrants so they conform to the dominant Canadian culture. In social work, Gray (2011) shows how under the neoliberal social investment regime, social workers are increasingly enlisted to discipline, blame, and target disadvantaged groups, especially single mothers, through welfare-to-work and child protection programmes. Similarly, McKeen (2007) criticizes the ways in which advocacy groups in Canada have been drawn into the National Children's Agenda's preoccupation with targeting 'at risk' groups. Understanding these informal mechanisms of regulation and control is central to analysing models of governance and creating a femocratic alternative.

What does femocratic childcare governance have to do with social work? Issues relating to femocratic childcare governance have direct relevance to and implications for critical social work. Like childcare workers, the majority of social workers are female. Like critical social work, femocratic childcare is social justice-oriented; favours anti-oppressive practice; champions the rights and needs of poor, marginalized, oppressed and excluded groups; and seeks to advance women's equality as mothers and workers, and recognition of children's rights. The integrated system of childcare services envisioned within femocratic governance would constitute a hub of family – welfare, healthcare and education – services in which social workers could play a vital role. Femocratic governance, like social work, resists complicity in neoliberal austerity measures resulting in, *inter alia*, individualized, marketized services; the devolution of responsibility on to individuals, families and communities (responsibilization), and targeted rather than universal provision (Gray, 2010, 2011). Like Foucault's theory of governmentality, Fraser's framework of redistribution and recognition and étatism and contra étatism deepens understanding of issues relating to childcare governance within neoliberal service provision and the possibilities to move beyond them.

Fraser's Framework: Redistribution and Recognition and Étatism and Contra Étatism

The 'redistribution-recognition dilemma' has been widely discussed (Olson, 2008). In *Justice Interruptus* (1997b), Fraser identified a dissonance between social movements engaged in material struggles for redistribution of economic power and resources and the 'newer' identity-based claims for cultural recognition around gender, race, ethnicity and nationality. With its roots in Marxism, redistributive justice is concerned primarily with socioeconomic inequality, exploitation of workers, poverty of the lower classes, and marginalization of disadvantaged groups in the labour market. Recognition justice is largely – though not exclusively – troubled by questions of representation, interpretation, communication and respect. Fraser's resolution was a 'critical theory of recognition' in which redistribution and recognition were mutually reinforcing rather than competing through transformative socialism (Marx) and linguistic deconstruction (Derrida and Saussure).

In 2009, Fraser raised another important paradox for feminism: étatism versus contra étatism. She traced the history of the second-wave women's movement in the USA in relation to four key characteristics of post-war capitalism: economism (the privileging of economic interests), androcentrism (the privileging of male interests), étatism (bureaucratic professionalism) and Westphalianism (nation–state sovereignty) (Fraser, 2009). By étatism, Fraser meant top-down bureaucratic organizational forms of welfare-state provision based on professional, technical expertise, where, 'far from being empowered to interpret their needs democratically, via political deliberation and contestation, ordinary citizens were positioned (at best) as passive recipients of satisfactions defined and dispensed from on high' (Fraser, 2009, p.

102). Being concerned about process, second-wave feminists sought alternatives to top-down, androcentric – masculine – forms of organization through democratic – participatory, anti-hierarchical and grassroots – organization, such as user-controlled women's shelters, health, legal aid and childcare services (Fraser, 2009; Gray & Boddy 2010). They did not reject the state, but rather 're-imagining the relation between state and society, they sought to transform those positioned as passive objects of welfare and development policy into active subjects, empowered to participate in democratic processes of need interpretation' (Fraser, 2009, p. 105). By joining with the self-help and service-user movements, their goal was to make state institutions more accountable to ordinary citizens.

Unfortunately, in unintended ways, the feminist critique of étatism – 'second-wave feminism contra étatism' – worked to reinforce neoliberal attacks on the welfare state and legitimize reliance on the voluntary sector to pick up the slack. Feminist arguments were used in the USA to justify President Clinton's welfare reform and in developing countries as NGOs worked to offset state retrenchment. Fraser (2009) noted it was 'but a short step from second-wave feminism's critique of welfare-state paternalism to Thatcher's critique of the nanny state', leading to a convergence of feminism and neoliberalism, or to 'feminist anti-étatism resignified' (p. 111). Feminist notions of democratic control were subverted to promote 'individual self-help and community networking' (p.111). Fraser (2009) proposed a 'post-neoliberal anti-étatism' to resist this merging of feminism and neoliberalism, suggesting 'a new organization of political power, one that subordinates bureaucratic managerialism to citizen empowerment ... not to dissipate but to strengthen public power [through participatory democracy]' (p. 116).

In confronting the redistribution–recognition and étatism–contra étatism problematic, Fraser (2009) provided an important framework for thinking about the organization of social services in an increasingly anti-welfarist environment. Her ideas resonate with the contemporary conundrum of childcare governance: how to avoid top-down, exclusionary control, neoliberal-state retrenchment and privatization. This puzzle is at the heart of contemporary debates on the role of the public and private – non-profit – sectors in the delivery of childcare services in Canada.

Public Childcare in Canada: A School-based Model

In autumn 2009, Canada's largest labour union, the Canadian Union of Public Employees (CUPE), launched a national campaign for public early childhood education and care (ECEC). On the face of it, this was uncontroversial and consistent with CUPE's broader anti-privatization efforts. For more than 40 years, the women's movement in Canada outside Quebec has argued for a national, public childcare system on the grounds of gender equality. However, the call for public funding *and* delivery was a significant strategic shift given that, until 2009, national and provincial childcare advocacy organizations had seen service delivery as either a public or not-for-profit activity (see, for example, CCAAC, 2004; CCCABC, 2007; Child Care Coalition of Manitoba (CCCM), 2001; Ontario Coalition for Better Child Care (OCBCC), 2008a; New Brunswick Child Care Coalition (NBCCC), 2007). However, CUPE's campaign challenged the status quo by defining not-for-profit delivery as 'private', thus putting the difficult question of public responsibility for childcare governance front and centre, especially since 'private' traditionally meant run for-profit as a business.

The trend internationally – in Iceland, New Zealand, Spain, Slovenia, Sweden, England, Scotland, Norway and the Netherlands – is to house childcare within Ministries of Education (Bennett, 2008; Neuman, 2008). Under this model, local municipalities or public school boards would be responsible for the direct delivery of ECEC. Based on recent developments, the school-based model follows international trends towards prevention and early intervention focusing on the importance of early childhood development (Gray, 2011; Neuman, 2008).

Canada's largest province, Ontario, seems to be moving in this direction, along with British Columbia and Prince Edward Island, at least in regard to preschool education for 4- and 5-year-olds. In November 2007, then Ontario Premier Dalton McGuinty appointed Dr Charles Pascal to the position of Early Learning Advisor to make recommendations on the best way to implement full-day learning for 4- and 5-year-old children in the province. Dr Pascal released his report in June 2009, recommending universal entitlement to government-funded, two-year, school-based, full-day early learning for every child who turned 4 by the end of December, delivered by existing school boards. The fragmented programmes for children and parents, including early learning and care, pre- and post-natal care, and family support, would be integrated within a system under the jurisdiction of a newly created Early Years Division within the Ministry of Education. Full-day learning would be provided by a combination of qualified teachers and certified early childhood educators (ECEs) (Pascal, 2009).

Advantages of the school-based childcare model

Some childcare advocates have long viewed the public-school system as the best vehicle to advance childcare services (Mahon 2004). The Pascal model unfolding in Ontario generated much praise from educators, childcare advocates, healthcare providers, municipalities, labour organizations, non-profit agencies and private business because the model was seen to have several advantages over Canada's market- or charity-based model of childcare delivery.

First, given that education in Canada has always been seen as a 'public good' and 'human right' to which all children are entitled, the school-based model effectively brought childcare into a quality, publicly-funded, universal system already focused on children with minimal parent fees (Friendly & Prentice, 2009), and carried political clout given the support of powerful teachers' unions (Neuman 2008). This distanced childcare from the welfare model in which it was seen as a targeted intervention for 'at-risk' and low-income communities. However, the Pascal model only proposed universal provision for 4- and 5-year-olds, which meant services for younger children might fall under a different Ministry, as in Sweden and Quebec, prior to their shift to preschool education (Mahon, 2004).

Secondly, the education model could better integrate early childcare and learning into a seamless system. In those jurisdictions where childcare has been moved to education ministries, policy silos between learning and care have begun to break down (Moss & Bennett, 2006; Neuman, 2008).

Thirdly, public delivery would likely resist the further corporatization of childcare and withstand international trade agreements, since the growth of large commercial chains elsewhere proved detrimental to service quality, accountability for public money, and women's equality (CUPE, 2009).

Fourthly, from a feminist political-economy perspective, the gendered implications of the school-based educational model were that parents, especially mothers, would have access to affordable services to support their labour-market participation, education and parenting responsibilities and the largely female childcare workforce would earn good wages and enjoy favourable working conditions in unionized workplaces (CUPE, 2009). Pascal (2009) maintained that his proposal addressed feminist concerns about the feminization and racialization of poverty.

Finally, in Fraser's (2009) framework, the educational model was redistributive because it was universal – making preschool education available to all children. However, Pascal's model allowed for public or private – non-profit – delivery of preschool education, before- and after-school care, and summer childcare, and Ontario's legislation did not explicitly rule out for-profit provision (Ontario, 2010).

Disadvantages of the educational school-based model

Despite its advantages, there are concerns about the school-based model. First, it does not take account of the needs of working parents. Ontario's early learning system would run only for the school day or year, meaning that working parents still needed to arrange – and pay for – before- and after-school and summer care for their children, though subsidies would be available for some families (Pascal, 2009). Although fees would be regulated, the Ontario Coalition for Better Child Care (OCBCC) (2009) wondered how a 'reasonable fee' would be defined, and warned that variations in fees across the province were likely. Therefore, only those children whose parents could afford care would have access to early care and learning opportunities outside the public programme, which was not designed to fit with parental working schedules (Chudnovsky, 2010).

Secondly, while promoting service integration, Pascal's (2009) model reinforced the division of learning and care by: (1) separating the school day from the extended day and summer days; (2) continuing to treat 'childcare' as income-tested and 'learning' as universal; and (3) splitting the delivery of services between the school board (school day) and contracting out before- and after-school care to 'local or regional governments, school boards, post-secondary institutions, or non-profit agencies' (Pascal, 2009, p. 14).

Thirdly, Moss and Bennett (2006) warned against 'schoolification' – 'the school imposing its demands and practices on other services, making them school-like' (p. 2) (see Neuman (2008) on Belgium, France and the UK). Canadian community-based childcare providers were anxious about the downward extension of the education paradigm and loss of early childhood education values and practices, such as a pedagogical commitment to play-based learning and partnership between caregivers and parents (Chudnovsky, 2010). This resonated with second-wave feminist critiques of hierarchical and paternalistic social services, in this case childcare providers, as outlined by Fraser (2009). Given the focus on learning, schools and parents, broader recognition of community knowledge, community care and representation of diverse experiences might be under threat.

Finally, community-based providers were worried about their place in Ontario's new early learning system. As positions opened up in the extended day or year services, staff retention in the non-profit sector would be a challenge. In other jurisdictions, such as New Jersey, USA, there were difficulties in merging public and community-based operators into one system, as there appeared to be a hierarchy of public and community providers. Whitebook et al. (2008) noted some disagreement between community services and the school district over the valuing of knowledge and collaborative governance: '[i]t's always [as if] the district knows everything, and the providers know nothing, but because the district has the money, providers don't want to complain or say anything' (p. 38).

This speaks to fundamental issues of recognition surrounding different understandings of community engagement, participation and democracy. Elaborated below is community-based childcare's long tradition of directly involving parents in services. In the face of Ontario's Early Learning Plan, the OCBCC asked: 'Will there be a Parent Engagement strategy? How will parents be welcomed into the classroom?' (OCBCC, 2009) It is at this level of 'everyday democracy' (Moss, 2007) that Fraser (2009) was working when she spoke of the desire for 'liberation from traditional authority' (p. 110), and is why some in the childcare movement are more inclined towards the community-based model.

Non-profit Childcare: The Community-based Model

The community-based model is difficult to define. For some, it acts as a default for anything that is not public. New Jersey, for instance, which has rapidly expanded its preschool system through a mixed-delivery model of public and 'community-based' providers, includes both non-profit and for-profit providers in the latter category (Mead, 2009). Due to the significant differences between non-profit and for-profit providers, this is not the definition adopted in this chapter (see, for instance, Crampton et al., 2005; Mahon, 2004). Following its usage by childcare advocates in Canada, 'community-based' refers only to non-profits, where collective ownership and control are central principles. In short, community-based childcare is about a philosophical stance that values local knowledge and experience in practice and positions parents, childcare workers and childcare advocates as active players in the policy field.

One of the most comprehensive descriptions of a community-based model can be found in Brennan's (1998) history of the Australian childcare movement, where community-based childcare first meant non-profit services run by parent committees. The Australian national government played an important funding and standard-setting function in this community-services childcare model to ensure equality of access across the country and developed an extensive system of community control, linking public funding to requirements for local management. National governments would allocate funds for childcare to local governments on condition they could demonstrate they had consulted with local residents. Local governments were expected to 'initiate community planning, make the final decisions as to which groups [would] be funded, disburse funds and co-ordinate the programmes in each area' (Brennan, 1998, p. 88). This was referred to as the 'submissions process' (Brennan, 1998). In addition, in the 1980s:

> planning committees were established in each state and territory to give advice on funding priorities and to represent the interests of each level of government as well as a range of community groups ... The composition of these committees varied but in addition to representatives from commonwealth, state and local

governments, they generally included members of community organizations, ethnic groups and women's advisory units. (Brennan, 1998, p. 175)

In Canada, the community-based model resonated for childcare advocates, such as the Child Care Advocacy Association of Canada (CCAAC, 2004), which released its strategy to promote quality, inclusive, accessible, publicly funded, non-profit childcare in 2004. The strategy laid out principles for community-based childcare, calling for 'community planning to determine the types of childcare services and their location' and for services 'responsive to the diversity of Canada's communities, promote social inclusion and provide for community and parental input' (CCAAC, 2004, pp. 26–7).

Some elements of community governance already existed in childcare in Canada, where parents in some childcare centres participated as board members, volunteers and fundraisers and comprised the majority of childcare boards in the province of Quebec (Mahon, 2004; Prentice, 2006). In certain Canadian jurisdictions, notably in Quebec and Vancouver, well-developed governance processes formed the foundation for Mahon's (2006) vision of a democratic childcare system. Beyond the basics of treating children as citizens, providing just wages and public, non-profit delivery of services, Mahon (2006) promoted the 'neighbourhood hub system' which, in addition to acting as networks of co-located, integrated services for children and parents, served as the locale for democratic control and accountability via elected boards and parental involvement. The hub system has been unfolding in Vancouver since the early 1990s. Their *Blueprint for Community Architecture for Early Childhood Learning and Care* envisioned a system in which:

> Hubs are operated by nonprofit community organizations, with Boards of Directors ... accountable to their constituents – members, families and other neighbourhood stakeholders. With resources in place for service infrastructure, hubs can also be accountable to help plan, coordinate and deliver a continuum of child development services. They can also develop a process for community input and feedback regarding programs and services. (Anderson, 2005, p. 6)

Expanding more concretely on the lessons from the Vancouver experiments, the Coalition of Child Care Advocates of British Columbia (CCCABC) developed a comprehensive plan for a community-based, non-profit childcare system. Elaborating what community-owned and controlled childcare might look like, the CCCABC (2007) called on communities to 'imagine an accountable governing body in your community with the mandate, power and resources to develop and deliver childcare' (p. 1). These bodies, either appointed or elected, would be democratically controlled by communities based on principles of participation, community ownership, non-profit, decentralized delivery, political autonomy, user–caregiver collaboration, and supportive infrastructure building on existing strengths, and would be empowered with a mandate, budget and accountability process (CCCABC, 2007). Childcare coalitions in the provinces of New Brunswick, Ontario and Manitoba have also emphasized community ownership, planning and control (CCCM, 2001; NBCCC, 2007; OCBCC, 2008b).

Advantages of the community-based childcare model

The advantages of the community-based model are less tangible than in the educational school-based model, invoking democratic values of recognition, popular control and user involvement. The principles underlying Australia's community-based childcare system stemmed from a context similar to that discussed by Fraser (2009) in the USA. Brennan (1998) explains, in childcare in the late 1960s, 'feminists expressed demands for new types of services which would be government-funded but managed and controlled by parents' and women's expertise was respected so that professionals were 'on tap, not on top' (pp. 66–7).

For Judy Rebick (2009), an activist in the Canadian women's movement, participatory democracy is the best strategy for resisting neoliberalism. Tracing democratic movements and experiments around the world, she focused on the political process. Like Fraser, she drew from the tradition of women's movements in the 1960s and 1970s, where the democratization of services through user control was emphasized. She explored the delivery of social services through missions in Venezuela, which offer a highly successful 'decentralised, democratic model for the delivery of social, health, and other community services' (p. 48).

She held that participatory processes – like participatory budgets or community organizing – served to engage traditionally marginalized groups, such as women, youth and indigenous people with some evidence that non-profit organizations were more effective in meeting the needs of multicultural communities. In their study of primary care services in New Zealand, Crampton et al. (2005) maintained non-profit governance boards represented and promoted the self-determination of minority groups, especially the indigenous Maori community, better than for-profits and government.

Disadvantages of the community-based childcare model

Important insights into 'community' have come from feminist and anti-racist literature on social capital and the social economy. Feminists have shown that 'social capital' and the 'social economy' are gendered concepts that make women's responsibilities for social reproduction in the family and the community invisible (Bezanson & Carter, 2006). They see the participation of families and the voluntary sector as pivotal to community-based childcare. On the one hand, this democratizing process is about empowering communities, while on the other, it advances reprivatization and neoliberal retrenchment by offloading state responsibilities on to 'communities' and reinforcing social hierarchies (Arneil, 2006; Bezanson & Carter, 2006). For instance, Rebick (2009) highlighted cases where participatory processes might inform thinking on governance, citing the example of Porto Alegre, Brazil, where the community identified childcare as a priority but couldn't afford it: 'Community groups stepped forward and offered to house the child-care centres for a fraction of the price it would cost in the public sector ... This compromise began to build trust' (p. 40). But there are reasons for caution, since it is problematic when the primary motivation for community involvement is cost-saving, rather than democracy, and cost-saving often comes at the expense of staff wages and training, and adding to women's unpaid work. When voluntary labour is a coping strategy, it is not empowering but 'coercive' (Prentice, 2006, p. 531), 'compulsory', 'oppressive, and non-reciprocal' (Bezanson & Carter, 2006, p. 435).

As seen in Australia, prior to welfare reform in the late 1990s, 'community management' was integral to the system, with a 'submission model of funding', where communities initiated projects (Brennan, 1998). While this empowered local residents, 'a vast amount of work (from overseeing the construction of centres through to advertising the service, hiring staff, administering the commonwealth grant and liaising with state agencies) was performed by unpaid volunteers' (Brennan, 1998, p. 127) and the community management approach overlooked the gendered nature of community. Further, the submissions process favoured better-organized services and intensified community inequalities. Providers had to be approved, legal organizations, and well-entrenched powerful voluntary organizations with professional grant-writing skills were best able to compete for funding. The most advantaged neighbourhoods benefited, resulting in regional disparities (Brennan, 1998). This affirms related research that inequalities in neighbourhood social capital translate into unequal access to services (Mahon & Jenson, 2006).

Other social inequalities and recognition injustices can result from the community-based model, and exemplify the notion of governmentality. Australia's history of philanthropy in early care and learning is similar to Canada's. Brennan (1998) refers to the early kindergarten movement's 'child-saving mission', where kindergarten was part of the early nineteenth-century social reform and philanthropic movement targeted at the poor and working class to impart middle-class values and morals. Aboriginal peoples also have a similar suspicion of child welfare in both countries, due to a history of intervention and apprehension (Brennan, 1998). This racial and cultural legacy continues to shape indigenous communities today.

In her interrogation of social capital, Arneil (2006) argued that romanticizations of the USA's civic past (à la Putnam) overlook the ways in which social capital has been used to meet harmful ends. Historically, women, the poor, and cultural minorities (immigrants, Aboriginal peoples, people with disabilities and sexual minorities) have been either excluded from organizations and social networks, or treated as 'charitable projects' by 'progressive' social reformers and welfare advocates, often led by Protestantism, the eugenics movement and the first-wave women's movement. Arneil (2006) demonstrated that attempts at building social capital during the Progressive Era in the USA through social welfare and education were intended to strengthen 'civic virtue, to morally uplift and to build civilization ... What appeared to be well-intentioned social capital building premised on the idea of creating civil communities with educated citizens instead caused profound cultural damage and pain' (p. 30), most deeply for Aboriginal communities. The social economy can provide powerful venues for knowledge production, misrepresentation and the reproduction of unequal social relations, so there may be a conflict between local democracy and social inclusion. Despite the recognition elements of the community-based model, universal access through public-school delivery may be more inclusive of immigrant, multicultural and urban Aboriginal communities than through voluntary organizations.

Community-based childcare poses a challenge because it exposes the strain between two central feminist concerns: the democratization of the welfare state and the reprivatization of social reproduction. For Fraser (2009), by embracing the voluntary sector with too little attention to this contradiction, 'second-wave feminism has unwittingly provided a key ingredient of the new spirit of neoliberalism' (p. 110) and risks subordinating redistribution to recognition (Fraser, 1997a). But she was optimistic about the future, seeking a 'post-neoliberal anti-étatism' that bolsters public services through participatory democracy (Fraser, 2009, p. 116) and a 'critical theory of recognition' that transforms social relations and identities. What might this look like in the case of childcare?

The Best of Both Worlds: A Femocratic Childcare System

In childcare, a 'post-neoliberal anti-étatism' and a 'critical theory of recognition' would need to combine the redistribution and universal entitlement of the school-based educational model with the recognition and popular control of the community-based model. This is not easy, but it is not impossible. The two approaches are not necessarily at odds. Feminism itself has been about forging common ground across liberalism and socialism, individualism and collectivism, institutional and grassroots, procedural and substantive democracy, decentralization and centralization and redistribution and recognition. This has been a major strength of the Canadian women's movement, and the unique contribution of feminist political economy in Canada (Luxton, 2006). This orientation can guide a femocratic re-envisioning of childcare governance to balance central authority with popular power in the interests of women. Femocratic childcare is both public and participatory.

There are already existing Nordic examples moving in this direction. Jenson et al. (2003) explained that what distinguishes the role of the voluntary sector in childcare in Nordic social democratic regimes from conservative, liberal ones is that community control is built into publicly provided services. However, what is being proposed would go much further in engaging citizens than what currently exists in the Nordic countries. According to the CCCABC (2007), community-based governance 'does not let senior levels of government off the hook!' (p. 10) (see also CCCABC, 2011). A participatory public childcare system must situate the democratic processes of community-based services within a pan-Canadian properly funded, carefully planned and regulated, non-profit, coordinated, universal, high-quality, affordable, accessible, inclusive and accountable childcare programme, where childcare workers were well paid (Anderson, 2005; Jenson, Mahon, & Phillips, 2003). This would require a social policy framework that strengthened social networks and made social reproduction a public responsibility (Bezanson & Carter, 2006). The federal government's role would be funding and the setting of standards, enshrined in legislation, and the provinces (preferably under one Ministry) would take on planning, regulation, monitoring and coordination and would make partnerships for public delivery with either school districts or municipalities (CCAAC, 2004; CCCABC, 2007; Mahon, 2004). The principal mandate of these local authorities delivering childcare services would be to engage with childcare workers, parents and community groups. This would be compatible with the hub model of integrated family services, and provide the opportunity for childcare workers, social workers, healthcare workers and educators to break down silos and coordinate their efforts.

This would not mean public participation was purely a local task. Citizens would have the right to engage at multiple levels. Mahon (2004) suggested that an independent national Early Child Learning and Care Council would perform data collection and analysis, provide advice and foster public engagement. Similarly, the CCAAC (2004) called for a federal department to 'develop and implement mechanisms to receive input from the childcare sector and stakeholders' (p. 17). The federal government could also promote local participation. Even though the submissions mechanism was problematic, one of the strengths of the Australian system was that the national government took a leadership role in requiring community involvement. In Ontario, Pascal (2009) saw potential in their Best Start community networks comprising municipalities, school boards, parents and community agencies, if they did not operate on a voluntary basis, and the CCCABC (2011) recommended a system of Early Years Centre (EYC) Networks. If federal legislation were to guarantee the fundamental principles of universality, quality and inclusion, surely the role of communities should be explicitly laid out as well.

Furthermore, community associations ought to have core public funding and training in civic engagement to make true partnership realistic (Bezanson & Carter, 2006) and break from the past federal practice of 'supporting more conservative advocacy organizations while marginalizing the more vocal critics' (Jenson et al., 2003, p. 152). Organizations in the voluntary sector are not simply service providers. Their most valuable contribution is their advocacy, representation and accountability. The YWCA Canada and Vancouver blueprint for childcare built support for community governance into its costing model (Anderson, 2005), and the CCAAC (2004) included funding for voluntary childcare organizations as a key part of developing the system. In addition to being the primary providers of parental and paid childcare, women are largely doing the organizing and advocating for childcare (Friendly, 2006). Federal funding for advocacy should be a basic right of citizenship and is vital for advancing gender equality and creating a femocratic childcare system.

Advocacy organizations and local communities must be involved at all stages of policy: agenda-setting, planning, implementation, monitoring and evaluation (CCAAC, 2004; Pascal, 2009). Pascal (2009) stressed that communities expected this consultation to be authentic and were fully aware when it was not. Of course, community control has to engage the whole community through inclusion and representation of diversity (Arneil, 2006), which will not happen without effort. Pascal (2010) recommended anti-oppression training throughout the early learning system and the CCCABC (2011) made First Nations and Aboriginal community control an absolute necessity.

Public officials would also benefit from education in citizen engagement processes and could learn from other jurisdictions, where participation was more integral to childcare services. It was seen earlier that the pre-welfare reform Australian childcare model made extensive use of multisectoral planning committees (Brennan, 1998), and childcare in Quebec is governed by local committees (Mahon, 2004).

Pascal's (2010) plan for Ontario incorporated some of these institutional elements for community democracy, such as engaging parents and the

Table 11.1   Fraser's framework of femocratic childcare governance

Public childcare	Community-based childcare	Femocratic childcare
Étatism	Contra-étatism	Post-neoliberal anti-étatism
Redistribution	Recognition	Critical theory of recognition

childcare community. However, there were differences of opinion in the community about the extent to which communities were engaged in the implementation of Early Learning in Ontario (confidential phone interview 1 & 2, 17 May 2010). Moving forward, existing Best Start Networks, including school boards, municipalities, public health, childcare, community partners and parents, could lend more permanence to these governance processes (confidential phone interview 1, 17 May 2010; Pascal, 2010). They provide a foundation on which to construct more responsive and community-driven childcare services as an antidote to 'schoolification' – scaling up the early childhood education pedagogical approach and its democratic principles, into the school system. It might mobilize the strengths of public and community-based governance and, in so doing, provide the opportunity to put Fraser's (2009) post-neoliberal anti-étatism and critical theory of recognition into policy practice (see Table 11.1).

Conclusion

Feminist political economy and critical social work highlight the tensions between structural constraints and agency – the importance of negotiating contradictions inherent in a neoliberal gendered order – so as to develop progressive alternatives. This analysis was guided by a concern with the ways in which power inequalities were institutionalized in governing structures, as well as with the agency of political actors and the potential for democratization or creating *femocratic* social services. This chapter sought to locate proposals for *public* ECEC within broader feminist debates about governance – how power, rights, responsibilities and accountability were organized in the provision of social services. Using Nancy Fraser's theoretical framework of étatism/contra étatism and redistribution/recognition as a starting point, it showed that two models for the governance of childcare represented opportunities and challenges for feminist thinking. The public, school-based model outlined by Charles Pascal (2010) in Ontario, Canada, defined childcare as a universal entitlement, valued women's work in the childcare sector and challenged the gendered division of labour, but might reinforce hierarchical and paternalistic tendencies. The non-profit, community-based model could facilitate popular control over childcare services, and value the experience and knowledge of parents, workers and community advocates in the policy process, while also sustaining neoliberal reprivatization. It argued that taking the best of each approach could build a participatory public childcare system: femocratic childcare, as part of a new politics of social work. Indeed, this is, as Fraser (2009) put it, 'a moment in which feminists should think big' (p. 117).

References

Anderson, L. (2005). *Lots to build on, more to do: Blueprint for community architecture for early childhood learning and care*. Toronto, ON: YWCA Canada. Retrieved 12 April 2010 from http://www.cccabc.bc.ca/res/pubs/pdf/YWCA_lots_to_build.pdf.

Arneil, B. (2006). *Diverse communities: The problem with social capital*. New York: Cambridge University Press.

Bennett, J. (2008). Early childhood education and care systems in OECD countries: The issue of tradition and governance. *Encyclopedia of Early Childhood Development*. Retrieved 20 March 2010 from http://www.ccl-cca.ca/NR/rdonlyres/BA90A19A-3D33-4F9FAE9D-CAA533A807B0/0/BennettANGxpCSAJE.pdf.

Bezanson, K., & Carter, E. (2006). *Public policy and social reproduction: Gendering social capital*. Ottawa, ON: Status of Women Canada.

Brennan, D. (1998). *The politics of Australian childcare: Philanthropy to feminism and beyond* (2nd edn). Cambridge: Cambridge University Press.

Canadian Union of Public Employees (CUPE). (2009). *Why public early childhood education and care?* Retrieved 10 April 2010 from http://cupe.ca/child-care/public-childhood-education-care.

Child Care Advocacy Association of Canada (CCAAC). (2004). *From patchwork to framework: A Child Care Strategy for Canada*. Retrieved 14 May 2005 from http://www.ccaac.ca/pdf/resources/framework_cc.pdf.

Child Care Coalition of Manitoba (CCCM). (2001). *Blueprint for Action: A Five Year Plan for Manitoba Childcare Policy Redesign*. Retrieved 6 June 2011 from http://childcaremanitoba.org/images/stories/docs/cccmpublications/CCM_Blueprint.pdf.

Chudnovsky, R. (2010). *Is full day kindergarten a good idea?* Coalition of Child Care Advocates of British Columbia (CCCABC). Retrieved 10 April 2020 from http://www.cccabc.bc.ca/cccabcdocs/integrated/files/alldayk_article_feb2010.pdf.

Coalition of Child Care Advocates of British Columbia (CCCABC). (2007). *The evolution of community-controlled childcare in BC*. Retrieved 10 April 2010 from http://www.cccabc.bc.ca/cccabcdocs/governance/ggcc_final_report.pdf.

Coalition of Child Care Advocates of British Columbia (CCCABC). (2011). *Community Plan for a Public System of Integrated Early Care and Learning*. Retrieved 10 June 2011 from http://www.cccabc.bc.ca/plan/Community_Plan_ECL.pdf.

Crampton, P., Davis, P., Lay-Yee, R., Raymont, A., Forrest, C.B., & Starfield, B. (2005). Is primary care what it claims to be? Does community-governed nonprofit primary care improve access to services? Cross-sectional survey of practice characteristics. *International Journal of Health Services, 35*(3), 465–478

Findlay, T. (2008). Femocratic administration: Gender, democracy and the state in Ontario. Ph.D. dissertation, Faculty of Graduate Studies, York University.

Fraser, N. (1997a). From redistribution to recognition? Dilemmas of justice in a 'post-socialist' age. In N. Fraser, *Justice interruptus: Critical reflections on the 'postsocialist' condition.* New York: Routledge. 11–39.

Fraser, N. (1997b). *Justice interruptus: Critical reflections on the 'postsocialist' condition.* New York: Routledge.

Fraser, N. (2009). Feminism, capitalism and the cunning of history. *New Left Review, 56*, 97–117.

Friendly, M. (2006). Why women still ain't satisfied: Politics and activism in Canadian child care, 2006. *Canadian Woman Studies, 25*(3 & 4), 41–46.

Friendly, M., & Prentice, S. (2009). *About Canada: Childcare.* Halifax, NS: Fernwood Press.

Gray, M. (2010). Social development and the status quo: Professionalisation and Third Way cooptation. *International Journal of Social Welfare, 19*(4), 463–70.

Gray, M. (2011). Social inclusion and what it means to the 'work' of social workers. Paper presented at *Leveraging Potential: Social Inclusion at Work and Play* International Conference, Monash University Prato Centre, Tuscany, Italy, 10–11 October.

Gray, M., & Boddy, J. (2010). Making sense of the waves: Wipeout or still riding high? *Affilia: Journal of Women and Social Work, 25*(4), 368–89.

Jenson, J, Mahon, R., & Phillips, S.D. (2003). No minor matter: The political economy of childcare in Canada. In W. Clement & L.F. Vosko (eds), *Changing Canada: Political economy as transformation.* Montreal and Kingston, ON: McGill-Queen's University Press. 135–160.

Larner, W. (2000). Post-welfare state governance: Towards a code of social and family responsibility. *Social Politics, 7*(2), 244–265.

Luxton, M. (2006). Feminist political economy in Canada and the politics of social reproduction. In K. Bezanson & M. Luxton (eds), *Social reproduction: Feminist political economy challenges neoliberalism.* Montreal and Kingston, ON: McGill-Queen's University Press. 11–44.

Mahon, R. (2004). *Early child learning and care in Canada: Who rules? Who should rule? Childcare for a change: Shaping the 21st century. Canadian Council on Social Development.* Retrieved 11 May 2011 from http://www.ccsd.ca/pubs/2004/cc/mahon.pdf.

Mahon, R. (2006). A real alternative: The Canadian election and childcare policy. *The Bullet, 12.* Retrieved 11 May 2011 from http://www.socialistproject.ca/bullet/bullet012.html.

Mahon, R., &. Jenson, J. (2006). *Learning from each other: Early learning and childcare experiences in Canadian cities.* Toronto, ON and Vancouver, BC: Social Development Canada, City of Toronto and Vancouver Joint Council on Childcare.

McKeen, W. (2007). The national children's agenda: A neoliberal wolf in lamb's clothing. *Studies in Political Economy, 80*, 151–73.

Mead, S. (2009). *Education Reform Starts Early Lessons from New Jersey's PreK-3rd Reform Efforts.* Washington, DC and New York: New America Foundation. Retrieved 20

March 2010 from http://www.newamerica.net/sites/newamerica.net/files/policy-docs/Education%20Reform%20Starts%20Early_0.pdf.

Moss, P. (2007). *Bringing politics into the nursery: Early childhood education as democratic practice.* Working Paper 43. Bernard van Leer Foundation: The Hague, Netherlands. Retrieved 19 March 2010 from http://www.ecdgroup.com/docs/lib_004343335.pdf.

Moss, P., & Bennett, J. (2006). *Toward a new pedagogical meeting place? Bringing early childhood into the education system.* Briefing paper for a Nuffield Educational Seminar. London: Nuffield Foundation. Retrieved 19 March 2010 from http://www.nuffieldfoundation.org/fileLibrary/doc/briefingpaper.draft3.august17.doc.

Neuman, M.J. (2008). Governance of early childhood education and care: Recent developments in OECD Countries. In E. Wood (ed.), *The Routledge reader in early childhood education.* New York: Routledge. 163–176.

New Brunswick Childcare Coalition (NBCCC). (2006). *About us.* Retrieved 20 May 2011 fromhttp://www.nbccc-csgnb.ca/about-e.asp.

New Brunswick Child Care Coalition (NBCCC). (2007). *Childcare in New Brunswick at the Crossroads.* Brief Submitted to the Department of Family and Community Services as part of the Early Learning and Childcare Public Consultation. Retrieved 20 May 2011 from http://www.nbccc-csgnb.ca/downloads/BriefNBCCC_elcc.doc.

Olson, K. (ed.) (2008). *Adding insult to injury: Nancy Fraser debates her critics.* New York: Verso.

Ontario. (2010). *Bill 242: An Act to Amend the Education Act and Certain Other Acts in Relation to Early Childhood Educators, Junior Kindergarten and Kindergarten, Extended Day Programs and Certain Other Matters.* 2nd Session, 39th Legislature, Ontario. Retrieved 3 June 2011 from http://www.ontla.on.ca/bills/bills-files/39_Parliament/Session2/b242rep.pdf.

Ontario Coalition for Better Child Care (OCBCC). (2008a). *Ontario Coalition for Better Childcare Annual Report.* Retrieved 3 June 2011 from http://www.childcareontario.org/wp-content/uploads/2009/03/ocbcc-annual-report-2008.pdf.

Ontario Coalition for Better Child Care (OCBCC). (2008b). *A transformational vision of early learning and care in Ontario.* Retrieved 3 June 2011 from http://www.child-careontario.org/wp-content/uploads/2008/12/ocbcc-full-day-learning-submission3.pdf.

Ontario Coalition for Better Child Care (OCBCC). (2009). *Implementing Early Learning – Bulletin #1.* Retrieved 3 June 2011 from http://www.childcareontario.org/wp-content/uploads/2009/11/Implementing-Early-Learning-1.pdf.

Pacini-Ketchabaw, V. (2007). Child care and multiculturalism: A site of governance marked by flexibility and openness. *Contemporary Issues in Early Childhood, 8*(3), 222–232.

Pascal, C.E. (2010). *Ontario's Commitments. Inspiring Innovation – Investing in Human Capital: Early Care and Learning Hubs.* 28 April. Asia Pacific Hall, Morris J. Wosk Centre for Dialogue, Simon Fraser University, Vancouver, BC.

Pascal, C.E. (2009). *With our best future in mind: Implementing early learning in Ontario. Report to the Premier by the Special Advisor on Early Learning.* Retrieved 10 April 2010 from http://www.ontario.ca/ontprodconsume/groups/content/@gopsp/@initiative/documents/document/ont06_018899.pdf.

Phillips, S.D. (2003). Voluntary sector-government relationships in transition: Learning from international experience for the Canadian context. In K.L. Brock & K.G. Banting (eds), *The nonprofit sector in interesting times: Case studies in a changing sector.* Montreal and Kingston, ON: McGill-Queen's University Press. 17–70.

Prentice, S. (2006). Childcare, co-production and the third sector in Canada. *Public Management Review, 8*(4), 521–536.

Rebick, J. (2009). *Transforming power: From the personal to the political.* Toronto, ON: Penguin.

Sainsbury, D. (1999). Gender, policy regimes and politics. In D. Sainsbury (ed.), *Gender and welfare state regimes.* Toronto, ON: Oxford University Press. 245–75.

Schram, S.F. (2012). Welfare professionals and street-level bureaucrats. In M. Gray, J. Midgley, & S.A. Webb (eds), *Sage handbook of social work.* London: Sage. 67–79.

Whitebook, M., Ryan, S., Kipnis, F., & Sakai, L. (2008). *Partnering for preschool: A Study of Center Directors in New Jersey's Mixed-Delivery Abbott Program.* Center for the Study of Childcare Employment. Retrieved 23 March 2010 from http://www.irle.berkeley.edu/cscce/pdf/partnering_preschool_report08.pdf.

12

Social Workers as Agents of Change

Iain Ferguson

In hindsight, very few radical social workers during the Progressive Era [the decade before the First World War] had consciously revolutionary goals in their daily work. A hundred years later, their achievements seem far more reformist than radical. Yet their emphasis on social justice, their analysis of socioeconomic conditions in structural or systemic terms, their focus on issues of social class, their links to movements organized by feminists and African Americans, and their ties to radical trade unionists and left-wing political parties represented a threat to the established political order that contemporaries could not ignore. (Reisch & Andrews, 2002, p. 35)

The world of early US social work, vividly captured as 'the road not taken' by Reisch and Andrews (2002) in their study of the radical tradition in the USA, seems far removed from the realities of contemporary social work practice. There are few parts of the world in which the activities of social workers can be seen as constituting a 'threat to the established ... order' (p. 35). Instead, the dominance of several decades of neoliberal welfare policies means, more often than not, that front-line workers in advanced capitalist countries are subject to managerialist regimes that leave little room for relationship-based casework, let alone radical collective approaches. Reisch and Andrews's (2002) description of the experience of early US social work remains important and continues to resonate with social workers in the twenty-first century. It reminds us that, while then as now only a minority of social workers would describe themselves as consciously radical or revolutionary, most people still come into the profession out of a desire to 'make a difference':

Most social workers come into social work either out of a desire to help others, or to challenge social injustice. What they all enjoy in social work is the opportunity

to build relationships with people, to work creatively with them, to make a difference in their lives, and perhaps even in society as a whole. They know that these
aspirations sound clichéd, and yet this is what keeps them going in social work.
(Cree & Davis, 2007, p. 148)

As argued below, the thwarting of these aspirations by 'neoliberal social
work' (Jones, 2004) is one factor that has contributed to a growing radicali-
sation of even supposedly 'non-political' social workers in recent years. This
chapter explores the extent to which social workers might still act as agents
of social change by basing their practice on social justice, which Fraser
(2008) defines as 'parity of participation':

> According to this radical-democratic interpretation of the principle of equal moral
> worth, justice requires social arrangements that permit all to participate as peers
> in social life. Overcoming injustice means dismantling institutionalised obstacles
> that prevent some people from participating on a par with others, as full partners
> in social interaction. (p. 16)

This definition has much in common with the Marxist notion of social
justice, which, according to Eagleton (1990), 'does indeed possess an
"absolute" moral criterion: the unquestionable virtue of the rich, all-round
expansion of capacities for each individual. It is from this standpoint that
any social formation is to be assessed' (p. 223). For social work, this
suggests a practice that seeks to promote the 'all-round expansion' of each
individual while challenging 'institutionalized obstacles' – poverty,
racism, sexism, and so on – preventing that expansion. A commitment to
social justice, informed by a critical understanding of the class-divided
nature of the world in which we live, is an indispensable element of such
a practice.

This chapter argues that the dominance of neoliberal approaches
through New Public Management – managerialism – over more than two
decades has significantly reduced professional autonomy, causing a growing gap between professional values and motivations and forms of practice
required. It explores some of the ways in which workers have responded to
managerialist constraints and the types of resistance they have employed
by drawing on discussions with experienced front-line workers. Crucially,
it suggests that the growing gap between professional values and motivations and the realities of contemporary practice can be a radicalizing
factor. Finally, it examines some ways in which social workers are developing collective responses to attacks on the living standards of the poor and
dispossessed with whom they work, as a possible basis for a renewed radical social work in the twenty-first century (see Chapter 2).

'Power of Circumstances'

An early episode of the 1960s BBC comedy series *Monty Python's Flying Circus* featured a sketch set in an East London launderette involving two local women, Mrs Premise and Mrs Conclusion. Mrs Premise informs Mrs Conclusion that she has been reading Jean-Paul Sartre's classic 1930s trilogy *The Roads to Freedom*, leading to a heated philosophical debate between them about Sartre's understanding of the meaning of freedom. At this point, Mrs Premise recalls that she and her husband had met the Sartre family on holiday in Ibiza the previous year when both families had stayed at the Hotel Miramar. As she had got on famously with Madame Sartre, she decides to call her from the launderette payphone to see whether Jean-Paul might resolve their dilemma. On being informed that Jean-Paul is busy at the moment, Mrs Premise responds, 'Never mind – when will he be free?' Cue for much chortling and great hilarity as she relays Madame Sartre's reply, 'That's the question he's been asking himself for the last 50 years!'

The meaning of freedom was, indeed, Sartre's central preoccupation for most of his life. What is also true, however, is that his views on the subject changed radically over time. He moved from an existentialism, which saw individuals as wholly responsible for their own lives with any attempt to blame others seen as moral evasion or 'bad faith', to an anti-Stalinist Marxism that envisaged a much more complex relationship between agency and structure. Explaining this shift in an interview in the *New Left Review* in 1969, Sartre (1969) suggested a 'simple formula would be to say that life taught me *la force des choses* – the power of circumstances' (p. 44). This did not mean Sartre ever denied the possibility of individual agency. Far from it: the belief that human beings were free to change their lives and, collectively, the world was at the core of his revolutionary activities during the social upheavals in France in May 1968 (Birchall, 2004). However, he came to see it as much more circumscribed than he had previously thought:

> For the idea which I have never ceased to develop is that in the end one is always responsible for what is made of one. Even if one can do nothing else besides assume this responsibility. For I believe that a man can always make something out of what is made of him. This is the limit I would today accord to freedom: the small movement which makes of a totally conditioned social being someone who does not render back completely what his conditioning has given him. (Sartre, 1969, p. 45)

The nature of the relationship between agency – the ability of human beings to act freely – and structure – the factors which shape and constrain that freedom – is one which goes to the heart of the social work project. On the one hand, an understanding of the often extremely limited life choices open to people who come into contact with social work services is the starting point for anti-oppressive practice. On the other, freedom for social workers to make choices about how they respond to the needs and wishes of service users – professional autonomy – is central to most notions of ethical practice. Where there is no choice – no discretion about how one might act – it becomes difficult to talk of ethical behaviour, for which the individual must assume personal responsibility. The great Italian novelist and concentration camp survivor Primo Levi argued that in the upside-down world of the camps:

> All that could be called good in the outside world, the normal world, was of little use for survival. This was a world in the grip of barbarism, where 'the law of the jungle' ruled, and starving prisoners learned to 'eat your own bread, and if you can, that of your neighbour'. (cited in Maitles, 2002, p. 242)

Fortunately, this is not normally the situation facing social workers. In fact, as Lipsky (1980) reported in his classic text *Street-level Bureaucracy*, despite – or perhaps because of – their location in large organizations, social workers were *bureauprofessionals*, who had considerable scope to interpret and make policy in their face-to-face interactions with clients. In other words, they were able to exercise discretion and make choices, including ethical choices, about how to direct clients and respond to their needs. Increasingly, however, that discretion has been restricted by the encroachment of managerialism over the past two decades. Lipsky (1980) argued that the uncertainty inherent in front-line decision-making means there will always be an element of discretion in the activities of street-level bureaucrats, with the face-to-face encounters of workers and service users shaped, to a considerable extent, by the ways in which workers understand and respond to their clients' problems (hence the importance of structural and anti-oppressive understandings: for an example from Greek social work, see Teloni, 2011). What is also true, however, is that discretion in social work is a dynamic, not a static, category (Bamford, 1989) that shrinks or expands depending on, among other factors, organizational culture, professional autonomy and workplace trade-union organization. What, then, have been the implications of managerialism for social workers' discretion and autonomy?

Managerialism, Discretion and Autonomy

Harris and Unwin (2009) summarize the key elements of managerialist discourse that sees management as a separate and distinct organizational function and measures progress in terms of increased productivity arising from advances in information technologies. Increased measurement and quantification shifts the focus from inputs and processes to outputs and outcomes. It holds that markets – or market-type mechanisms of supply and demand – and contractual relationships are the best way to deliver services. It places a customer orientation – and consumer choice – as central, and blurs the boundaries between the public, private and voluntary sectors.

In relation to worker autonomy and discretion, three aspects of managerialism are particularly noteworthy. First, performance management is promoted, typically in the form of managerial regimes driven by key targets and performance indicators and underpinned by inspection, regulation and audit. In respect of the UK experience, driving the introduction of this regime in the 1980s was a discourse of failure, shared by Conservative and New Labour governments alike. Welfare professionals, including social workers, motivated by a public sector ethos, could not be trusted to provide the kind of services successive governments wished to see. Instead, a greater role for the market in social care and top-down regulation was required for the delivery of efficient social services (Harris, 2003). Performance management has had a major impact on professional practice and worker morale. According to Munro's government-commissioned review of child protection in England and Wales:

> A dominant theme in the criticisms of current practice is the skew in priorities that has developed between the demands of the management and inspection processes and professionals' ability to exercise their professional judgement and act in the best interests of the child. This has led to an over-standardised system that cannot respond adequately to the varied range of children's needs. (UK Department of Education, 2010, p. 5)

Similar views were expressed by groups of experienced workers in Scotland in Ferguson and Woodward's (2009) study:

> We live in a performance framework where outcomes have to be seen to be measured. I think we all know that outcomes are really very, very difficult to measure but nevertheless they are measured, a lot of them are measured in such meaningless ways ... The managers control day-to-day practice, which is just chasing numbers and ... targets. (p. 69)

These managerial regimes also have implications for ethical practice. In Munro's useful phrase, an overarching emphasis on preparing for inspections, meeting targets and addressing performance indicators has led to a procedural ethos, where workers have become preoccupied by individuals 'doing things right' rather than 'doing the right thing' (UK Department of Education, 2010, p. 14). Perhaps, not surprisingly, performance management has also led to poor worker morale. In an Audit Commission (2002) study into the reasons why public-sector workers were leaving their jobs, more than 50 per cent said they were 'overwhelmed by bureaucracy, paperwork and targets' (p. 22).

Besides subordinating professional knowledge and expertise, managerialism and the marketization of services have shifted the balance of power within many social work settings, resulting in a situation where it is increasingly difficult for front-line workers to challenge management decisions. Following a presentation to a group of front-line workers in 2010, for example, some of those present informed the writer of a training session on the operation of a new computerized assessment system in which they had recently participated. When they had objected that the new system made no provision for recording unmet need and described this as poor practice, their managers told them in no uncertain terms to 'just do it'. They were instructed to complete the assessments or clearly implied negative consequences would ensue for those who continued to object.

Several factors contribute to this oppressive climate, including the need to meet rigid targets; the weakening of collective cultures (both professional and trade-union) within many workplaces; the subordination of worker expertise to the requirements of new technology; and the expense of new software systems. These factors have resulted in a growing chasm between the priorities of politicians and managers on the one hand and those of practitioners on the other: 'There's a huge gap between managers ... who are trying to implement what we've been talking about and their understanding of what actually good social work practice is' (Ferguson & Woodward, 2009, p. 72).

Managerialism is precisely the application of private-sector priorities to social care, so it is scarcely surprising that social work and social care are increasingly shaped by market forces, not least the pressure to drive down costs, to do 'more for less', through the introduction of competition. This pressure has been felt most keenly in the voluntary and private social-care sectors in the UK, where it has led to a race to the bottom when it comes to wages and working conditions. A social worker in Ferguson and Woodward's (2009) voluntary sector focus group commented:

> My experience has been that workers' conditions have gone down and down and down, the wages have gone down, the hours have gone up ... We started working 37 and a half hours instead of 35 hours a week and the staff accepted it. We didn't get our annual increments. So that is how they managed to stay in business ... There is something about being professional in an organisation but how on earth do you provide empowering practice if workers are totally disempowered? I don't think it's possible. (p. 93)

In a context of austerity, there is growing pressure on workers to find ways of cutting costs and reducing care packages. At a Social Work Action Network (SWAN) Conference in Birmingham in 2011, worker after worker spoke of being forced to review client care packages with a view to reducing their costs. According to some contributors, the definition of a good social worker was the person most successful at cutting packages and saving the department money!

Challenging managerialism

Given this conflict-laden managerial context, to what extent and in what ways might it still be possible for front-line workers to act as agents of change in the lives of those with whom they work? To what extent is a radical, or at the very least, an ethical practice still possible? Ferguson and Woodward (2009) explored these questions with groups of front-line local-authority and voluntary-sector workers and service users and carers.

Retain a commitment to good practice

For some respondents, radical social work in the current period meant, above all, retaining a personal commitment to a model of good practice and not allowing oneself to be ground down. For Amy, qualified for more than twenty years:

> If we don't take some kind of personal responsibility then we just becomes more insulated, more depressed and more demoralised and to me, that's kind of what radical practice is, it's not allowing yourself to get demoralised and maintaining a sense of focus. (Ferguson & Woodward, 2009, p. 75)

While this was primarily an individual task for Amy, other respondents were perhaps more fortunate in belonging to teams where there was still a strong, collective value base. For Kathryn, who had been qualified for eight years:

> Our team has very strong social work values ... we're unafraid to challenge the internal system and we have an excellent manager as well so we can see ourselves as a force ... insisting on creating that kind of dialogue. (Ferguson & Woodward, 2009, p. 74)

One view, then, is that value-based work prioritizing a worker–client relationship, once regarded as *traditional – mainstream – practice*, has now become radical in contemporary managerial environments.

Work alongside service users and carers

The vision of a different, more equal, relationship between social workers and clients based on solidarity and shared struggles was a key theme of 1970s' radical social work (Bailey & Brake, 1975). The reality of 'service-user involvement' as it has emerged over the past 15 years has often had little in common with that earlier vision. Too often, it has involved tokenistic and consumerist forms of involvement with the service user cast as customer, albeit without any money, often in opposition to the worker (Cowden & Singh, 2007). In its current incarnation of personalization or 'cash for care', moreover, there is concern consumer choice is being used as a cover for cuts (Ferguson, 2008; Lymbery, 2010). Nevertheless, for several of Ferguson and Woodward's (2009) respondents, especially those involved in voluntary-sector projects, good practice meant above all challenging the lack of power of service users and stigma they experienced. For Doreen, an experienced worker in a mental health project this meant:

> Not being as far removed from service users as I certainly felt when I was a social worker and in terms of trying to involve them in more meaningful ways in the work and the way in which projects are run. (p. 90)

Mount 'guerrilla warfare' and small-scale resistance

Other respondents alluded to radical practice as 'guerrilla warfare' and small-scale resistance. Referring to the ever-longer assessment forms workers and service users were obliged to complete to obtain even the most basic resources, front-line worker Conor, qualified for 30 years, claimed:

> Written assessments ... are not for anyone's benefit apart from the system ... they've actually designed it to capture information that's needed for performance indicators – that much has been admitted by management. So what's happening is that there's a kind of guerrilla warfare practice developing amongst staff. There's whole swathes of these huge, long documents, about sixteen pages, just for one review – ridiculous! But people are just ignoring them and getting on in their own way, and doing it in a way that's friendly to service users and useful for staff. (Ferguson & Woodward, 2009, p. 158)

Murray, qualified for 16 years, who managed a youth service, argued:

> By repeating at every management meeting ... that young people who offend are just young people who have needs and who are damaged, [eventually] they just invested more money in our generic childcare ... so you do have room to manoeu-vre ... there is some hope even within the doctrine of managerialism. (Ferguson & Woodward, 2009, p. 158)

While the concept of 'guerrilla warfare' might sound subversive, it is far from new. Histories of the early Charity Organisation Society in the UK contain many examples of volunteers who rejected the stigmatizing distinction between 'deserving' and 'undeserving' clients and were prepared to turn a blind eye to minor infractions of law or Society regulations (Jones, 1983; Pedersen, 2004, Webb, 2007). In the 1970s, Pearson (1975) described social workers as 'middle class bandits' for whom the main task was 'doing the job properly':

> do the job, that is, for which he was prepared by his [*sic*] education to believe that he was paid and trained to do – was through the breaking and bending of rules that would not allow him to do the job properly, rules which were antagonistic to the profession's redemptive scheme. (pp. 36–7)

White (2009) refers to these as actions of 'quiet resistance' and identifies the most common types as 'dressing up assessments' or strategic manipulation of knowledge and information about service users; bypassing decision-making procedures by deliberately delaying paperwork; overt cooperation with tasks which conceals resistance; 'resistance through distance' by escaping or avoiding managerial authority; cynicism; and withdrawal from active participation in the workplace, through sickness and stress, moving jobs, or leaving the profession. These tactics are reminiscent of covert resistance adopted by subaltern groups throughout history, as discussed by James C. Scott (1992) in his classic text *Domination and the Arts of Resistance*, where he refers to them as 'hidden transcripts' aimed at challenging the 'public transcripts' or official views and practices of dominant groups. Among the many examples Scott (1992) provides is the apposite Ethiopian proverb: 'When the Great Lord passes, the wise peasant bows deeply and silently farts' (p. v).

Most of the strategies White (2009) describes should be celebrated and supported as workers' attempts to protect clients from harmful state policies or secure resources they might not otherwise have obtained. In addition, they provide workers with a way of 'doing the job properly', of maintaining a degree of professional integrity in the face of a managerialist ethos that seeks to reduce everything to cost. As a means of achieving real change, however, they suffer from some obvious limitations. Leaving the job, for example, while often an understandable response to an intolerable situation, is clearly not an effective way of improving the situation of service users. Cynicism might lead to concealment of forms of illegal behaviour, which might place both the individual worker and client at considerable risk. The main limitation of these strategies, however, necessary as they might be, is that they are *individualist* responses. Unless they are part of a wider collective strategy, they leave oppressive policies and structures intact (which is why the suggestion by some writers that such 'deviant social work' represents an advance on radical or structural approaches seems both misguided and naïve (Carey & Foster, 2011; see Chapter 1).

Engage in collective activity and political campaigning

The responses described above represent necessary attempts at ethical practice within ever-shrinking discretionary spaces and the constraints of dominant individualism. A fourth response, however, goes further: collective activity and political campaigning involve challenging the constraints imposed by managerialism and moving from the 'power of circumstances': 'We should be getting in alongside people in other agencies and people in communities to challenge oppression and ... the way our lives are run for us by politicians (Conor)' (Ferguson & Woodward, 2009, p. 75). Two decades of managerialism have limited the scope for radical approaches. There are reasons to believe, however, that the tide is turning once again.

First, even though social workers do not have a strong record on political participation, alienation and powerlessness – arising from the imposition of neoliberal values and priorities very different from those that brought social workers into the profession in the first place – can also give rise to anger and resistance (Ferguson & Lavalette, 2004). Where opportunities are provided to give collective expression to such feelings, as SWAN in the UK has attempted to do through the organization of annual conferences, campaigns and publications, new forms of organization and resistance can ensue (SWAN, 2011b). The main role of action networks is to: challenge the isolation and powerlessness felt by many workers; bring workers, service users and movement activists together to share ideas and experiences; and campaign around specific issues, whether they be attacks on the rights and conditions of service users or the scapegoating of workers over issues of child or adult protection.

While campaigning is likely to be a central element of any new radical social work, it is also possible that new forms of direct practice will emerge from the collective discussions between workers, users and carers. Elsewhere, justified anger over official responses to refugees and asylum seekers fleeing conflicts relating to the 'war on terror' in the past decade has been a powerful factor in fuelling political campaigning by social workers as far afield as Slovenia (Zorn, 2007), Greece (Teloni, 2011) and Australia (Briskman, Latham, & Goddard, 2008).

Secondly, the appeal of radical perspectives is likely to increase in the face of a global crisis of capitalism, which began in 2008 and shows no sign of abating (Callinicos, 2011; Harvey, 2010). In 2008, ruling classes throughout the world responded to this crisis by shifting the huge costs of bank bailouts on to the poor, elderly and sick through austerity programmes that effectively ended the post-war welfare settlements. How social work as a profession responds to these attacks on the living standards of the poorest sections of the community will shape the character and public perception of the profession for decades to come. Fortunately, in at least some cases, social workers have risen to the challenge. On 8 October 2011, radical social workers in Hungary and supporters of the New Approach to Community Work Group assembled in central Budapest to protest against a bill passing through the Hungarian Parliament, which would criminalize homeless people by threatening rough sleepers with up to 60 days in prison and making 'dumpster diving' (raking through bins for food) an offence. The social workers involved acted in accordance with the Hungarian Social Work Code of Ethics (New Approach to Community Work Group, 2011) to defend the rights of vulnerable homeless people:

> It is the social worker's responsibility, as well as a right and duty of the undersigned professional organizations, to call the attention of decision makers and the general public to their respective responsibility for the emergence of poverty and suffering as well as for their obstruction of the alleviation thereof (point 10).

> Social workers facilitate social change through their activities and professional stance (point 11).

Unfortunately, the Hungarian state saw things differently. Following the rally and demonstration, one of the social workers, Norbert Ferencz, was charged with 'incitement' and sentenced to three years' probation. However, the fact that social networks publicized this event and news of the demonstration reached audiences that rose to his defence (SWAN, 2011a; International Federation of Social Workers (IFSW), 2011) suggests it may serve as an inspiration for protest action of this nature in the future.

Finally, a third factor fuelling a renewed radical social work is the growth of global resistance to neoliberal capitalism. In the past, the social work profession has been renewed and transformed through its contact with wider social movements, such as the 1970s women's movement (Thompson, 2002). In recent times, social workers in Greece, Croatia, Slovenia, the USA and the UK have been engaged in the Occupy movement that emerged in 2011 in protest against global economic inequalities. Inspired by the revolutions in North Africa, and under the slogan 'We are the 99%', by October 2011 Occupy protests were taking place in over 95 cities across 82 countries, and over 600 communities in the USA. In Slovenia, social workers involved in Occupy Ljubljana established a new organization, *Direct Social Work 15o* [15 October], which issued the following statement:

> Not to be servants of financial capitalism, supervisors of expenditure of the poor! To become an advocate for the people, join the movements today. Social work emerged from working class movements for social justice – and became in time a

mediator between the state and the people. Social workers became expropriated, too. With neo-liberalism social work has become a global profession – to mend and reduce the harm done. But social work is also an opportunity for those who are pushed into the shadow of silence to speak, for those who have become dependent on others to take the things in their own hands. We need to relinquish roles in which we treat people as things, in which paper is more important than deed, and by which we serve disablement and not empowerment. Enough of the indirect social work, enough of the paperwork, enough of the closed institutions, enough of social cripples. 15o is an opportunity for social work, an opportunity to become directly responsible to the people. (SWAN, 2011c)

Conclusion

Since the early 1980s we have seen a global social work profession often in retreat, lacking in confidence, and unable to resist a neoliberal restructuring of welfare, undermining the very foundations of ethical practice. It has been a period in which even the very modest conceptions of social workers as agents of change promoted in 1970s ecological models have sometimes seemed unrealistic and unattainable. In some respects, the crisis of global capitalism and the imposition of ever-more oppressive austerity measures will make the struggle to preserve an ethical, let alone radical practice, even more challenging. But, as shown in this chapter and elsewhere in this book, there is also evidence that the experience of alienation produced by managerialism, coupled with growing outrage at the way in which ruling classes everywhere are seeking to shift the costs of the crisis onto the poorest, most oppressed sections of the population, is fuelling a new radicalism among social workers in some quarters of the world. One important source of that new radicalism is the emergence in 2011 of powerful new social movements in opposition to austerity. Encouragingly, there is evidence that social workers in some countries are seeking to forge links with, and learn from, these new movements (including, in some cases such as Greece and to a lesser extent Britain, a re-energized working-class movement). As Lavalette has argued (2011), in the past, as part of their daily praxis, such movements have sometimes developed forms of 'popular social work', based on solidarity and social justice, which stand in marked contrast to official, top-down social work. To the extent that social work as a profession is able to engage with these developments and movements, stand with them in their struggle to defend the rights and living standards of the poorest and most oppressed in society, and promote forms of practice for individual flourishing and collective solidarity, it remains a profession worth fighting for.

References

Audit Commission. (2002). *Recruitment and retention*. London: Audit Commission.

Bailey, R., & Brake, M. (1975). *Radical social work*. London: Edward Arnold.

Bamford, T. (1989). Discretion and managerialism. In S. Shardlow (ed.), *The values of change in social work*. London, Tavistock/Routledge. 135–154.

Birchall, I. (2004). *Sartre against Stalinism*. New York: Berghahn Books.

Briskman, L., Latham, S., & Goddard, C. (2008). *Human rights overboard: Seeking asylum in Australia*. Brunswick, VA: Scribe Publications.

Callinicos, A. (2011). The crisis of our time. *International Socialism, 132*, 3–17.

Carey, M., & Foster, V. (2011). Introducing 'deviant' social work: Contextualising the limits of radical social work whilst understanding (fragmented) resistance within the social work labour process. *British Journal of Social Work, 41*, 576–593.

Cowden, S., & Singh, G. (2007). The 'user': Friend, foe or fetish? A critical exploration of user involvement in health and social care. *Critical Social Policy, 27*(5), 5–23.

Cree, V.E., & Davis, A. (2007). *Social work: Voices from the inside*. London: Routledge.

Eagleton, T. (1990). *The ideology of the aesthetic*. Oxford: Blackwell.

Ferguson, I. (2008). *Reclaiming social work: Challenging neo-liberalism and promoting social justice*. London: Sage.

Ferguson, I., & Lavalette, M. (2004). 'Another world is possible!' Social work and the struggle for social justice. In I. Ferguson, M. Lavalette, & E. Whitmore (eds), *Globalisation, global justice and social work*. London: Routledge. 207–223.

Ferguson, I., & Woodward, R. (2009). *Radical social work in practice: Making a difference*. Bristol: Policy Press.

Fraser, N. (2008). *Scales of justice: Reimagining political space in a globalizing world*. London: Polity Press.

Harris, J. (2003). *The social work business*. London: Sage.

Harris, J., & Unwin, P. (2009). Performance management in modernised social work. In J. Harris & V. White (eds), *Modernising social work: Critical considerations*. Bristol: Policy Press. 9–30.

Harvey, D. (2010). *The enigma of capital and the crises of capitalism*. London: Verso.

International Federation of Social Workers (IFSW). (2011). *IFSW writes to the Hungarian Government*. Retrieved 27 November 2011 from http://www.ifsw.org/p38002346.html.

Jones, C. (1983). *State social work and the working class*. London: Routledge & Kegan Paul.

Jones, C. (2004). The neo-liberal assault: Voices from the front-line of British state social work. In I. Ferguson, M. Lavalette, & E. Whitmore (eds), *Globalisation, global justice and social work*. London: Routledge. 97–108.

Lavalette, M. (2011). Social work in extremis: Disaster capitalism, 'social shocks' and 'popular social work'. In M. Lavalette & V. Ioakimidis (eds), *Social work in extremis: Lessons for social work internationally*. Bristol: Policy Press. 1–14.

Lipsky, M. (1980). *Street-level bureaucrats: The dilemmas of individuals in public service*. New York: Russell Sage Foundation.

Lymbery, M. (2010). A new vision for adult social care? Continuity and change in the care of older people. *Critical Social Policy, 30*, 5–26.

Maitles, H. (2002). Surviving the holocaust: The anger and guilt of Primo Levi. *Journal of Genocide Research*, *4*(2), 237–251.

New Approach to Community Work Group. (2011). *Blog*. Retrieved 20 December 2011 from http://ujszemlelet.blog.hu/.

Pearson, G. (1975). Making social workers: Bad promises and good omens. In R. Bailey & M. Brake (eds), *Radical social work*. London: Edward Arnold. 13–45.

Pedersen, S. (2004). *Eleanor Rathbone and the politics of conscience*. Yale, CT: Yale University Press.

Reisch, M., & Andrews, J. (2002). *The road not taken: A history of radical social work in the United States*. New York: Brunner-Routledge.

Sartre, J-P. (1969). Itinerary of a thought. *New Left Review*, *1*(58), 43–66.

Scott, J.C. (1992). *Domination and arts of resistance: Hidden transcripts*. New Haven, CT: Yale University Press.

Social Work Action Network (SWAN). (2011a). *Statement on sentencing of Norbert Ferencz in Budapest on 4/11/11Call for International Solidarity*. Retrieved 27 November 2011 from http://79.170.44.81/socialworkfuture.org/index.php/articles-and-analysis/news/178-norbert-sentencing-statement.

Social Work Action Network (SWAN). (2011b). *Social Work Action Network*. Retrieved 20 December 2011 from www.socialworkfuture.org.

Social Work Action Network (SWAN). (2011c). *Occupy Ljubljana: Statement from social workers in Slovenia*. Retrieved 20 December 2011 from http://www.08.socialworkfuture.org/index.php/articles-and-analysis/international-articles/168-occupy-ljubljana.

Teloni, D. (2011). Grassroots community social work with the 'unwanted': The case of Kinisi and the rights of refugees and migrants in Patras, Greece. In M. Lavalette & V. Ioakimidis (eds), *Social work in extremis: Lessons for social work internationally*. Bristol: Policy Press. 65–80.

Thompson, N. (2002). Social movements, social justice and social work. *British Journal of Social Work*, *32*(6), 711–722.

UK Department of Education. (2010). *Munro Review of Child Protection: Part One. London: Department of Education*. Retrieved 11 October 2011 from http://www.education.gov.uk/munroreview/downloads/TheMunroReviewofChildProtection-Part%20one.pdf.

Webb, S.A. (2007). The comfort of strangers: The emergence of social work in late Victorian England (Part One). *European Journal of Social Work*, *10*(1). 39–54.

White, V. (2009). Quiet challenges? Professional practice in modernized social work. In J. Harris & V. White (eds), *Modernising social work: Critical considerations*. Bristol: Policy Press. 129–144.

Zorn, J. (2007). Borders, exclusion and resistance: The case of Slovenia. In M. Lavalette & I. Ferguson, I. (eds), *International social work and radical tradition*. Birmingham: Venture Press. 117–143.

13

The Speculative Left and New Politics of Social Work

Mel Gray and Stephen A. Webb

Modern-day politics has much to learn from social work values. It is well understood in our field that cooperation is a craft and its foundations lay in learning to listen well and discuss rather than simply win an argument. Social workers know that dialogue does not erase differences, but amicably puts them into play. They know that sharing is valued over selfishness: it is a form of generosity, a way of giving that may mean a loss to oneself. As social workers, we have the skill set to deploy practical methods by which to cement a social glue and weave connections through our common ties. In order to confront the dilemmas and tragedies of the contemporary political situation, however, more must be done. Much more. How does social work exemplify and construct possible ways to live together? As the chapters in this book have shown, it starts by taking a stance and exerting itself in fresh and meaningful ways. In this final chapter, we sketch a framework for what taking a stance in social work might look like under the banner of what we call the 'New Social Work Left'.

Social workers know that David Cameron's 'Big Society' model of UK private-sector, volunteer-led social welfare is a sham. They have worked for far too long in poor areas ruined by competition, where petrol poverty and the siphoning of petrol from tanks of cheap second-hand cars is an everyday occurrence, of places where 'the local community, like the colony, is stripped of wealth, then told to make up for that lack by its own efforts' (Sennett, 2012, p. 24). 'Your lack is my gain' is the modern mantra of neoliberalism. Social workers think differently. They find ways of connecting the community to the outside world, of joining people together. In *Together*, Richard Sennett (2012) praises those who, like social workers, take the hard route of maintaining their distance while keeping up their caring commitment. He celebrates the woman who works at a local family centre, putting in the hours often without pay, to help her clients in the best possible way, with her lightness of touch rather than scolding blame. This takes years to learn. It is an attunement to a subtle way of being together. A good social worker is moved by and in turn moves others through personal reciprocity and portrays ethical principles and the promise of a better shared life.

The story of the 'I' is not the whole story. In laughter, tears, love and orgasm, we are reached and sometimes overwhelmed by intimate others. In collective anger at injustice and heartfelt times of solidarity, we dissolve in waves of being together in the smooth space of *the common*. In the language of Gilles Deleuze and Félix Guattari (1987), the self is constantly 'deterritorialized' (p. 10), whereby one person opens up to the external flows of another. Neoliberalism will have none of this. It insists on a perverse liberal individualism of the person. The individual should literally become like a market calculating every social transaction to their own benefit. As Michel Foucault (2008) explained, 'we must act on the market milieu' (p. 259) in which the individual *homo oeconomicus* is making his or her decision, in order to guide people towards economically and socially desirable behaviours. With this violent calculating regime, as Marx famously wrote, 'all that is solid melts into air', all firm foundations, whether for law or for self, are hollowed out. Social work has dared to imagine a good life, where things shine forth, or, in the evocative words of David Kishik (2012), a place with vitality, 'a landscape built of sheer life' (p. 119) comes to pass.

Cooperation and sharing is hard when modern politics actively encourages rivalry, deceit, greed and selfishness. This muck eventually gets inside your head. The neoliberal rationality of competition, consumption and the marketization of everything, including personal relationships and state-owned enterprises, is the very opposite of social work's core values. This kind of individual neoliberalism endorses, based on a flexible bundle of acquisitive skills whereby the self is reflexively managed as a business, creates morally bankrupt relationships. As Jameson (1991) urges, '"the market is in human nature" is the proposition that cannot be allowed to stand unchallenged; in my opinion, it is the most crucial terrain of ideological struggle in our time' (pp. 263–4). It is worth remembering that the market is kept alive only by dint of political interventions. Unless social work confronts this ideology, if the only 'social profession' continues to let it pass, or worse still accepts it, our citizen clients will continue to suffer from the worst excesses of poverty, injustice and environmental decay.

Modern politics is in urgent need of repair, and this repair starts in our own backyard, then moves over the fence. Much good work has been achieved recently in progressive left politics. Michael Lavalette's (2011) *Radical Social Work Today* and Iain Ferguson's (2008) *Reclaiming Social Work* are fine examples of how the long night of the social work Left is drawing to a close. The development of the Social Work Action Network (SWAN) in Europe is an example of social workers on the Left organizing against the impact and cuts of neoliberalism. The launch of the new Policy Press journal *Critical and Radical Social Work* is also an important development to be supported. In this vein, a new politics of social work is a *renewed politics* building on radical trajectories that have been persistent in the profession at least since the 1970s (see Chapter 2). The stakes are high, but what is of paramount importance is the necessity of *thinking a new politics*, thinking afresh while having courage, keeping the faith and working in solidarity. Repairing our own political stance means making a commitment to secure a critical measure of and *distance* from a pernicious economic rationality that is undermining our values without the slightest sense of remorse.

Is Anti-capitalism Enough?

So what is to be done? In Chapter 1, we showed that a 'New Social Work Left' entails a politics and an ethics articulated through a radical epistemology and critical, if not militant, confrontation with its adversaries – capitalism and neoliberalism. This new politics was expressed as a proposal rather than a manifesto – it does not assert what ought to be but what might possibly emerge from a critical thinking that rests on a core set of principles relating to justice, equality and freedom. This proposal is about *provoking thought* in concrete situations where social workers operate.

We find ourselves proposing a new politics of social work at exactly the moment that neoliberalism is suffering from severe setbacks associated with the global financial crisis and capitalism is experiencing one of its most uncertain times (Harvey, 2011). However, as a political economic system, neoliberalism is far from done in its global ambitions for profit and accumulation. While one of the main achievements of neoliberalism has been a marked increase in inequality (Harvey, 2005; Wade 2003), its continuation and diffusion shows no sign of slowing down. In spite of financial crises and the fragile state of national economies worldwide, neoliberalism remains in ascendancy across the globe. Briefly, the backdrop to this state of affairs is that falling profits in the late 1970s generated a new form of finance capitalism that ultimately led to governments removing regulatory barriers to borrowing and the rapid transnational flows of capital. At the same time, production moved to cheaper labour markets such as China. As David Harvey (2011) shows, to solve the problem of demand, this new finance capitalism poured rivers of credit to increasingly cash-strapped consumers. A historic real-estate boom resulted, but when the bubble burst, so did this new financial edifice. As the banks and credit system were shored up by governments with taxpayers' money, the people were abandoned and subjected to the most severe austerity measures in the history of capitalism. Austerity is an occasion for a further attack on the standard of living of working-class people. In Britain, the Cameron government is using the debt crisis to go after the social welfare programmes so unpopular with neoliberals. This is a class assault – succouring the rich and screwing the poor.

The net effect of the global financial crisis has been to shift the brunt of the crisis from banks to state debt. Unemployment remains the big problem and the banking system is insolvent (Marazzi, 2011). In Marxist terms, this amounts to the fundamental contradictions of capitalist accumulation and 'the long-term systemic risks that capital poses to life on planet earth' (Harvey, 2011, p. 262). The effects of dismantling what is left of the welfare state through the politics of austerity have a direct and harmful impact on social work and its fellow citizen clients. The austerity measures also run the risk of provoking major social unrest. The irrationality of the system is now clear. There is a mass of capital and a mass of unemployed labour, sitting side by side, in a world of social need. What could be more ridiculous than this?

Springer (2012) introduces a formal definition of neoliberal violence, arguing that 'the hegemony of neoliberalism positions it as an abuser, which actively facilitates the abandonment of "Others" who fall outside of "neoliberal normativity"' (p. 3). He pulls no punches:

> To continue to embrace the maligned doctrine of neoliberalism and the malevolence it unleashes is to stay the course of battery, exploitation and assault, and to abandon those most embattled by its exclusions, and most scarred by its exceptional violence (i.e. the poor, people of colour, the unemployed, women, the lesbian, gay, bisexual and transgender community, ethnic minorities, the young and old, disabled peoples, the homeless) to the full fury of its wrath. (p. 4)

In 'Down with Existing Society', Alain Badiou (1987) similarly rails against the present state of affairs:

> If the lamentable state in which we find ourselves is nonetheless the best of all real states this simply proves that up to now the political history of human beings has only given birth to restricted innovations and we are but characters in a prehistoric situation. If, in terms of political thought and practice, of forms of collective life, humanity has yet to find and will not find anything better than currently existing parliamentary states, and the neoliberal forms of consciousness associated with them, this proves that as a species, said humanity will not rank much higher than ants and elephants. (p. 3)

Taking up Springer's (2012) exhortation, we recommend that the continuing violence and coercion of neoliberalism should be a call to action for social work. It should incite militant intervention and energize a collective strength with an urgent need to redress its terrible wrongdoings. From a social work perspective, what is required is a more detailed examination of power relations at work: how they are configured as part and parcel of capitalism and how social relations and control structures are managed. The discussion below shows that a key focus for social work is managerialism, marketization and regulatory practices distilled in front-line practice. As Ferguson persuasively demonstrates, management and managerialism are the enemies of critical social workers (see Chapter 12).

Eve Boltanski and Luc Chiapello (2005) identify the main stalwarts of the neoliberal capitalist apparatus as its managers. Management is crucial in accepting, legitimating and authoritatively delivering the new justifications for profit and greed in this phase of capitalism (see Chapter 6). For Boltanski and Chiapello (2005), management discourse does the most decisive work in the economy. In effect, if state law and the military are always ready in reserve, it is managers who are the glue that hold the new capitalism together, delivering its command and regulatory structure at the level of the everyday. As such, it is the rationality of management, its agenda and practices that must be a central target for a sustained social work critique and radical confrontation. Have no doubt, social services management supports, maintains and deepens the neoliberal apparatus. As Carey (2007) demonstrates, without resistance, the deskilling and marginalization of front-line practice will continue to be inflicted by care managers and bureaucrats. According to the Invisible Committee's *Coming Insurrection* (2008), it is time to get organized and sabotage management as the representative authority of capitalism.

A 'New Social Work Left' develops counter-acts and oppositional tactics against the totality of neoliberal domination. In identifying with those excluded from community, social work thus helps identify the reach and content of the abused, abandoned and oppressed as political in character. That is, identification with groups such as poor slum dwellers or migrant workers, or what is being called the 'precariat', should be mobilized as a *political community* involving social work and those excluded (Standing, 2011). Equality must remain centre stage and be cast in relation to emancipation (O'Brien, 2011). This is not a naive or reductionist notion of equality but one based on an active commitment and process enforced by various means and constant effort.

The violence of neoliberalism, aided and abetted by its policing state and law, has led other commentators to claim that we live in dangerous and unprecedented times. Indeed, Italian historian and political philosopher Giorgio Agamben (2005) maintains that we live under a *state of exception* whereby the power of decision over life is unmatched in comparison with other times. This present state of exception means that law can be suspended to preserve a juridical state order at any time, and this is predicated on the blurring of legal and illegal, public and private, citizen and criminal, terrorist and freedom fighter. With the advent of George W. Bush's US presidency in 2000 and the subsequent strategies of detention, interrogation and control used in post-9/11 camps, such as Guantánamo Bay, the state of exception reached new heights. Stephen Graham's (2010) *Cities under Siege* addresses the rapid transformation of militarized forms of law enforcement used to subdue dissent and criminalize behaviour. He critically examines the subtler and more familiarly overt modes of social control and surveillance that are being put to use in troubling ways in modern cities. Journalists were surprised and shocked by police methods used to subdue various 'Occupy' demonstrations across the USA and Europe. There is an increasing dependence on methods of local policing that is eerily similar to how Western militaries behave on the battlefield.

While sovereign states claim the entitlement to 'decide the exception' or to classify people according to identity cards, the risk of detention camp is permanently with us. Here the state, especially during times of emergency or crisis, abandons all pretence to embody popular democracy and takes on a militarized, legal mode, often against its own citizens. With Guantanamo Bay very much in mind Agamben (2005) argues:

> Indeed, the state of exception has today reached its maximum worldwide development. The normative aspect of law can thus be obliterated and contradicted with impunity by a governmental violence that – while ignoring international law externally and producing a permanent state of exception internally – nevertheless still claims to be applying the law. (p. 87)

Badiou (2001) regards the present situation of global neoliberal violence as 'evil' in its attempts to impose particular 'truth' regimes, such as the 'war on terror' and the universalization of the market, as the only viable economic model and salutary social order. Where does social work situate itself in relation to the evil of neoliberal capitalism and, if it is not for, but against, then what stance does it take in constructing new political forms of life and ideas? In the words of the World Social Forum, 'Is another world possible', or is capitalism the only game in town? Where is the vanguard of a progressive alternative politics in all of this? Who will magically work the transformation of subordination and exploitation into political agency? And where are the sustained acts of resistance that writers from Althusser to Foucault tried to console us with?

What most diagnoses fail to offer, including postmodern social work, is any working-out, in a meaningful fashion, of concrete *forms of resistance*. We may speculate, however, whether it is possible to identify a *rising* opposition to confront the situation that has been imposed upon us. Moreover, does a radical alternative inhere in Marxism and, by implication, a Marxist social work when 'Marxist literature, although plentiful in quantity, has a depressing air of sterility and helplessness' (Kolakowski, 1978, p. 29)? Does this suggest a deep structural fault line in the thinking of the Left that should be avoided at all costs in developing any new politics? British Leftist historian, political scientist and one-time editor of the *New Left Review,* Perry Anderson (2000), thinks so. In confronting present forms of neoliberal violence, he urges us to avoid what he calls the 'consolation' of the Left, which is based on the need to have some message of hope and has a 'propensity to overestimate the significance of contrary processes, to invest inappropriate agencies with disinterested potentials and to nourish illusions in imaginary forces' (p. 10). As we discuss below, we are often left with a pluralistic politics resting on the activation of new social movements that embody a hesitant and weak critique of advanced capitalism. Does this best capture the uneven journey and immediate prospects for a new politics of social work?

The question of a militant political agent – Foucault's subject of resistance – antagonistic to the supposed inevitability and universality of capitalism – sits at the very centre of this seemingly bleak state of affairs. As C. Wright Mills (1960) said over forty years ago, this must be *'the* political problem which *we* must [turn] into issue and trouble' (n.p.). This question is just as pressing for social work as it is for any other agency of progressive change. Indeed, any attempt to construct a new politics of social work must confront the question directly.

There is little doubt that social work reflects this wider impasse in contemporary politics and political activism: 'There are innumerable blueprints for utopian futures that are, in varying degrees, egalitarian, cosmopolitan, ecologically sustainable, and locally responsive, but no solution to the most intractable problem of all: who is going to make it happen?' (Bull, 2005, p. 19). This absence of agency is a structural effect conditioned by the disappearance of a politically influential working class. In the context of contemporary capitalism, the alternative appears to be between various forms of 'spontaneous' market-driven agency – those indirect effects of the 'invisible hand' – and populist reactions asserting state or communal sovereignty. Perhaps, better examples of social movement-focused politics are the mass movements, such as 'Occupy Wall Street', 'The Global Justice Movement' and 'Ecofeminism'. The vexed issue of identifying a primary agent of radical change has led Wendy Brown (2011) to ask, 'do humans want freedom?' and 'do we want them to be free?' For us this fundamental question links explicitly to the agenda of social work because of its foundational consideration of equality, justice and emancipation. Brown (2011) is concerned:

> all the indications of the past century are that the seductions of the market, the
> norms of disciplinary power, and the insecurities generated by an increasingly

unbounded and disorderly human geography, the majority of Westerners have come to prefer moralizing, consuming, conforming, luxuriating, fighting, simply being told what to be, think, and do over the task of authoring their own lives. (p. 55)

For Brown (2011), this state of affairs is hardened by people who are largely oriented 'towards short-run gratifications rather than an enduring planet, towards counterfeit security rather than peace, and disinclined to sacrifice either their pleasures or their hatreds for collective thriving' (p. 56). Have the workers sold out completely, or have they been ideologically duped? Must we, in the words of Žižek (2009), await a 'new form of Terror', as a necessary condition for the mobilization of a contemporary emancipatory politic? How much voluntary servitude must we endure? If, as Brown (2011) suggests, humans do not want the responsibility of freedom, and are neither educated for, nor encouraged in the project of political freedom, what does this mean for social work, the very basis for which rests on this desire and orientation? How can social work actively pursue an agenda of emancipatory politics orientated towards freedom, justice and equality, let alone do so on behalf of others? Indeed, to accomplish this, our international professional associations – the International Federation of Social Workers and International Association of School of Social Work – would pretty much have to rewrite their definitions of social work from top to bottom.

Ideological Justifications for Capitalism

The response to Brown's (2011) question about freedom is complex, but best approached by taking into account how this current state of affairs has come about. As Boltanski and Chiapello (2005) brilliantly demonstrate in *The New Spirit of Capitalism*, acceptance of neoliberalism no longer rests simply on material incentives or coercion by the politicians and the media in persuading people to buy in. Instead, it requires justifications that link personal gains from involvement to some notion of the common good. People have to believe in capitalism because they think it works for them and others, and because they have been led to think there is no better alternative since the demise of communism. According to Boltanski and Chiapello (2005), this legitimating exercise is what contemporary and flexible capitalism does extremely well. The moral promises made by capitalism are a critical feature of how it defends and sustains itself. They show how capitalism absorbs aspects of anti-capitalist critiques and finds new ways of legitimating itself in the eyes of society (Davis, 2005) by holding out the prospect of participation and discretion – through reducing bureaucracy and permitting greater flexibility – as part of its new moral ideals. The new capitalist superhero is a teamworker, who embodies acute vision, listening powers, intuitive feelings, networking skills and cultural aspirations. Indeed, the inculcation of the service-user movement and programmes of empowerment can be read as features of this new spirit of capitalism in social work (see Chapter 9). McLaughlin (2008) has made some useful mileage out of this by suggesting that contemporary forms of hegemonic power and governance have assimilated the language of social work and, by implication, contributed to the sustainability of capitalism as a feeder discourse. In an otherwise confused analysis, he makes the salient point with capital Ps that 'we are seeing the Political gaze looking inward towards the personal, with Politics becoming overtly concerned with the micromanagement of people's personal and interpersonal lives' (McLaughlin, 2008, p. 148). As Davis (2005) notes, 'drunk on the dreams of independence and networks, we no longer challenge capitalism on grounds of equality or justice' (p. 3).

In reviewing the conditions of justification at work with the new spirit of capitalism, Budgen (2000) highlights how the primary focus is its ability to satisfy a desire for *autonomy*, that is, exciting new prospects for self-realization and freedom, and *security*, that is, durability and generational transmission of advantages gained. He summarizes:

> Boltanski and Chiapello proceed to outline a model of the new moral framework of this emergent order, whose ideal figure is a nomadic 'network-extender', light and mobile, tolerant of difference and ambivalence, realistic about people's desires, informal and friendly, with a less rigid relationship to property – for renting and not absolute ownership represents the future. (p. 153)

The iconoclastic imagery of the new spirit of entrepreneurial capitalism is embodied in the likes of David Cameron and Richard Branson, the former running a national government and the latter a multinational company, issuing soothing, touchy-feely language about reform in open-necked shirts, united colours of Benetton pullovers and Croc shoes. The net result of the new spirit of capitalism, with its emphasis on personal autonomy and security, has meant it has been able to disarm elements in the Left's critique of it as essentially dehumanizing and oppressive.

It is worth recapping the main emphases drawn so far to show how these dovetail into considerations of a new politics for social work. If we lay Agamben's (2005) state of exception, with all its unrivalled pernicious powers of control and violence, alongside the way in which capitalism has formulated a new spirit by accommodating the logic of personal security and autonomy, it sets in focus the sharp edge of a new politics. This enables the identification of the primary agent of change for an emancipatory politics, which is at the centre of a juncture of considerations about what a new politics might look like. However, as Badiou has often remarked, anti-capitalism cannot be directly the goal of political action; in politics, one opposes concrete political agents and their actions, not an anonymous 'system'.

Badiou has defined the critical project in terms of the attempt to account for the abandonment and betrayal of the revolutionary impetus in the 1970s. These two strands from a progressive social theory and political philosophy demonstrate how a new politics in social work must be concerned primarily with the invention of new political forms. Given the overarching concentration on the construction of new creative ways of thinking the political, strategies and tactics for engagement will be entirely speculative. The violence of neoliberalism requires a new critical combination against it, capable of bringing together demands for justice and solidarity with those for equality and authenticity. In social work, we should renew and expand on the radical tradition of the 1970s, developing a more essential base for political and intellectual work. In order to begin this important work, it is necessary to cast aside certain obstacles and hindrances that have distracted us from a politics of social work.

Beyond the Malaise of Postmodern Identities

Some social work researchers are fascinated and seduced by the aura of postmodernism. Let us be clear, postmodern politics is not in the slightest bit concerned with equality, justice and poverty. Postmodernism is not cool. The vagaries found in the postmodern social work literature, and often associated with 'identity politics', celebrations of diversity and the Othering of difference, is a self-defeating exercise that can only lead to a political blind alley (Noble, 2004). Postmodernists, such as Derrida, Deleuze and Baudrillard, who were supposedly at the forefront of critical thought, are partly responsible for emasculating critique against neoliberalism.

Back in 1990, Habermas dubbed thinkers like Foucault, Deleuze and Lyotard 'neo-conservatives' because they lacked a theoretical justification for an alternative to the political *status quo* in capitalist society. In a televised debate with Chomsky in 1971, Foucault refused to offer an alternative to capitalism on the grounds that the task of the 'revolutionary is to conquer power, not to bring about social justice' (Merquior, 1985, p. 148). Rancière, too, is critical of Foucault's political stance. In outlining their differences, he says, 'it's a question of equality – which for Foucault had *no theoretical importance* – that makes the difference between us' (in Guénoun & Kavanagh, 2000, p. 5). Unlike Rancière and Badiou, Foucault was interested in the prisoner, the sexual deviant and the insane, not the poor. Social work is ethically interested in all four categories of the social. Social work research has too often focused simply on the most popular of Foucault's output –

Discipline and Punish – and other secondary-source material. As a result, too much credence has been given to the effectiveness of formal techniques of surveillance and disciplinary power by 'petit Foucauldians' in social work. The mistake has been made to interpret disciplinary power in terms of 'control', which is not a Foucauldian concept at all (McBeath & Webb, 2004). Moreover, despite Foucault's insistence on the centrality of resistance to all power relations, he rarely analysed the concept empirically. Unless social work research is prepared to take account of the more complex later work on biopolitics and governmentality, we may have reached an impasse whereby it is most instructive to forget Foucault for social work (Garrity, 2010).

Remarking on the anti-politics of Deleuze, Badiou (2000) notes: 'Deleuze's fundamental problem is most certainly not to liberate the multitude (*the mass poor*) but to submit thinking to a renewed concept of the One (*Being as Becoming*)' (p. 10; emphasis added). Indeed, this is a perfect shifter for showing the condition of postmodernism not only as a 'neoliberal postmodernism' but also as an 'apolitical postmodernism' or even an 'anti-political – out of this world – postmodernism'. The uptake of postmodernism in social work has merely served to exacerbate this at a different level of engagement. The postmodern social worker takes on identities that look and act much like commodities – identities of difference become neoliberal hippy fetishism. The stress on multiple identities, celebrations of difference and codes and narratives that need to be deciphered in order to expose the surface appearance of simulations are deprived of critique of the real apparatus of power, the economy, and state have no capacity to put forward an alternative political world-view.

Postmodern social work denies the hard political core of any emancipatory project – an agent of radical change. As Boltanski and Chiapello (2005) argue, 'if everything without exception is now nothing but code, spectacle or simulacrum, from what external position can critique denounce an illusion that is one with the totality of what exists?' (p. 455). Claire Colebrook (2003) argues that the whole question of 'how one thinks of oneself *without* identity politics, or *without* individualist politics' (p. 145) has never been more relevant. Sociologist Paul Gilroy (2000) goes further to argue that identity-based discourses are rooted in the same romantic historicism that led to European fascism. In fact, the politics of identity sets social groups against one another, often through 'rights claims', and thereby helps to protect neoliberal capitalism and its partner state from potentially threatening popular alliances (Webb, 2009).

Does social work really want to have any involvement with the consequences and hidden effects of the identity politics agenda? One very serious problem with identity politics becomes apparent in conceptions of citizenship and human rights in the social work literature. Attempts to engage critically with citizenship, within critical and human rights theory, often underline how the status of the citizen has ceased to be perceived as a privilege and is, instead, viewed in terms of access to political rights and political participation. The political subject is thus constituted by his citizenship and not the other way around. A consequence of this is that the emphasis on the universal rights of human beings has been replaced by the particular rights of the neoliberal citizen. The net effect is that the political claims of particular groups are denied their potentially universal character. Celebrating diversity in social work amounts to nothing more than particularistic and relativist identity claims that have no connection whatsoever to issues of equality, poverty and injustice, but instead connect to the neoliberal conception of individual agency as a market of consumer relations.

The Winds of Change

The practice of social work inevitably operates within a 'grand tension' of refusing the dominant order while at the same time being contaminated by and maintaining this order. For radicals the tensions to which this situation gives rise are best dealt with by political discipline, developing local clusters of solidarity and being critically reflective (see Chapter 5). These entanglements will enable social workers to live with these tensions and sustain their refusal of neoliberal management practices. Radical interventions in social work are tactically best suited to specific issues via small groups. In our recent empirical work on community engagement, we were most surprised to discover just how multinational corporations and local state bureaucrats are scared stiff of social protest and radical mobilization. This is especially true when a public issue gains salience with the media. Many protest groups are not aware of the panic they excite in the minds of the bosses. Big business and their state bureaucrat allies are utterly risk-aversive about inciting public protest. They neither understand nor can account for what they see as the 'emotive and irrational public'. This small unknown fact may be a striking tactical lesson for the New Social Work Left. Talking about and organizing around social inequality and injustice is a threat to political power – the capitalist class. Badiou constantly reminds us that successful protests and uprisings in different domains have often taken place because of the actions of minorities (see Hewlett, 2010).

Social work can become a politics of refusal. It can discover a new sense of promise and negate and react against the violence of neoliberalism. In the introductory chapter, it was shown that Badiou's *The Communist Hypothesis* (2010) rests on a simple, yet important conviction: we need to be able to envision something other than capitalism and the concept of communism

– as shared community – makes this possible. There is little doubt that the potency for social work in these new creative ways of thinking by writers on the left, such as David Harvey (2005, 2011) and Jean-Luc Nancy (2000), will face enormous, perhaps insurmountable obstacles before they can translate across to front-line practice.

The first task of adherents to the New Social Work Left must consist in militant opposition to this lie of neoliberal capitalism in all its manifestations, or what Agamben (1999) refers to as an 'I would prefer not to' strategy. These dark times of neoliberal violence can be overcome and social workers can contribute to its downfall, connected, together and in solidarity with a fresh optimism. Each of us on the social work Left has this to do: *stand together in fraternal solidarity*. Jane Jacobs (1993) gives a feel for how we might imagine new forms of collective life:

> Imagine a large field in darkness. In the field, many fires are burning. They are of many sizes, some great, others small; some far apart, others dotted close together; some are brightening, some are slowly going out. Each fire, large or small, extends its radiance into the surrounding murk, and thus it carves out a space. But the space and the shape of that space exist only to the extent that the light from the fire creates it. The murk has no shape or pattern except where it is carved into the space by light. (p. 490)

The metaphoric space defining the fires gives life in the murk. Life attracts life. The fires are places where people share, giving each other close-grained and homely support. The lights from the fires signify the common. The conditions that make up the thing we call the 'world' can only exist at all as a consequence of the gift of belonging-to-one-another. This is what theologians called the spirit of community – the *donum dei*. The gift that gives the relationship is the sense of the influx of each of us into each other. Or to be less elegiac, this communization of life is what Nancy (2000) calls an essential sharing of the world which is foundational (Noys, 2011).

What new forms of collective life are possible, and how will social work contribute to the conception and practice of new forms of life? What radical alternatives are available for a social work politics? Will social workers take part in a fresh demand for equality, justice and universal emancipation and be galvanized in a call to arms? Let us leave the last words to Badiou (2010), and ask you to consider whether or not he is correct:

> *We know that communism is the right hypothesis.* All those who abandon this hypothesis immediately resign themselves to the market economy, to parliamentary democracy – the form of state suited to capitalism – and to the inevitable and 'natural' character of the most monstrous inequalities. (p. 6)

References

Agamben, G. (1999). *Potentialities: Collected essays in philosophy*. Stanford, CA: Stanford University Press.

Agamben, G. (2005). *State of exception*. Chicago: University of Chicago Press.

Anderson, P. (2000). Renewals. *New Left Review*, *2*(1), 5–24.

Badiou, A. (1987). À bas la société existante! (Down with existing society). *Le Perroquet*, *69*, 1–3.

Badiou, A. (2000). *Deleuze, the clamour of being*. Minneapolis: University of Minnesota Press.

Badiou, A. (2001). *Ethics: An essay on the understanding of evil*. Trans. Peter Hallward. London: Verso.

Badiou, A. (2010). *The communist hypothesis*. London: Verso.

Boltanski, L., & Chiapello, E. (2005). *The new spirit of capitalism*. London: Verso.

Brown, W. (2011). We are all democrats now ... In G. Agamben, A. Badiou, W. Brown, & J-L. Nancy (eds), *Democracy in what state?* New York: Columbia University Press.

Budgen, S. (2000). Review of *Le Nouvel esprit du capitalisme*. A sequel to Max Weber's *Protestant Ethic and the Spirit of Capitalism* from contemporary France. *New Left Review*, *1*, 149–156.

Bull, M. (2005). The limits of the multitude. *New Left Review*, *35*, 19–29.

Carey, M. (2007). White-collar proletariat?: Braverman, the deskilling/upskilling of social work and the paradoxical life of the agency care manager. *Journal of Social Work*, *7*, 93–114.

Colebrook, C. (2003). *Understanding Deleuze*. London: Allen & Unwin.

Davis, W. (2005). *Review of 'The New Spirit of Capitalism'* – Luc Boltanski & Eve Chiapello. London: Verso. Retrieved 4 April 2012 from potlatch.typepad.com/weblog/files/renewal_boltanski_review.doc.

Deleuze, G., & Guattari, F. (1987). *A thousand plateaus: Capitalism and schizophrenia*. Trans. B. Massumi. Minneapolis: University of Minnesota Press.

Ferguson, I. (2008). *Reclaiming social work: Challenging neo-liberalism and promoting social justice*. London: Sage.

Foucault, M. (2008). *The birth of biopolitics: Lectures at the College de France*, 1978–1979. Basingstoke: Palgrave Macmillan, http://www.amazon.com/Birth-Biopolitics-Lectures-Collège-1978-1979/dp/0312203411.

Garrity, Z. (2010). Discourse analysis, Foucault and social work research: Identifying some methodological complexities. *Journal of Social Work*, *10*, 193–210.

Gilroy, P. (2000). *Against race: Imagining political culture beyond the color line*. Cambridge, MA: Harvard University Press.

Graham, S. (2010). *Cities under siege: The new urban militarism*. London: Verso.

Guénoun, S., & J.H. Kavanagh (2000). Jacques Rancière: Literature, politics, aesthetics: Approaches to democratic disagreement. *SubStance*, *29*(2), 3–24.

Habermas, J. (1990). *The philosophical discourse of modernity*. Cambridge, MA: MIT Press.

Harvey, D. (2005). *A brief history of neoliberalism*. Oxford: Oxford University Press.

Harvey, D. (2011). *The enigma of capital and the crises of capitalism* (2nd edn). Oxford: Oxford University Press.

Hewlett, N. (2010). *Badiou, Balibar, Rancière: Re-thinking emancipation*. London: Continuum.

Invisible Committee, The (2008). *The coming insurrection*. London: Semiotexte.

Jacobs, J. (1993). *The death and life of great American cities*. New York: Vintage Books.

Jameson, F. (1991). *Postmodernism, or, the cultural logic of late capitalism*. Durham, NC: Duke University Press.

Kishik, D. (2012). *The power of life: Agamben and the coming politics*. Stanford, CA: Stanford University Press.

Kolakowski, L. (1978). *Main currents of Marxism*. Oxford: Oxford University Press.

Lavalette, M. (2011). *Radical social work today: Social work at the crossroads*. Bristol: Policy Press.

Marazzi, C. (2011). *The violence of financial capitalism*. Los Angeles, CA: Semiotexte(e).

Merquior, J.G. (1985). *Foucault*. Berkeley, CA: University of California Press.

McBeath, G.B., & Webb, S.A. (2004). Post-critical social work analytics. In J. Fook, S. Hick, & R. Pozzuto (eds), *Social work: A critical turn*. Toronto, ON: Thompson Publishers.

McLaughlin, K. (2008). *Social work, politics and society*. Bristol: Policy Press.

Nancy, J-L. (2000). *Being singular plural*. Stanford, CA: Stanford University Press.

Noble, C. (2004). Postmodern thinking: Where is it taking social work? *Journal of Social Work, 4*, 289–304.

Noys, B. (ed.) (2011). *Communization and its discontents: Contestation, critique, and contemporary struggles*. Retrieved 10 January 2013 from http://www.minorcompositions.info/wp-content/uploads/2011/11/CommunizationDiscontents-web.pdf.

O'Brien, M. (2011). Equality and fairness: Linking social justice and social work practice. *Journal of Social Work, 11*, 143–158.

Springer, S. (2012). Neoliberalising violence: Of the exceptional and the exemplary in coalescing moments. *Area*. Article first published online 24 February, http://onlinelibrary.wiley.com/doi/10.1111/j.1475-4762.2012.01084.x/abstract.

Standing, G. (2011). The precariat: *The new dangerous class*. New York: Bloomsbury Academic.

Sennett, R. (2012). *Together*. New Haven, CT: Yale University Press.

Wright Mills, C. (1960). *A letter to the Left*. Retrieved 4 April 2012 from http://www.marxists.org/subject/humanism/mills-c-wright/letter-new-left.htm.

Wade, R.H. (2003). Is globalization reducing poverty and inequality? *International Journal of Health Services, 34*, 381–414.

Webb, S.A. (2009). Against difference and diversity in social work: the case of human rights. *International Journal of Social Welfare, 18*, 307–316.

Žižek, S. (2009). How to begin from the beginning. *New Left Review, 57*, 43–55.

Index

Printed in China